LAND BELOW THE WIND

"Land Below the Wind" is a literal translation of *Negri De-Bawa Angin*, which is the native Malayan term for Borneo.

EMPIRE BUILDER AT EASE

Land Below the Wind

BY

AGNES NEWTON KEITH

Sketches by the Author

BOSTON
LITTLE, BROWN AND COMPANY
1939

Published November 1939
Reprinted November 1939 (five times)
Reprinted December 1939 (three times)

THE ATLANTIC MONTHLY PRESS BOOKS
ARE PUBLISHED BY
LITTLE, BROWN AND COMPANY
IN ASSOCIATION WITH
THE ATLANTIC MONTHLY COMPANY

17865

To my Mother and Father

Green Pasture in the U.S.A. — 1934

A LION lay down with a lamb one day, and the lamb was never the same. Neither was she at ease and content with the fold, nor could she hunt in the wild. Her heart, which had been a good lamb's heart, wasn't even liver for a lion's mate.

There was no solution, and the lamb never discovered what to do about it, so she just went on that way.

But the things lamb saw when hiding behind lion, when crouching with fright in the jungle, when peeking out from the bush, when looking over her shoulder because she was running away! The things she saw when in attitudes of abject, lamblike trepidation she was scuttling back to the flock! Ah, even a lamb knew a stronger beat of her domesticated heart for the galvanizing delight of those things!

North Borneo — 1939

CONTENTS

Part IV

WINDS OF HOME

ILLUSTRATIONS

Part I

THOSE WHO WERE NOT BORN THERE

1. " *Look Up the Facts!* "

For four years now I have drunk the toast to "Absent Ones" with people whose hearts turn back to a different land from mine, whose thoughts are of another country, whose children play on a different soil. We have spoken of "home," and home to them was England.

In my heart these people are mine, as I hope in their hearts I am theirs. But when we open our mouths to speak, as I do, or when they do not open their mouths to speak, as they do not, there is no mistaking who comes from the United States of America. As an Englishman's wife I think too much has been written on the question of Understanding the English. When my husband removes his pipe I can understand him almost perfectly, and when he ex-

3

presses his views on publicity his meaning is all too clear. If for the moment then I call the attention of strangers to the Conservator of Forests and Director of Agriculture of North Borneo, it is because my only business in Borneo is as his wife.

North Borneo is a British Protectorate which is administered by a Governor and Civil Service appointed by the British North Borneo (Chartered) Company, and it is the sole remaining country in the British Empire to be administered by a chartered company.

Here my husband stopped me for discussion. I said North Borneo was the only country in the world administered by a chartered company, and he said, No! and why did Americans always want to say that a thing was the only one in the world? And I said it was for the same reason that English people said a thing was the only one in the British Empire, the world and the B.E. being of comparable size in our respective minds. After which we turned quickly to latitudes.

The state of North Borneo lies between four degrees and seven degrees north of the equator, and covers the northern tip of the island of Borneo, which is the third largest island in the world. It has a population of about 270,000 and its Civil Service numbers, all told, some seventy persons.

Singapore and Hong Kong are both about seven days distant from us by steamer when wind and sea are favorable, but it is my prejudiced opinion that wind and sea are never favorable between Hong Kong and Borneo. Northeast of Borneo lie the Philippine Islands. East of us are the Celebes Islands, and beyond them lies our successful rival, New Guinea, the second largest island in the world. South and southwest of us lie Java and Sumatra, which have produced, according to my very fortunate experience, some delightful and attractive young Dutch civil servants.

The length of time required for a person to come from the United States to Borneo is approximately the same as for my mail. When we came out in 1934 we left Southern California on September 27 and arrived at Sandakan, North Borneo, on November 10, forty-four days later, or just over six weeks.

The climate of North Borneo is warm, as day in and day out the temperature averages about 88°, and the humidity is very high. It is not a distressing climate, but it makes one too content to sit and do nothing. If you go to bed tired at night you wake up so in the morning. There is never anything in the air to make you breathe deeply and throw out your chest and say briskly, "How invigorating!" One may say, "How delicious, how fragrant . . ." but one sits down and relaxes even while saying it.

Our home is in Sandakan, the capital of North Borneo, which is situated on the east coast and is the largest town in the state. It has a population of approximately 14,000 persons. About seventy-five of them are Europeans, 10,000 are Chinese, and the rest are natives of Borneo, natives of Netherlands East Indies, Philippine Islanders, Malays, Indians, and Japanese. The Chinese predominate in the coast towns, but are seldom found in the interior.

The natives of North Borneo are a brown-skinned people of less than average height whose features show a Mongoloid influence. That is as far as I can safely go, for students of ethnology tear each other to pieces and retreat on crutches after a discussion of the identity and origin of the

5

earliest North Borneo inhabitants. The natives have no written language and therefore no written records, and their only history is tradition and folk tale. Mr. Owen Rutter in his volume *British North Borneo* roughly divides the native pagan peoples of North Borneo into Dusuns and Muruts, the Dusuns being people of the plains and the coasts, and the Muruts people of the hills and the interior. The Dusuns are generally speaking a farming people, while the Muruts are a hunting, and formerly head-hunting, people. These are the aborigines of North Borneo, and both Muruts and Dusuns are believed to have come from a common stock. These two large classifications, of course, cover a number of differentiated tribes, all of whom speak different dialects and have different customs. Distinctly apart from these aborigines of North Borneo is another group of its inhabitants, the Bajaus. These people comprise a large portion of the coastal tribes, are generally conceded to be of pure Malay stock, and are Mohammedans, not pagans.

The principal exports of North Borneo are timber, rubber, tobacco, cutch, dried fish, birds' nests, used by the Chinese for bird's-nest soup, and seed pearls. Borneo forests produce a number of fine timbers, among which is a very fine, soft hardwood which is used for decks in the British Navy, and general construction.

My husband has been in Government service here in North Borneo for fourteen years. As well as being Conservator of Forests and Director of Agriculture he is Honorary Curator of the State Museum, Game Warden, collector of strange beasts for distant scientists, patron of pauperized natives, and the repository for unwanted animals. He collects old Chinese porcelain, writes papers on scientific subjects, is recording a Murut vocabulary, speaks Malay well enough to be distressed by mine, and cites Oxford Dictionary English to the confusion of my American.

WHITE MAN RESISTING THE LURE OF THE TROPICS

Before we were married he told me that he hated cats, letters of introduction, leftovers, people who cut down trees, coeducational schools, bombastic phrases, and women in shorts.

I like cats and leftovers, and I think that a good bombastic phrase and a woman in shorts can go a long way at the proper time.

7

Those Who Were Not Born There

Since I have been married to an Englishman I have come to believe that the profane words "all Englishmen are . . ." and "all Americans are . . ." usually precede a libel, and the greater the truth the greater the libel. But one thing is true: an Englishman's wife is *his* wife, and I like that possessive pronoun. When I left the United States it was difficult to tell whose wife anyone was. As my husband's wife I have tried to cultivate an appreciation for the beauty of plain facts. But I have been in Borneo only four years as against his fourteen years, and my statements sometimes shatter him. When he looks at me dispassionately and says "Look up the facts!" I feel as chilled as a fish on ice, but I do look up the facts.

Without my husband my story of Borneo might have been more what people think Borneo ought to be, and less what it is. But when I see a shudder shaking him I quickly reduce my adjectives and multiply my qualifying clauses. In fact we have almost collaborated — I to enthuse, and he to refuse.

And so I acknowledge with gratitude his criticism, which, while it distresses me, does me good.

2

Like most Californians I wasn't born in that state, but was carried in at an early age. I grew up in Southern California, in fact in Hollywood, and this may be one of the reasons why the actions of the natives of other continents have neither surprised nor alarmed me. I spent four years at the University of California at Berkeley during the flapper decade. There I acquired a certain amount of scholastic knowledge in spite of the fact that I belonged to various organizations whose social activities required attention. It was collegiate in those days to be sophisticated, and to sigh aloud that life was futile, even while we whispered to ourselves that life was thrilling. I spent four very happy years there, sighing and thrilling; such happy years that I came to believe that happiness was a common state of affairs, and not, as I now know, an occasion for comment.

After I received a university degree, I decided to be a newspaperwoman. For days I sat perseveringly in the outer office of the *San Francisco Examiner* until I finally wore down the resistance of the editor and was hired for one month's trial. There was at that time in the city room a very beautiful young blonde woman who was nicknamed Kissy-wissy. She ran the Beautiful Baby contests and the Thought Symposiums, and irate parents and persons who thought their characters had been maligned were turned over to her to be placated because she was fluffy and sweet. Her body was molded in beautiful curves, and mine was not, and we were known in the city room as "Spareribs and Gravy."

At that time Annie Laurie Bonfils, or Winifred Black as she was known in the East, was a significant voice on the Hearst newspapers, especially the *San Francisco Examiner*. She said to me once, "Kissy-wissy is too beautiful for the newspaper business. But I think you'll do very well, Agnes." I did not mind the inference about my beauty at all, I was so intoxicated at the suggestion that I would make a newspaperwoman.

That year I made out my first income-tax report, and

was perhaps the only person in the United States who was really grateful to do so. And then, just as I felt the world at my fingertips, I became involved in a violent scene which nearly destroyed me. At noontime one spring day I stepped out of the revolving doors of the Examiner Building in San Francisco to be met by a temporarily crazed drug addict. He smashed my skull in with a two-foot length of iron pipe which he wielded like a baseball bat, and then continued to beat my head until he was literally pulled away by the traffic policeman. He didn't kill me, but during some of the ensuing years I almost wished that he had.

After the case had been dealt with in the courts and the man had been committed to prison, I left San Francisco to go south to my home in Venice, and recuperate. It was not a triumphant return. As a result of the injuries to my head I suffered a partial loss of memory. Then as I began gradually to remember again I had constantly to fight the belief that I was losing my mind. Owing to the severity of the skull fractures I had lost all power to concentrate and my thoughts shifted about like a kaleidoscope, and trying to grasp an idea was like trying to pick up a piece of wet soap. During those years when my mind was distracted and my nerves were broken I learned that happiness is never to be taken for granted.

I must have had a naturally thick skull and a strong constitution, because in time I began to recuperate, and my father sent me to Europe with my brother. The plan was that I should go to the French Riviera to rest and grow strong, while my brother, a civil engineer, engaged in a more exciting project of skipping about southern

Europe while he tried to persuade the Albanian Government to build a railroad. But by the time we reached the Riviera I was, for the first time since my injury, beginning to feel a zest for life again, and I refused to be left behind. So we wandered about southern Europe, where we discovered bedbugs and expatriate Americans, and King Zog in Albania, and Rose Wilder Lane in Tirana. We drove over the mountain passes of Montenegro in a Ford, and crossed the inland sea of Skutari in a small boat, and were marooned on the Adriatic coast by a seaquake.

By the time we returned to America I was beginning to have trouble with my eyes, a trouble which in diagnosis proved to be a result of the old frontal skull fracture. For two years then I lost the use of my eyes, and was unable to read even a page in a magazine. During that time I used my energies in a futile fashion, dancing, modeling clothes, doing small bits in plays and pictures, and planning political publicity stunts; for with my temporary handicap, which the doctors told me would only be remedied with a gradual healing of my nerves and a return to strength and health, I could do none of the things which I wished to do. Only the wisdom of my family and the tolerance of my friends made that fruitless period endurable.

Those were the early years of the depression. The one stable feature that I knew in that fast-moving, high-pressure America was my home, of which my father and mother were the body and soul. I have never met any other persons like them. They proved to me what love can make of human beings. Against the dignity and beauty of their relationship the marital dissatisfaction of my generation was pathetic. Their love was the same, yesterday, to-day, and forever. But my generation was not only married, it was divorced and remarried to each other's husbands. That was 1934.

Then a young Englishman, a friend of my brother's who had been for a time at school in the United States, and whom I had first met when I was eight years old, came to visit us on his leave from Government service in British North Borneo. Several times in the past we had almost married each other, but each time events which I thought at the time were more important had occurred to prevent us. But as soon as we met again in 1934 we both knew that nothing more important than marrying each other could occur to us.

We decided to be married immediately. We could and would see no obstacles. We procured a license, waited the necessary three days, and were married.

I had three months then to prepare for Borneo. I first located a doctor who agreed to perform an operation on my head which might prove a final cure for my eyes, and for the injuries from which I still suffered. I believed, because I had made up my mind to believe, that it would cure me. It did.

3

The life, as my husband described it to me, of the British inhabitants of North Borneo seemed to have little to do with the Wild Man from Borneo as advertised by Barnum and Bailey. I decided that I should need more dinner gowns than safari clothes, for if there were only twenty European women in Sandakan, where we were to be stationed, what those women wore must be noticeable.

"What do the Englishwomen wear in Sandakan?" I asked Harry.

"I never noticed. Frilly things, I suppose."

"I don't like frilly things on myself."

"Oh, women always wear frills. And take several garden-party dresses and big hats for Government House teas."

"I look ridiculous in big hats."

"Well, everybody in Sandakan wears them. Take things like that dress you have on now. I like that."

"This isn't a dress, it's a negligee."

I ended by taking everything I had, as no European dresses may be purchased in Borneo. In the four and a quarter years since I have made and remade, copied and created, on the basis of that wardrobe. I am far from the mode of *Vogue* and *Harper's Bazaar*, but here in Borneo where we dress from leave to leave we have standards of our own which enable us to look with an understanding eye upon rejuvenated clothing.

Before we left the United States I discovered that most people didn't know much about Borneo. The advice of my friends was confusing. Although no one knew about Borneo, everyone knew about The Tropics. I was advised not to take silk underwear as it would rot in the tropics. This I did not find to be so. I was advised to take many pairs of silk stockings, as I could not purchase them in the Far East. Later I discovered that American silk stockings may be purchased more cheaply in Hong Kong than in the United States. When sold in the United States the minimum price is protected, whereas in Hong Kong the article is unprotected and also duty-free. However, I took a bathtubful of stockings with me, soaking them all overnight in a tub of cold water before leaving. I still have them, as I have never worn stockings in Borneo.

Friends advised me to take beach costumes and shorts, saying that in the tropics I should live in such things. But I discovered the answer to that was — *not* in conservative Sandakan!

I was advised to dispose of jerseys and knit goods. However, in the wet season I still huddle gratefully into a jersey, and when traveling in the mountains of Borneo I have sometimes slept in all of my clothes under five blankets, and shivered still, so penetrating is the perpetual dampness.

My mother advised me to take her electric heating pad. I humored her and took it, not really expecting to find a use for it. But that pad has since visited all about Sandakan comforting people who have sciatica or rheumatism, ailments which are aggravated by the dampness here.

I was advised to have inoculations against smallpox, typhoid, cholera and plague, and anything else anyone could think of. It was better, people said, to Get It All Over With Now. But when I consulted the list of things that my friends thought I should get over with before I left the United States, the program left time for nothing but recuperation. I disregarded advice and sailed without inoculations. I do not advise others to do so.

One friend suggested that I should have my appendix out before venturing in the wilds, as a prophylactic measure. Never having had any unpleasant relations with it, I hesitated. My husband saved me by saying that I must keep my appendix, as an attack of appendicitis in Borneo meant a trip to Hong Kong for the operation, a pleasant break in a four-year Borneo tour. He had had his own appendix removed in Hong Kong several years before, and had enjoyed the holiday. However, my chance for a Hong Kong appendectomy has since vanished, as North Borneo has advanced in medical efficiency.

The problem of how I should occupy myself during the long indolent hours of being a white woman in the tropics was worried about by my friends. They advised me to take fancywork, embroidery, knitting, anagrams, puzzles, art materials, learn hooked-rug making, and study French. I should like to do all of those things, and perhaps when I am home on leave I may have time for them, but my life in Borneo has so far been too busy.

The last night before we left the United States I stayed

up all night packing. At intervals my husband awoke to ask me why I did not come to bed. The answer was in our twenty-three pieces of luggage. Not until the shore line was out of sight the next day and the agony of saying good-bye was over did I look about me on the ship. The other passengers apparently saw nothing extraordinary in us; they did not know that there stood before them the phenomenon of two perfectly happy people. It was surprising to me that they didn't point at me and whisper, "She's been dead for years, but look at her now!"

I turned to my husband and said, "I will never forget this moment. I am doing what I would rather be doing than anything else in the world, with the person I want to do it with. Some people may live a lifetime and never have a perfect moment like this."

"I hope you still feel that way after four years in Borneo," my husband said soberly.

That was almost five years ago, and I still feel that way to-day.

2. *Outpost of the Empire*

IF we are to believe the poets, the Empire Builders of to-day, when compared to those of Victoria's day, are only as men among gods; but the gods are gone and the men still live.

If I were a British-born wife I should not write the following paragraphs. Not because, although the quality of despotism is inferred to be common among British husbands, I had been silenced or intimidated by Harry. But I should keep silent for a better reason, one for which Britons do keep silent: I should keep silent because I should wish neither to condemn nor to compliment my own family to strangers. But I am an American, and I was a stranger in North Borneo. These Britons are mine by acquisition, and I have the right to plead for or boast of them.

There are now about seventy men in the North Borneo

Civil Service. In Kipling's time they would have been called Empire Builders. Mud, blood, guts, and boots they had then, with a white man's burden on every page, an old tradition in every line, and an old-school tie to mark the place where the body lay. Men with a magnificent gesture then, a magnificent gesture which will not come again until another Kipling finds the words to make of our husbands heroes, where to-day we make of our heroes husbands. Empire Builders then; "men in the Stud Book" we call them now. (Look him up in the Stud Book! Name, age, qualifications, years of service, salary, allowance, and class.)

For four years now we have studied each other's idiosyncrasies. We know each other well, and I speak truly when I say that the honesty and integrity of purpose of this group of men is beyond question, their ability and manner of life are above average, and their kindness and hospitality are such as I shall remember all my life.

I think if after four years of a similarly close scrutiny of those who administer government in the United States the same conclusion is arrived at, then no subject of the United States will feel himself any more ill-governed, oppressed, or abused than do the subjects of North Borneo.

Too puny a voice mine to say, like Queen Victoria, "Let empires be built!" — and, come hell or high water, they build 'em. Likewise too untutored a mind mine to attempt the argument, "Let empires be destroyed!" — and, come hell or high water, they blast 'em. Foolish I, if I deal in the theory of empires.

But if empires are to be built, then I think that these Britons of North Borneo with whom I have laughed, loved, lived, and been happy, will build them well.

Outpost of the Empire

Around-the-world journalists often pass through Sandakan. They seldom stop because the matter may be dealt with in passing through. There are only seventeen miles of paved road and this may be driven around in three quarters of an hour, with a passing glimpse of the golf club, Paupers' Home, the wireless station, and the agricultural station. At one end of the road is the jungle, and a more sensational description of the jungle may be given by those who do not travel in it. At the other end of the road is the Sandakan Club, and bachelors may be located there who will tell good elephant stories, both in size and in subject. The local color, and the social characteristics of an Outpost of the Empire, may be picked up on the run by studying the characters of Somerset Maugham or Kipling, according to which public one writes for. A week-end is enough for the whole problem.

At a safe distance, and not, one imagines, expecting to be seen in Borneo again, the author sends his book to press. One chapter of compendious paragraphs covers the complete canvas of life in North Borneo, both wild and administrative. The authors have not been reticent in printing what they think about us. We, perhaps, are at a disadvantage inasmuch as our thoughts about the authors have so often been unprintable.

The unusual form of the government of North Borneo always excites these galloping geographers. The fact that we are administered by the appointees of a *chartered company*, under the protection of the Crown, would seem to suggest to them that the subjects of North Borneo punch time clocks like store clerks, only without benefit of trade-union hours. The shareholders in the Chartered Company

are usually pictured as a group of coupon clippers barter-
ing the souls and bodies of wild men for a 2 per cent divi-
dend.

One writer has described North Borneo as the place
"Where There Ain't No Ten Commandments," and attrib-
uted this blasphemous state of affairs to the "iniquitous
character of the administration of the country." This
author devoted two chapters and considerable emotion to
describing the "shocking" condition of North Borneo. A
few months after publication this book was withdrawn
from circulation by its publishers, with an apology to the
British North Borneo Company for the "grossly libelous
and untrue statements" therein.

Less septic but no less remarkable are the experiences of
our big-game hunters. One intrepid hunter recalls having
shot a rhinoceros in the front garden of the Residency at
Tawau. He explains that the Resident had sent for him to
do this, but as he was unlicensed for shooting rhino the
Resident confiscated the carcass. This so enraged the author
that he almost shot the Resident, perhaps would have done
so had he been licensed for shooting Residents. People in
North Borneo remember this doughty visitant well, and
rumor has it that other details of his visit are in the official
files, but no one has yet been found to recall the shooting
of the rhino.

Another writer describes an elephant hunt in which a
slim, steel-nerved young Englishman fearlessly pursued a
rogue elephant and shot him through the ear and brain. The
young Englishman assures me that he shot the elephant
through the tail because the elephant was running away.

Possibly the author became confused by some similarity of appearance between the ends of the elephant.

In these bold stories of the Borneo wilds, it seems to me that the adventurers have passed over the most melodramatic scene of all, and the one which needs no exaggeration. Here is a jungle background almost as wild as our chroniclers picture it. Here are the aborigines, as fierce or as mild as they seem. Here is the tangled green of the jungle creepers which have constantly to be beaten back, and the wild which awaits to engulf again the clearing we call Sandakan. And here, living in astounding peace and security, following a social pattern as formal, as pleasant, as gently inflexible, and as uniform as the design on a set of teacups, are the European households of Sandakan.

A few miles out elephants may be seen upon the road, and orangutans and gibbon apes are one jump away in the jungle, and crocodiles are caught off the customs wharf, but at four o'clock in the afternoon we are drinking our afternoon tea.

Then, just as the rural pattern falls indelibly on us, and background and scene seem unalterably at odds, Sandakan is translated into terms of Graustark and played to an operetta score. There are medals and uniforms, and guns and saluting and feathers in hats, singing and dancing and native chiefs. There are Headmen and Orang Tuas, and Suluks and Bajaus and Dusuns and Muruts, and Hajis and Imams, and Chinese and Filipinos and Japanese; there are the pagan tribes of Borneo and the *ladies of Sandakan*, drinking tea and eating cakes together on Government House lawn to celebrate the crowning of a British King.

And there in that scene too fantastic for fiction breathes the real heart of a non-racial empire that mankind could, if he would, build to-day.

2

When I first arrived in Borneo we were assigned to the same small, well-preserved, pleasant, but very warm bungalow in which my husband had lived as a bachelor. It was a house which was popular with bachelors because of its secluded position behind tall bamboo hedges. This secluded position, however, made for warmth, and the bungalow was never popular with wives who had to spend the hot hours of the day in it.

Harry recklessly advised me to do what I wished with the house. I did. Partitions fell, hangings went into closets, weapons went into corners, and fringed lamp shades disappeared. I liked it, he exhibited admirable self-control, and apparently we were about to settle down. Just then we discovered that a Government house was about to be vacated on the hill. I had always wanted to live on a hilltop.

The people who were leaving the house invited us up to inspect it. When we sat in that house and looked out through its open doors the harbor of Sandakan with the dark mangrove swamps in the distance became a background to our entire world. I knew then that was where I wanted to live.

When the possibility of our moving was discussed everyone reminded me of the violence of the wind on that hilltop, of the age and enfeebled condition of the house there, of the superior condition of paint and polish in the house which we still occupied, of the hillside garden without top-soil where flowers would not flourish, and of the difficulty of coercing a vigorous enough stream of water up the hill to gush through a water closet.

I worried about the last. Only people who have lived both with and without plumbing can appreciate it. Finally I decided that I would not allow the lack of a w.c. to keep me off the finest hilltop in Borneo.

First my husband had to be persuaded. He said he wanted me to have what I wanted to have, but . . . the house we were already in had just been painted, the partitions had just been taken out for us, the plumbing had just been put in, the garden was in bloom, the trees were coming on to flower, *and* it was the house that he had always found large enough, cool enough, and breezy enough as a bach-elor. . . .

But women are very tenacious when it comes to the mat-ter of moving. In time my husband was persuaded, the Government department which assigns houses was per-suaded, and our friends who thought we were foolish were persuaded.

Then moving day came, and went, but not with the ease which the words imply. It was a grievous revelation of the hidden frailties of our household goods. When we took the bed apart it disintegrated into predigested termite food, the cupboards had no backs when moved from the wall, and the tables that had crossed their legs at ease in corners toppled over. The whole was a sad exposure of clay feet. Only the Martin Johnsons' refrigerator, standing cold and efficient, a monument to man's conquest over decay, was all it had seemed to be. I was proud indeed to walk up the road behind it, while ten Chinese *kuli* women trundled it up the hill.

When the furniture had limped into the new house and lain down in new corners, when the dog had found a new divan, and the *wah wahs* [1] new trees, and the orangutan the

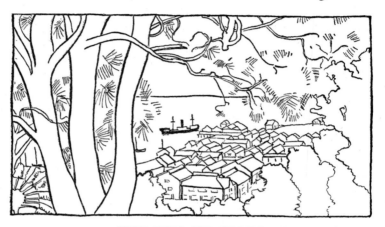

VIEW FROM OUR HILLTOP

new godown, I stood looking down at Sandakan Bay from the hilltop which now was ours.

The harbor of Sandakan lay below me. It was morning, and the water of the bay was motionless and flat and chromo blue as on a picture postal card. The roofs of the Chinese town were very red in the sun, and the tree-covered cliffs of the coast very green, and in the distance the mass of the jungle was a deeper, duller green. The coconut trees, where they fringed the shore, were drawn in with meticulous attention to detail, and the mushroom

[1] *Wah wah* — Dyak name for gibbon ape.

islands which skimmed on the water were so small and perfect it seemed that I could capture one and send it home with "Greetings from Borneo."

Native boats took the wind and leaned with it, their colored sails abandoning themselves to it; launches cut pale scallops on the flat blue surface, and Chinese junks rocked restlessly. Only the Hong Kong steamer was dignified and discreet. Ponderously she lay in mid-harbor, with her only finery a crimson stomacher about her funnels.

And thus we came to live in a house with an amiable disposition but negligent manners. Every winter it grows shabbier and shabbier, and more resigned to be so. When the northeast monsoon blows from the Sulu Sea it comes to us over five miles of jungle, sweeping up the damp breath of the trees and hurling it on us till the skirts of the house whirl upwards, and she braces herself and screams. And when the southwest monsoon drives the black clouds up from the bay and the wet sheets fold over us, there's not a garment the poor house wears that isn't soaked in the rain.

But when the sun comes, how she steams and sweats, how her pores open while she stretches and relaxes, and then grows brisk again. Then I think with fright of the well-disciplined houses at home, with double doors and well-fitting windows, efficient radiators and tiled bathrooms, houses that are despots to be catered for. No cracks in them for the wind and the sun, no carved niche for a favorite goddess, no bare beams for lizards to sleep on, and no place in the rafters for Georgie the musang.

I have recently read the statement of a journalist in the

tropics that he could not bear the sight of another bougainvillea against a blue sky. I have sometimes felt that
way about journalists but never about bougainvilleas.
All day in the sun the sides of our house, the doors and
windows, lie open to let the beauty in, to embrace and
absorb the fecund warmth, the deep strong scent, and the
lazy, lovely languor.

Royal Sulu sarongs hang at our doors, chrome yellow,
cerise, and purple. They blow out into the color of the
garden, and suck it in again with them in a deep exciting
breath — yellow grapes of the *Cassia fistula*, cerise and cop-
per of bougainvillea, lipstick lips of the African tulip,
crimson petals of flame-of-the-forest, and the stealthy scents
of frangipani, *chempaka*, *kenanga* tree, and *sundal malam*.
The outdoors is our only adornment, the only one that
can stand against the insects, the sun, and the rain.

Once we had a very nice woven-grass Shanghai mat. It
was so large it covered the living-room floor of chipped cement, and so new it wasn't paid for. The white ants came
up through a crack in the floor and ate their way across
the mat from corner to corner. Between the hours of
8 P.M. and 8 A.M. they ate, digested, and excreted the mat.
I remembered then the words of Government House
Nanny, who had just come out from England: "The
whole of Borneo is nothing but an anthill!"

But when the rain comes . . .
Barefoot activity runs through the house, while mats,
tables, lamps, and chairs are hauled away from leaking
doors and windows and unshutterable verandahs. Everything that will close is closed, but it is impossible to con-

trol the ventilation space between the top of the wall and the roof, and the rain blows in.

Charcoal braziers are lit in the bedroom to dry the bedding, and glow under the bed itself. My shoes in the wardrobe are wet, my clothes on their hangers wilt, the cough-drops melt in the corked bottle, and the envelopes in the desk all seal themselves.

Sandakan Harbor has vanished, and our house drifts alone in a cloud of rain. We have one place to go for comfort. Over a burning brazier we sit in the one dry room where we keep our books.

"Aren't we having more rain than usual this season?"

"No. We always have rain from September to March."

"But perhaps we are having a record rainfall this year." I always feel sure of this each rainy season.

"Don't be ridiculous. Our annual rainfall is only one hundred inches. Besides, we need rain for the garden."

"I should think with a rainfall of a hundred inches we could live in a house that wouldn't leak."

"Any house that is built to be cool is bound to leak."

This book room is built inside an extra upstairs bedroom, with sealed walls and screened doors and windows. Cockroaches, mud wasps, silver fish, and bookworms are outlaws here. After the lights are lit in the evenings it is the only place where flying ants, beetles, mosquitoes, and cicadas do not make fun of you.

There is mental energy in this room, discharged and accumulated from the past, which seems to exhilarate you when you enter it. Not only is it a good place to work in, but it is a good place to stop while the bath water runs, or when dressing for dinner or waiting for breakfast, for there is always something unfinished to be gone on with there.

The bedroom is the next place of importance. Like a ship beached by a high tide, our bed stands in the middle of our bedroom floor. All the other pieces of furniture have washed away from it to the outer edges of the room, where they will not intercept any breeze. We made our bed and we certainly like to lie in it. Six-foot-six both ways it is, made of heavy Borneo timber, and constructed after a picture we drew. For coolness' sake it has a wooden bottom and a hard mattress. I hated such beds at first, and thought that I faced four years of sleepless nights on hard beds, panting for breath in the warm air, longing for home leave, and wondering why I left America.

The climate is like that — unbearable at first, then forgettable, then comfortable, and before leave comes you get chilly. My grandmother always told me that I couldn't change the weather, but perhaps that was because we lived in California then, and it wasn't necessary.

However, one soon becomes accustomed to the warmth, which is not extreme for a tropical country. The worst that can be said about the climate in Sandakan is that it is never invigorating, and the warm, humid air seems to promote longevity in germs. Germs never die here, they are passed about from person to person like poor relations visiting, and colds and influenza, and various fevers carried by mosquitoes, are prevalent. But nobody gets run down by motorcars, or trampled to death in crowds, or beaten up by policemen, or falls out of skyscrapers, so perhaps it evens up in the end.

28

Outpost of the Empire

When I take my bath I stand by an open window and look through the tall bamboos past the European houses on the hillside, across the jungle, to a distant blue horizon. That is the Sulu Sea. There is an island there, which looks like a dog's head swimming in the water. Its name is Taganak, and it belongs to the Philippine Archipelago. My husband has explained to me that it has nothing to do with America, but I still look toward it with the sneaking feeling that it is a compatriot of mine.

Inside the bathroom the view is not so inspiring. There is one faucet in the side of the wall, and a small zinc tub for bathing. The accepted manner of bathing is to stand on the floor and dip water over yourself from the tub. However, I still feel there is nothing to take the place of reading in your bath, even if all you can get into it is your bottom, while your legs hang over the edge. The cement floor in the bathroom slopes to an open drain in one corner, and is always wet.

The small closet off the bathroom is the toilet, or w.c. as it is known in Borneo. It is well to speak about it be-

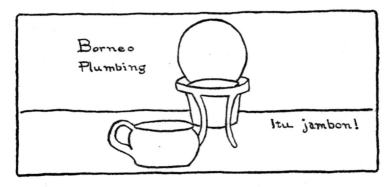

Borneo Plumbing

Itu jambon!

cause a w.c. is not to be taken for granted. It has a mentionable luxury value, like air conditioning or an outside swimming bath. For years the w.c. has been a topic of polite conversation here. People like to recall the old days before the houses had water "laid on," when every drop used was brought up the hill by prisoners from the wells in the settlement, and when *jambons* were good enough for Government House itself. Not such old days, either, for our own w.c. has only been in a year, those of Government House are within my memory, and in North Borneo there are still no town systems for running water outside of Sandakan and Jesselton.

3

I soon learned that it requires five servants to take care of my husband and myself. Our household grows and dwindles with unemployment in Sandakan, but usually it consists of two Chinese amahs, Arusap, our Murut houseboy, one Dyak-Murut small-boy, a Javanese gardener, three to a dozen semi-Siamese cats, one dog, two gibbon apes, and sometimes an orangutan, jungle animals as they come and go, and my husband and myself.

The food for all of us is prepared in the cookhouse, which stands slightly apart from our bungalow. Half the floor of the cookhouse is occupied by a cement mausoleum which functions as a wood-burning stove. Here fish heads, buffalo stomach, pickling octopus, gamy wild pig, and barking-deer stew simmer in amity beside less gustful kettles which provide the food for Harry and me. A huge iron basin is always steaming with water for the baths, and two smaller kettles bubble with the drinking water. Tap water in Sandakan is safe, but as we frequently travel in districts where everything must be boiled as a precaution against dysentery, we continue to boil our water in order to establish an unbreakable habit with the servants.

I have cooked over our stove, and that is literally true, for I myself cooked more readily than the food did. I have turned omelets, and produced soufflés, and baked cakes in its oven, and they were good but I was miserable. Now I confine myself to cold desserts and advice.

The bread is what I marvel at. Made from tinned flour, raised with tinned dried yeast, kneaded by a Chinese girl who never tasted bread until she learned to make it for me, baked in an oven which a cook at home would scorn, eaten with cold-storage butter months removed from the cow which produced it, it is the best bread that I have ever eaten.

The lower compartments of the stove are used by Wimbush, the Siamese cat, for her kittens, and by Thomas, the semi-Siamese, for voluptuous living, and the back of the stove is used to ripen the mangoes and to dry shrimp paste and tins of salt and red peppers and herbs and the skulls of the animals which Harry collects.

Scrambling down the hill about fifty yards distant from the house are the backquarters. Here live our Chinese amahs and Arusap. Ah King's room is first. It is the corner room, with two windows; a wardrobe is used to close one, and shutters are nailed over the other. Ah King has a large ironing board in her room, the symbol of her trade, and a small stretcher bed. From what I know of Ah King I imagine that she sleeps on the ironing board and irons on the bed.

Ah Yin's room is the place of discarded possessions. The old floor mat with the pink flowers, the dressing table with the fancy headdress, the broken mirror, the empty ginger jars, the dog-bitten sarongs, the faded cretonne curtains, the sea shells painted with the Woolworth Building, and the old wooden wardrobe that always smelled — we threw them out. Down the back stairs they were hurried, and now they crowd into Ah Yin's room. The wardrobe has ceased to smell, the ginger jars have flowers, and the Woolworth Building holds pins.

Arusap's room is the last. It will always be the abiding place of an aborigine whose people are accustomed to live in a house till the roof falls in, and then move on to another house. On the wall of Arusap's room there is a large photograph. This is a picture of Arusap, posed for in a store suit. One would not know to look at this stylish Arusap with the broad lapels and the striped tie that he is the brother of Mensaring, the Murut chief, whose naked likeness is on the picture postal cards that tourists send to the folks at home to show them wildest Borneo.

Close by Arusap's mat sleeps Usit, youngest and most useless member of the household. His eyes are glued shut and his soft mouth is just open, as he sleeps the close, deep sleep of all small boys.

And last of all a small room connects with Arusap's room, and this is where the Muruts who visit Sandakan may stay. Six stayed with us for Coronation week.

Our furnished living quarters are supplied to us by Government and upkept by the Public Works Department. As is usual with landlords and tenants, our point of view is sometimes at variance. P.W.D. furniture in its natural state arouses uncontrollable impulses in me for surgery. Legs, fancy backs, flourishing arms, malignant growths, humps, and decorational deformities I deal with like a surgeon.

Our personal furniture is of Borneo timber made after our own design. There is something peculiarly your own about a piece of furniture which to begin with was a tree in your forest, then was a picture drawn on a sheet of paper, then was a log in a timber mill that you saw every day, then was a piece of smoothed timber that you told the Chinese workman what to do about, and now is the shining, flawless top of the long dining-room table.

The day relaxes into evening, with a warm deep breath. The grinding of an anchor chain at sea, the striking of a clock in town, the tap of wooden clogs upon the road, sound faintly. Arusap steps softly with the dinner plates, and small-boy steps precariously with the bowls, his eyes on us and not on what he carries. The tall emerald goblets sparkle on the table, the rose hibiscus float in the celadon bowl, the candles burn like topaz eyes in the fat brass fish that hold them, the tall Malay lamps flicker behind my husband's head, and his bare feet touch mine under the table. All that is uncouth is hidden in dusk, and now in the gentle evening the glowing candles tell the truth.

4

Before we arrived at Sandakan Harry had told me about Arusap, the Murut boy who had lived with him for ten

33

years. Harry warned me that Arusap might not stay after we were married, for newly arrived wives had the reputation of installing unwelcome efficiency in bachelor households, and of expecting the native boys to work diligently, which is the last thing that a native is by nature equipped to do. Native servants will only work for the masters they are fond of, and if displeased with their employers they "resign" and return to their villages to live on their relatives.

The first face that Harry picked out for me among those of the persons standing on the customs wharf to greet us when we arrived at Sandakan was that of the friendly and smiling Arusap. He was holding in his arms a large and very old porcelain jar which he had brought down from his village as a wedding present to us. He presented it to Harry, and inside the jar was a note written in Malay. The note said: —

GREETINGS, TUAN,

I know that the Tuan likes such ancient and valuable things as this jar, but the Mem I do not know about. If she does not like the jar, please give it back to me, because I do like the jar.

ARUSAP

I did like the jar, and it has always been kept in a place of honor.

During the years since I first saw Arusap smiling on the wharf he has resigned many times, but never with any intention of leaving us, for he soon discovered that I did not install efficiency in the household, and I did not expect him to work too diligently. Although I should like him to work diligently I am a person who accepts facts, and I have accepted the fact that Arusap is Borneo's gift to us, and that he is subsidized by ourselves to represent one pure-blood native survivor of a now vanishing Murut tribe.

When I do not know where Arusap is I can usually find him sitting quietly in the pantry smoking rank black Dusun tobacco. If he did nothing but sit and smoke, as he usually does, he would still be worth it, for Arusap is child and parent, philosopher and friend, but he is not a good house-keeper.

Ah Yin, our number-one amah, is known to us as the Pearl without Price, for among the local amahs of Borneo she is the jewel of the Orient set in the ear of the sow. Ah Yin is young, attractive-looking, scrupulously well-groomed, and she has two expressions; one is that of smil-ing very happily, and the other that of weeping sadly. Thus the impassive Oriental.

We first discovered her four years ago in Hong Kong when she was working for friends of my husband, and we asked her to come to Borneo with us then. She said that she would, but that she must go first to Canton to say good-bye to her mother and father. This she did. That farewell was, we now believe, a last good-bye. The small village near Canton in which her parents lived has since been destroyed by the Japanese, and when we telegraph for news of them there is no answer.

When Ah Yin arrived at our home in Sandakan, having followed us from Hong Kong one month later, she pre-sented me with an attractively wrapped gift. The package had been addressed for her in English by a Chinese letter writer, and it said, "Wedding gift for Mr. & Mrs. Keith.

A happy wedding to you." Inside was a pair of silk bloomers.

Coming down on the Hong Kong boat Ah Yin established several invaluable contacts. One was with the Chi-

AH YIN

nese pantry steward, and consequently we have always been able to purchase Hong Kong vegetables and meat from the ship's larder when the boat comes in port.

Contact in the East with European women so often becomes superficial that my contact with Ah Yin fills a need in my life. I prefer to have her speak Malay, so that

I may use my vocabulary, but she prefers to speak English so that she may use her vocabulary. The result is intelligible to ourselves only. But the words of our lips hide nothing, because we know what is in our hearts.

Ah Yin is very feminine, very wily, very yielding, and very forceful. She is immaculate, she gives grace to each duty, and performs every service with a craftsman's hand. There is no job in the house which she does not have better ideas about than anyone else, which she cannot perform better than anyone else if given an opportunity to, and no job in the house which she does not sternly dictate.

Far behind Ah Yin in importance comes the number-two amah, Ah King from Canton, who is known to us as Elephant Foot. When the door bangs, the stairs creak, and the house shakes, they herald the slippered approach of the Silent-footed Oriental. Ah Yin said to me once about her, "I think Ah King not very smart; he only very good."

Ah King left Canton two years ago in answer to a letter from her friend Ah Yin, which cited the prosperity and the full stomachs of the Borneo Chinese. Ah King may not have been very smart, but she knew enough to catch the first Hong Kong steamer for Borneo after receiving that letter. She arrived in Sandakan to occupy the position of wash amah in our household. Before Ah Yin would allow Ah King to appear before me she first taught her to say "Good morning, Missee" and "Good night, Missee," both of which Ah King obediently produced in one phrase, "Good-morning-Missee-good-night-Missee," when presented to me. She learned that two years ago, and she has not learned much since.

37

One thing only Ah King can do well. With her tar-black pigtail tied around her waist she squats on her haunches by the tubs, humming, tittering, sniffling, belching, stealing a puff on her cigarette, and sopping her arms in and out of the tubs till the dirtiest clothes emerge spotless. And then, standing barelegged in her underpants at the ironing board, with the loosened black pigtail spanking her bottom, she can iron perfection into them.

When Ah King is careless in the housework Ah Yin attacks her in such scathing Chinese that her thin form withers like seaweed on the sand. Five minutes later, wiping the tears from her eyes with her pigtail, Ah King titters with laughter as she steps on the cat, drops the thermos jug, and falls downstairs with the tea.

Ah Yin, with her quick, perceptive mind, performs the mental processes for both, banks Ah King's money for her, gives her salts and quinine, takes her to the dentist, and makes her clothes for her. And she has just now to our distress bobbed off the long black plait of hair which was Ah King's only beauty. Ah Yin says that Ah King spent too much time plaiting it.

There is also on our payroll small-boy Usit, the offspring of two Borneo natives. It is difficult to explain in sensible terms just why we employ Usit, or what his duties are. One duty, for instance, is to laugh very hilariously in a high, sweet baby voice, and another is to stand with his small bare feet apart and whistle fuzzily, and another is to cry and have to be comforted. I think in the first place we got Usit because we had a dog, and no one should ever own a dog without getting a small boy to go with it. This afternoon I see that Usit has affairs to attend to in Sandakan at the football field. He may return in time for tea, or possibly dinner, or — well, whenever he is free.

Outside in the garden there works Husin, a Mohammedan with two wives lurking at home. Before him was Amat with three wives, one divorced and remarried to him three times. Strong, silent men of the fertile soil, these, men of the great outdoors!

And behind these five persons present to-day there passes in my mind's eye a long white-coated, Chinese-trousered procession of individuals whom I have in the past employed as cooks.

5

My first experience with Chinese cooks in Sandakan began with Lim Sang, who was an authority on Americans. I think that in his mind he classified us with these two characteristics: we shook hands with our servants, and we didn't know when we were being cheated. Lim Sang had learned about Americans in the Philippine Islands, long before I ever met him. There he had overworked his belief in our national credulity, and had had to leave Manila quickly and quietly. He arrived in Sandakan at the same time as I did.

When he heard that an American had come to town he hurried up to shake hands with me and apply for a job. My husband had never before had an English-speaking servant in the house, and it was against his principles, but Lim Sang sold himself to us on the strength of his ability to manage the electric refrigerator and to speak English, as I had not then learned Malay.

39

Oddly enough Lim Sang could cook. This prejudiced our judgment, and when he asked us to advance the money to bring his wife and five children from the Philippines, we did so. They arrived. They were fine children with large appetites and Lim Sang was a good provider. The seven Lims lived on the best that our cupboard offered. Malted milk, Klim, cold-storage butter, tinned wholemeal flour, Bovril, cocoa, tea, coffee, and sugar slid from our shelves. The disappearance of leftovers and opened tins could be condoned, but not the usurping of unopened tins, some of which I later learned were traded back to the store for cash.

The infant Lims grew round and rosy, while I studied Malay and spent little thought on the household management, which, as long as it didn't intrude on me, I was satisfied to leave alone. But I did occasionally stop to wonder at the capacity which Harry and I had developed for absorbing tinned foods.

Ah Yin did not stop to wonder; she went into action. She checked up on all food supplies, and examined into the closed hampers which the Lim children innocently conveyed away. As a result of her disclosures we locked up the pantry supplies, and I began purchasing everything possible by written chit, instead of allowing Lim Sang to shop for me. I made up my mind then to be rid of him as soon as he had worked out some of his debt to us.

But Lim Sang guessed that this was my intention, and he kept the debt well in advance of the salary cuts, for I did not have the heart to be too drastic when he had a family.

In the end I realized that contact between Lim Sang

and ourselves was profitable in one direction only. We canceled the debt, and told Lim Sang to go.

He asked me for a letter of recommendation. I didn't wish to prevent his obtaining another position when he had a family to support, but I wondered what to put in the letter. Finally I wrote, "This man can cook," and let it go at that. It was the only cook's reference I ever wrote that mentioned cooking.

The next several cooks were moderately efficient, and only legitimately dishonest. I showed them how to cook a few special dishes, and gave up eating the dishes that they couldn't cook. Left to myself I might have retained any of them indefinitely, for I had soon learned to be philosophical about the cooks making their squeeze, and as long as they stayed within the legitimate percentage I preferred to be oblivious of it. But Ah Yin was oblivious of nothing, and would not be philosophical about our being cheated. She persisted in faithfully unveiling all the minor thefts and major squeezes of each cook, until feuds existed which could only be satisfied with blood.

Later a quite respectable person, Chan Yu, came to us, and when he proved to be inoffensive and to make his squeeze in an unobtrusive manner, I decided that he should stay. But not so Ah Yin. She came to me one morning with her usually smiling face woeful, and her words injected venom into the body of a peaceful day.

"Cookie no good! He no clean, he no honest, he no cook nice, he cheat Missee, he take away food! I tell him, No! He say never mind, Missee rich. I tell him, Stop! Then he say he make much trouble for me. This cookie stay here I no can work. Very much I like Missee. If Master no have money sometime, never mind, I work without money. But if this cookie stay, I no can stay. Next Hong Kong boat I go."

"But Ah Yin, many times I send other cookie away because Ah Yin say no good. I no can do this all the time. If Chan Yu go, who cook for me? New cookie come, more trouble come."

"I think good you have Master Burton cookie, Ah Pu."

"I no can steal other Master's cook."

"Ah Pu like to come. Master Burton have got many women in back, all time tell Ah Pu do this, do that. One wife only, more good. I tell Ah Pu come."

"No, Ah Yin. Have got much trouble if I steal other Master's cookie."

"Missee not steal cookie. I can do."

I knew it was iniquitous in theory to allow a servant to influence my staff personnel, but I preferred Ah Yin's efficient dictatorship to an inefficient democracy in which no one was the boss. Besides, I was fond of her. Yet I knew that even if I condoned the stealing of Ah Pu a closer relation between him and Ah Yin in our house would probably terminate that friendship also.

"Never mind, Ah Yin. I talk to cookie. I think all men can work here happy."

"No, Missee. This cookie tell market men Ah Yin bad woman."

This was the familiar deadline. When the cooks blacked the amah's faces in market the crisis was reached, and it was useless to counsel amity.

"I talk to Master to-night." These words solved problems. After speaking them I could go into communion with myself, and then produce a weighty verdict hiding behind "Master says."

I talked to Harry that night. "If I'm to keep hiring and firing until I find an honest cook it will be a life's work. But I must have peace in the household. What shall I do about it?"

"If Ah Yin won't keep peace with any cook tell her she will have to do the cooking herself." And thus, quite casually, Harry solved the problem.

The next morning I told Ah Yin what the Master said. I would give Chan Yu a month's notice, and then she should become cook. She said she did not know how to cook as the other cooks in Sandakan did. This, I said, was an advantage. She looked very doubtful, and I knew then that she wished to consult her friends as to the etiquette of and omens surrounding this change of occupation. Three days later she came to me looking very happy.

"I think very good I cook. All men say amah can do," she said.

"Very well. Finish one month, then cookie go," I said. "Then Ah King do all the washing and the upstairs work, and Arusap do downstairs work, and Ah Yin cook. If cookie go I will pay other men here more money. But tell Ah King that she *must* learn to speak Malay now."

That day I told Chan Yu that he must go. I think he had already recognized the quality of Ah Yin's determination, for he accepted his notice of dismissal so peaceably that I wrote him a good letter of recommendation. In my letters for departing cooks I always discussed abstract qualities such as cleanliness, willingness to learn, quietness, sobriety. In my letter for Chan Yu I commented at length

43

upon the pleasure of associating with one of his pacific disposition. It was the quietest cook's departure we ever had. Departed with him the egg beater, the carving knife, and the best enamel pots, but these were only the legitimate perquisites of departing cooks.

Ah Yin was then established as ruler of the cookhouse, and earned the wage of the vanquished Chan Yu, a princely wage for a Chinese woman servant, and in time she came to provide the best meals in the history of our household.

Ah Yin and Ah Pu, the friendly cook of our neighbor, soon began to coöperate in their marketing, and came to control the choice of the fresh foodstuffs. They formed a beef trust which monopolized the best portions of the steer that was occasionally slaughtered. By leaving a standing order with the butcher for a large portion of the animal they were always able to obtain the "sweet meat," or beefsteak cut. They kept the meat in their masters' refrigerators, and sold the less choice cuts to other cooks.

Shortly after the first pay day of our new regime an epidemic of gold teeth appeared in our household. Ah Yin took herself and Ah King to the Chinese dentist, and they returned with several prominent teeth gilded. Arusap, with one splendid gesture, had all his front teeth capped with gold. I asked Ah Yin the cause of the dental magnificence. She answered: "Have got plenty money now. We get gold tooth like Master. If Master have got I think very good."

Before we came to Borneo cleaning day was an event which required mental and physical heroism on my part. But in our Sandakan household both mental and physi-

44

cal strain have happily been shifted to others. Now Ah Yin supplies the remedial state of mind, and Arusap and Ah King supply caustic activity, and I stay out of the way. This is not the way it is done in all Borneo households. Immaculate housewives do the downstairs on Monday, the upstairs on Tuesday, the brass on Wednesday, the curtains on Thursday, the floors on Friday, behind the pictures on Saturday, and inventory the drinks and food on Sunday, and wash the dog. This is a very good way. But it can be done my way.

Arusap has just laid a letter on my husband's desk.

GREETINGS, TUAN,

I know the Tuan does not like to lend money to the servants, and I hope the Tuan will not be angry with me, but I ask to borrow five dollars to send to my wife Kuta at Kampong Pau. I promised to send my wife five dollars in the seventh month, and five dollars in the eighth month, and five dollars in this month, the ninth month. I did not do so because the Mem has not yet paid the wages for the seventh month, the eighth month, and the ninth month. I hope the Tuan will not be angry with me, but I ask with many thanks if the Tuan will lend me five dollars to send my wife Kuta at Kampong Pau.

With greetings and salutes, Tuan

ARUSAP

"Agnes! Haven't you paid the servants their wages for three months?" Horrified voice of my husband.

"I *must* have paid them! . . . At least I suppose I paid them. I always do pay them at the end of the month when

45

the salary check is credited. I don't actually remember paying them, but, well . . . Perhaps I didn't pay them. . . ."

I think backwards. This would explain the bank balance which I noted with smug approval the other day. I had thought it was because I had been too busy to do catalogue ordering from Singapore. My mind went back to the sixth month. Yes, I remembered paying them for June because we had just returned from a jungle trip and I remembered adding seven dollars extra to Arusap's wage for traveling allowance.

But the seventh month? A blank in my mind. What had I been doing at the end of the seventh month when I should have been paying servants? July, that was . . . OH! It was in July that I started to write!

It was in July that I started to live in the book room surrounded by loose scraps of paper. My physical likeness came out to meals, and went for walks, and talked with people, and told Ah Yin what we wanted for dinner. But my mind remained in the book room, sniffing nervously, hopefully, disconsolately, excitedly, but persistently, among those fluttering papers.

"Arusap?"

"Mem?"

"Haven't I paid any of the servants their wages for three months?"

"That is right, Mem. Nobody has been paid *gaji* for three months."

"Why didn't you tell me, Arusap? I forgot about it."

"We saw that the Mem was busy writing her story.

46

Never mind, Mem. It makes no difference, Mem. I only wish to borrow five dollars to send to Kuta."

Shall we ever again be served like this?

And so we have the servant problem.

6

Life in the early days before I arrived in Borneo must have had a Gargantuan lustiness, or so it seems to me when I listen to the old-timers' talk.

"Gone are the days when we rode to the races on buffaloes, and went out to dinner in sedan chairs," says the Principal Medical Officer. "It used to cost me and my wife eight dollars to go out to dinner. We had two sedan chairs and eight *kulis,* four to each chair because we were so heavy."

"And twelve courses to each dinner," says my husband.

"I remember," says the Captain, "when everybody in Sandakan drank a man off when he went on leave, and he still owed chits for the drinks when he went on next leave."

"Men went down to office at ten, and went to the Club at eleven. Some of them couldn't sign their names before ten in the morning, and they didn't know them after six in the evening."

"What a book could be written about those days!"

Nostalgic silence. I wait hopefully.

"Most of the men were bachelors then. Ah, well, we're all domesticated now."

How truly, I thought, may the decline of all glories be laid to women, either the presence or the absence thereof.

"Speaking of the old days, Keith, where are the Murut heads that used to hang in your living room when you were a bachelor?"

"We keep them in the hall now."

"How about that big rice-beer jar that used to stand on the verandah?"

"My wife put the umbrellas in it, so I loaned it to the Museum."

"What became of your game trophies?"

"They're on the verandah now."

"This place doesn't look the way your old bachelor house used to. That was as good as the Museum. You must have had as many native weapons on your walls as there are in the whole of Borneo now."

"I say, why did you move from that other house? Nice, cozy little place it was."

"My wife liked the view from this hill."

But now that wives have found their way in it is useless to listen longer. The Gargantuan lustiness of the old days is gone.

48

3. *What Do the Women Do?*

BACHELORS say that bringing a wife out here is not even a gamble — the chances are ten to one against success. This may be a barricade behind which the eligibles crouch to avoid the onslaughts of the women, but the barricade is built upon some truth.

The men have their jobs to do, but the wives have to make theirs for themselves. If a woman does not adjust herself to the life here, to hours of solitude, and to isolation from the modern world, there is nothing to take her mind off her own discontent, and no one to hear her complaint except her husband, who soon learns to say yes without listening. There is too little to do, and it is too easy to do it.

If a woman has children their care and responsibility are to a great extent taken over by Chinese amahs. And at the age of four or five they must, in any case, be sent home to England, as there are no European schools in North Borneo and the tropical climate is not a healthy one in which to raise a family.

There are seldom more than twenty European women here, and the only unmarried English woman resident is the Hospital Nurse Matron. The rest of us all belong in one group, So-and-Sos' Wives. Being one twentieth of the white female population, each one of us comes in for considerable comment.

As men in tropical service are not eligible to marry until after eight years of duty here, our husbands, before becoming our husbands, have had this period to observe the mistakes of So-and-Sos' Wives. They have had leisure and opportunity to observe the indiscreet, irrational, injudicious, and obtuse actions which So-and-Sos' Wives always commit. Our husbands, being kind men, are anxious that their wives shall not make these mistakes, and in addition there are some new ones that they have thought of themselves. They chart a course carefully for the wife to follow, with red lights on the danger spots.

"Don't play morning bridge — it's nothing but gossip. Don't visit the women in the morning — there's too much scandal talked. Don't get mixed up with the dramatics or the music crowd; they're always having split-ups, and you don't want to get mixed up in it.

"Don't call people by their first names — there's too much quick intimacy. Don't accept invitations until you know people well; go slow at first. Don't let the women advise you about your household, or start managing your servants. Don't be motherly to young cadets or you'll be talked about. Don't go in the Club on Saturday or Sunday

— the men don't like it. Don't play games in shorts. Mrs. So-and-So looks ridiculous in them.

"And don't" (this with great emphasis) "ask Public Works Department for repairs to the house. The house is allocated to the Government servant, not to his wife, and P.W.D. has no authority to take orders from the wife."

OUR HOUSE

This last "don't" alienates the wife from her place which she had just decided, by the process of elimination, must be in the home, and at the same time elevates household repairs to the realm of diplomatic relations with a foreign power. If you want a leaky water faucet fixed or an electric light repaired you ask your husband to ask P.W.D. Your husband forgets it the first day, and you ask him the second. He has a busy day at the office and forgets it again, and you ask him the third. By then it has developed into nagging, which is annoying and inexcusable in the face of the more important things which your husband has to do. You realize this also, and early the next morning you quietly employ private labor to repair the water faucet and the light, and by ten o'clock everything is in working order.

By noontime P.W.D. men arrive at your husband's suddenly remembered instigation, and you try to explain matters to them. It seems simple to you — you did want them and now you do not. But P.W.D. has been given an order, and supplied with materials, and it is down on an official form, and unless the men carry out the commission it may take months of official communications to arrange for an orderly retreat. The best solution is to supply them quietly with another water faucet and light fixture to work upon.

But this may not occur to you the first time. You continue to try to explain to P.W.D., and at tiffin time to your husband. He then has to explain to P.W.D. that his wife changed her mind, which is embarrassing for the husband, as the wife had no place in the deal anyway, but just wormed her way in.

The mystery of it is that despite the network of cause and effect, of Government minutes and official channels, if the water faucet continues to leak and the lights still refuse to function, somehow by some subtle course of deduction the wife seems to have been to blame.

2

In the beginning I found the pattern of Sandakan social life difficult to follow: the significance attached to doing and saying the right thing irked me. To wear tails when one should wear a dinner coat, or dinner coat when it should be a sack suit, was not one of the major problems in America when I left. The men here also dislike wearing coats, ties, tails, mess jackets, but nothing except death will prevent their being found in them at the proper times. In theory this chafes me, but the result is attractive to the eye.

In justice to the Empire Builder at home, let me draw another picture. It is dinnertime. My husband wears a Malay sarong and *baju* and I am wearing *kebaya* and sarong. The heat of the day has gone and the outdoor night creeps quietly in, while we sit with bare feet and relaxed bodies looking out on the black of the harbor and drinking Bols gin. There's not much at that moment that London or Paris, New York or Chicago, could offer to entice us from our outpost.

In the daytime the men use numberless white wash suits, for which there is no substitute in a tropical climate. Women rely exclusively on wash dresses for daytime wear, as materials demanding dry cleaning must be sent to Singapore, an expedition requiring three weeks' time, and export and import customs permits. At intervals some enterprising Chinese opens a dry-cleaning establishment in Sandakan, and I optimistically experiment by sending my husband's flannels, and consequently he has no more flannels.

For evening wear we preserve from the cockroaches, the moths, the mildew, and the rot, several silk gowns. These are known among us by the occasions they have celebrated, as "the Coronation Day lace," "the Charter Day pink," and "the white I wore to the wedding."

The second year of residence here a woman begins to wear her uniform. This is the dress the Chinese tailor copies for her after the style which she brought out from home. This uniform goes through various editions in local cottons, the editions corresponding to the number of years before her next home leave arrives. By that time she is so wedded to the style that it may endure for a lifetime. I started on culottes two years ago, and am now standardized in them. They are known here as "Mrs. Keith's culottes," and I imagine that my tailor issues licenses to other users. I doubt if my fashion sense ever advances now beyond the culotte era.

Styles of the season are nothing to us. By the time we have read in the magazines what the smart women are wearing, the smart women are not wearing it. But hats destroy complacency. It is unbelievable, seeing them in magazines, that human beings wear those things. And yet after you see the new hats pictured, your own old hat looks like the kind that only Royalty can wear and get by with. Many a Borneo shelf hides a stylish hat, mail-ordered from home, that its owner has never had the temerity to wear.

Beauty culture occurs once a year when Mrs. Africa arrives from the Philippines with the permanent-wave machine. Three years ago on her first visit she had four curlers, and a permanent wave took all day, but now you can get it done in three rounds, if the electricity holds out.

The first Sandakan sitting blew out the lighting system, but the second attempt took place successfully at the rear of the especially wired Filipino barbershop, with myself as patient. It was like being operated on in a public clinic, as all the Chinese, Malay, and native children of the town

54

crowded into the open front of the shop to watch. All through the long hot hours the watchers kept their vigil, and when the time came for the patient to be wheeled out, they ran home and returned with parents and grandparents. We all came out of the anesthetic together, and looked with mutual anxiety at the result. When my hair emerged in tight pigtails a hush of disappointment swept the audience, and their eyes went in disparagement from me to the picture on the barbershop wall of the Filipina with the wavy coiffure.

I was slow at first about learning the Sandakan food regulations. I used to eat lamb without peas, roast beef without Yorkshire pudding, eggs without bacon, toast without marmalade, and I would sponsor without a shudder the mixed marriage of vegetables and fruits. I know the combinations now, can use the proper condiments, and no longer baste mutton with mustard or use Worcestershire sauce with scrambled eggs. I do not ask for sherry when I should have taken a long drink, or whiskey straight, or gin neat. But on my return to America I shall go and sit by the service door of a restaurant and watch the trays go by, where sausages mate with sauerkraut and baked beans furnish a meal and a half, where ice cream is a labor of love and lettuces have hearts and aren't ashamed to show them.

3

In Sandakan there is a game played with visiting cards. Every married woman has a small card box with her name lettered on it, planted at the entrance to her garden path. Spiders and lizards live in this box and in the wet season a very small snake, so care must be taken in opening the door not to snap off the end of the lizard's tail or flatten the snake in the hinge. At intervals, among the lizard's droppings, if you remember to open the box, various cards will appear. These you scrutinize, forget about, and some days later find under the ash tray. You then disinter your own and husband's cards, stealthily approach the friend's card box, and offer a return sacrifice to his lizards. The rule as to who drops the first card is as mystifying and inexplicable as the use of a subjunctive clause, and I have never really understood either of them. The rule has something to do with the sex, length of domicile, and matrimonial alliances of the parties involved, but the whole thing is best enjoyed if regarded as a game. The really important rule to remember is that when calling on the person you should not meet him in the flesh.

Sometimes newcomers do not understand about this game, or play it with a different set of rules in the outer world from which they come. This creates an impasse in social relations, for not until after the first round of cards can people meet in person. The impasse continues until somebody quietly hands the newcomer a printed slip containing the laws of the Medes, the Persians, and the Game of Cards.

There is a growing tendency now to modify the rules of this game, and I believe that in the near future it may be played by tangible human beings whom one sees and greets, instead of unseen robots who drop cards silently and disappear on oiled wheels along greased grooves into the cosmic vacuum.

The men play another game in Sandakan. My husband is not an enthusiastic game player — in fact it was two years before I saw him come in contact with a game, and even then he seemed to be staying as far as possible away from any of the activity. On that occasion the married men were to play the bachelors of Sandakan in a cricket match. As I had never before seen cricket, or my husband playing it, I thought I should attend.

I went down to the *padang* at ten o'clock with my best hat on, as I knew the women would be there too, and we all sat under a canopy with cold drinks, and waited for the game to begin. At least I thought we were waiting for the

game to begin. The men were on the field in smart white flannels, moving about in such a leisurely manner and with such gentlemanly courtesy and good feeling, and such apparent desire for the opponent to make the best shots, and such well-modulated remarks of "Well bowled, sir," that I, accustomed to American football, thought they must still be practising.

My husband was sitting (he says he was standing, but he wasn't) in the extreme corner of the field looking at the sky. I thought he was a substitute and waiting for his turn to come.

Meanwhile the gentlemen on the field continued to

exchange courtesies about the weather, and to applaud each other's plays, and occasionally one would trot good-naturedly off the field towards us, and we would pat-a-cake amiably. The trotting off the field was about the only violent movement there seemed to be. Every time someone retired I expected to see Harry flash nobly into the thick of the action, or what would have been the thick of the action if it hadn't been cricket. But he remained with dignity at the corner of the field looking at the sky.

As I had been warned that the game might continue all day I thought I would just walk over and ask Harry if he couldn't sit in the shade until his turn came to play. I strolled down the edge of the field to his corner, and although he seemed still to be looking at the sky he saw me out of the corner of his eye, and he looked around with disapproval at me for making myself conspicuous. Just then a ball got away from one of the quiet gentlemen who were talking about the weather in the middle of the field, and came towards Harry. But as he was looking with disapproval at me instead of the sky, the ball had the field to itself.

I went home then because apparently Harry had been playing cricket all the time, and that was what his job was, to sit in the corner of the field and look at the sky, and not, even with good cause, to turn and look with disapproval at his wife.

4. *Government House*

No story of Colonial life in the British Empire paints the picture as it is without a view of Government House standing in the shade of the trees, surrounded by a garden of English flowers, with a stretch of green turf for the tennis, with a secluded back garden for tea, and with His Excellency the Governor's wife glimpsed behind the hedge doing a bit of surreptitious and energetic digging in the garden between social events. No matter where in the British Empire the Government House may be, I feel sure it will be recognized by these features. Government House, Sandakan, is no exception.

If one paints the picture in more detail one sees, inside, rooms which are large and dignified and always made gay with flowers, tables with *Tatler*, *Punch*, the London *Times*, the *Manchester Guardian*, and the framed photographs of the children who are at home in their English nurseries. Chinese servants in long white gowns will be bustling in

with gin and bitters and whiskey and soda, and native servants in sarongs and wound headcloths will be smiling brilliantly and moving languidly, and women in flowered evening dresses will be talking about the weather, and men in
mess jackets or tails will be standing erect and presenting
a more handsome than comfortable appearance. And if
one listens at the open doors of such a gracious room there
will be heard the soft tones of pleasant voices.

The hospitality of Government House, North Borneo,
is traditional. Night after night the lights burn there, while
visitors from every part of the world meet those of us
who call Sandakan home. Meeting in this spot thousands
of miles away from our native lands, with people coming
from every direction and going in every other, we begin
to lose all sense of space or distance.

"G.H.," as Government House is more airily referred
to in private, is not only the international meeting ground,
but it is the promulgator of local social custom. Functions
at Government House are dignified and formal, and the
guests are expected to dress accordingly.

Long columns sometimes run in the Singapore newspapers to determine the exact state of public opinion in
regard to the dress-suited Briton in his Empire exile. The
advent in an English colony of some prominent American
visitor who has forgotten or discarded his dress suit and
appears at a formal function in an open shirt usually brings
up this question. In a tropical climate it is easy to relax
and be sloppy, and it seems to me that it is better to be on
the side of excess formality than the contrary. I know that
this requires an effort, for there is no use in pretending that
a dress suit in a tropical climate is comfortable, but the

result is attractive. We women have less than the men to contend with in dress discomfort.

His Excellency the Governor and his wife extend an unceasing hospitality to the Europeans of our community, a hospitality which we cannot return, as it is the accepted custom that the Governor should not dine away from Government House. The only social return which we can make is to remember to "sign in the book." At the entrance to Government House grounds is a small sentry box where may be found "the book" of the Governor and his wife. To sign one's name in this book is the equivalent of leaving cards or calling on the Governor, and one is expected to make a dinner call within twenty-four hours of being entertained at Government House. Those who do not do so are not invited again.

It is also the correct thing for all visitors to Sandakan, which is the seat of government, to sign in the book within twenty-four hours of their arrival. After this courtesy call is paid on the Governor the visitor will be invited to Government House so that his acquaintance may be made, but unless he signs in the book his acquaintance will probably not be made. It is a simple custom to conform to, and one whose benefits in hospitality received it is usually beyond the powers of the recipient ever to return.

2

In Westminster Abbey one May day a King was crowned.

"O God, the crown of the faithful; bless, we beseech thee, and sanctify this thy servant George our King: and as Thou dost this day set a crown of pure gold upon his head, so enrich his royal heart with thine abundant grace, and crown him with all princely virtues, through the King eternal Jesus Christ our Lord. Amen." [1]

And at the sight of the King's head being thus crowned the people cried, "*God Save the King*," the Peers put on their coronets, the trumpets blew, the great guns of the Tower were shot off, the women wept and prayed, and the British Empire throughout five continents echoed with the sound.

In Sandakan we celebrated the Coronation with as much enthusiasm as if we had been in Westminster Abbey, instead of nine thousand miles away. The first royal breeze came when the British cruiser *Adventure* steamed placidly into the tepid waters of Sandakan Bay. Past the silent leper settlement of Berhala she crept, picking her way among the tiny islands, and then in the early morning freshness settled peacefully at anchor close to the mainland. Her guns saluted the fort, and the fort returned the salute, and with that seventeen-gun salvo Sandakan stepped into a pageant.

The opening scene was the garden party at Government House. All those on the calling book had been invited, and as this included aborigines of Borneo, Malays, Chinese, Japanese, and Filipinos, local color poured over Government House lawn as profusely as if it had been a Hollywood set. Native chiefs had come in from all parts of North Borneo, and many a pagan head-hunter ate pink cakes and drank orange squash amidst Sutton's best bal-

---

[1] Prayer spoken by His Grace the Lord Archbishop of Canterbury, at the Coronation of His Majesty King George the Sixth, May 12, 1937.

sam and salvia which bloomed in the garden that day.

Suluk Chief Tuan Haji Abdul Samat, with rancid coco-
nut-oil-scented hair, and tight bright trousers, moved with
a rocking-horse gait on his high-heeled Malay slippers.
Penglima Sura, Chief of the Orang Sungei, who had traveled for three days down the rapids of the long river to
be present at the fete, watched with interest the passing
European pageant. Across his consumptive chest a brilliant
pinch-busted bolero was fastened by one button, and his
emaciated legs were clad in henna-colored native trousers
which fitted him like wrinkled skin. Under a headcloth of
rust and purple shone his barklike face, and his blackened
teeth showed startlingly in his blood-red betel-juice smile.
All of the natives were chewing *sireh*, with the red juice
trickling from the corners of their lips.

Of the many pairs of tight native trousers present Datu
Agasi, Suluk chief, wore the pair most precariously so. Only
a man of his courage would have dared to sit down in them.
Perhaps his impeccable black patent-leather shoes gave him
confidence.

Kiang, chief of the lazy Idahans, wore loose-wrapped
Bajau trousers which allowed him to relax comfortably,
and when he walked he moved with the confident grace
of a marauding tomcat. Old Bagat, the Murut chief, was
disappointingly dressed in khaki. His aboriginal costume
consisted only of a *chawat*, or loincloth, and this he would
not wear among Europeans. The *imam*, priest of the Mohammedan mosque, was a dignified figure among his followers, dressed in a long, flowing gray robe and a fusty-
smelling black turban. In contrast to the native groups
the rest of us looked pallid. Although the natives stayed

shyly to themselves, they looked happy and amiable and rallied with enthusiasm for refreshments, accepting the unfamiliar hospitality of European food with dignity.

The Chinese citizens of importance remained slightly withdrawn from the general festivities, forming an almost immovable, and socially unmixable, black and white frieze. Their wives, gowned with the perfection of neatness and

CORONATION DRAGON DANCE

grooming of the Chinese dress, made the European women seem overdressed by contrast.

The Coronation garden party was an event which we women had premeditated months before with the ordering of new gowns from home. During the preceding weeks our besetting topic of conversation had been, "Will my new dress arrive in time?" Apparently they all had. Certainly it was exciting to see so many new gowns all at once, and although it was difficult to examine each other without appearing to, we all managed to do so. In addition to the confidence-restoring effect of our new gowns, our conversational powers were rejuvenated by contact with the newly arrived navy personnel. It was delightful not to be struck dumb in the middle of a conversation with the realization that you had said exactly the same thing in those very words the last time you had conversed with that person.

The Seaforth Highlanders had come with the *Adventure* and they serenaded us with bagpipes, and danced the sword dance on the smooth green turf of the tennis courts. The native chiefs received even this with polite impassivity. When the afternoon was nearly over people drifted towards the Governor to be ready for the farewell line. Women adjusted their expressions and men relaxed theirs, for the strain of the performance was nearly over.

Then the ship's band struck up "God Save the King," and I found to my surprise that my eyes were full of tears and my heart was throbbing. I may not be an Empire Builder, but I discovered that day that there was something strong and real in the flood of feeling that was pouring over the British Empire on five continents, and I was proud to be engulfed by it. For even old Bagat, the Murut chief, even Haji Samat, even Kiang of the Idahans, could understand from his own tribal rule that with the birth of every ruler there comes the death of an individual. And we all shared one desire that day, to pay tribute and respect to the death of Albert Frederick Arthur George, the man, and the birth of King George the Sixth, the Ruler.

Following the garden party came a week of festivity.

Never have I seen such intensive social activity in Sandakan. Even in the backquarters of the European homes celebrations were held, and meals and drinks were brewed all night over the kitchen fires. When we would return to our bungalow after midnight we would find that our household had moved surreptitiously into the front garden and its members were looking down with an untiring admiration at the unusual fireworks and electrical display in the town below.

All week Arusap entertained six brother Muruts who had come in from their village in the interior. They all slept in his room with him, as an aftercrop of lice and ringworm attested. My trips to the backquarters were triumphal entries, with naked natives springing to their feet and saying in Malay, "Greeting, Mem," which they had been instructed by Arusap to do. We donated oddments of food to their entertainment, and I disposed of a large decanter of whiskey and sherry which had been accidentally mixed together, and for which I had long been trying to find a use. I wondered at the time if I was a wicked white woman plying the natives with drinks, but at the same time I remembered the rice beer with which I had in the past been plied by the natives, and I thought that if I could stand up to rice beer with cockroaches in it, whiskey with sherry would be mild for them.

Every night there floated up to us on the hill the mingling of many melodies from the native and Chinese town below. The skirl of the Highlanders' bagpipes, the insistent drums of the Chinese dragon dance, the plaintive thread of Malayan *keronchongs*, the throb of native chants, all these wove in and out of the staid beat of "The Land of Hope and Glory" like the glinting golden cords in a woven native cloth.

The final night of celebration came. After the good-bye dance at the Club Harry and I stopped in the cool darkness of our garden and looked down at the harbor below. The *Adventure* had not yet extinguished her fairy lights, and against the midnight background of sky and water she glowed in perfect miniature outline. An imperial crown outlined with electric jewels shone amidships.

"God save the King!" I said.

And if an American citizen, and one who by marriage is also a British subject, may with reverence and sincerity feel those words, I felt them then.

Then the lights blacked out, and Sandakan Harbor became an indigo pit. To-morrow we should again be just a far-flung outpost of the British Empire.

5. Visitors

ONE can pay back the loan of gold, but one dies forever in debt to those who are kind — so says a Malay proverb. In Borneo we must be both debtors and creditors, for there is much here which money cannot buy.

There is a hotel in Sandakan, and there is also a Government Civil Hospital. The hospital charges one dollar per day less than the hotel, furnishes better meals, offers the use of modern plumbing and the attention of nurses and doctors. It is my experience that people go to the hospital with less complaint than they go to the hotel.

When guests come to North Borneo not only their housing but their transportation usually becomes the responsibility of the people who are resident here. There are 124 miles of railroad track, including sidings and switches, in the entire state of North Borneo. This railroad connects Jesselton on the west coast with Melalap, towards the interior. There are 102 miles of metaled roads in the entire state, of which roadage Sandakan, the capital, boasts as its own about seventeen miles. Consequently we do not take buses and streetcars when we travel in North Borneo. We go in either launches or small native-manned boats up the rivers, or walk through the jungle, or if there is a bridle path, and there usually is not, we may ride small native ponies from the like of which my own feet dangle almost to the ground. These forms of travel are not only slow but they require that we transport our living accommodations with us, which necessitates the employment of native *kulis* who carry the luggage on foot. The arrangements for these carrying *kulis* are best made through the auspices of the Government, as the natives are not enthusiastic about carrying luggage even although paid to do so. Consequently the travel of visitors in the state of North Borneo is almost entirely dependent upon the coöperation and personal assistance of the Government.

Borneo is frequently visited by expeditions both popular and scientific. Until recently little scientific work has been carried out here, and the island is of growing interest to students of anthropology, ethnology, zoölogy, and geology. These visiting expeditionaries fall into two groups — those who take care of themselves, and those whom we take care of. Osa and Martin Johnson were the shining examples of visitors who took care of themselves, and who left many of us in debt to them for their kindness.

For some months whenever I opened an American pictorial I would come upon the picture of our refrigerator surrounded by Osa and seven Muruts eating ice cream. The text of the pictures would advise me that this well-known brand of kerosene-burning refrigerator had manufactured ice for the pagans of North Borneo, and added ice cream to the diet list of the head-hunters.

Retired from public life now, the refrigerator stands in our pantry and relaxes comfortably into middle-aged obscurity. It is a valued and respected member of the community, but its day for the headlines has passed. In our home it has never produced the same ice cream which it did under Osa's hand, for there isn't the same fine enthusiasm in my touch. Osa, who had a way with food, and whose camp pantry made my home godown look like scraps from the rich man's table, did things with a magnificent gesture. I have never forgotten the size of the soda biscuits from which we ate caviar, sitting on campstools in their jungle camp at Abai.

Abai Camp (known as Johnsonville) was created by the Martin Johnsons in 1935 as a headquarters for the moving pictures they made of the Borneo jungle. The camp was on the Kinabatangan River, about fifty miles from Sandakan. They cleared the jungle there and built a small village, with its own electric light plant, half a dozen bungalows, and vegetable and flower gardens planted by Osa. There the Johnsons, the film sound engineer, the airplane pilot, half the unemployed of Sandakan, and all the animals obtainable by capture or purchase in North Borneo or Malaya, spent almost a year.

The animals were everywhere, either in cages or loose, according to their supposed state of amiability. Osa was always being chewed up by various ones because she would embrace them without paying attention to the animal's mood. Osa, with her cheek against a large Siamese ape, tickling it and saying "Koochi-koochi-itsy-bitsy-muvver's baby!", telling Martin what to do about a reel of film, shouting to the cook how to mix the butter in the cake, and telling me that she was going to buy a mink coat as soon as she arrived in New York, while the ape was obviously making up his distracted mind to wallop her one — Osa was an awesome sight. She was completely without fear of the animals, and sometimes, I thought, without discretion. However, she was the one to get bitten, and she never complained.

One day at Abai they were photographing five orangutans in an artificially erected tree in camp. A boy stood beneath the tree with the end of an electric cord which was wired to carry a slight charge of electricity. When the orangutans grew restless in the tree and started to climb down, the boy would reach up and shock them with the wire. At each success the boy gained confidence and the orangutans lost it.

Finally the largest and most influential of them decided to be fooled with no longer, and began a determined descent. The boy climbed up the tree toward him, not realizing that the wire must be grounded on earth to carry the electrical charge. When he reached the orangutan he found he was tickling the angry beast with a powerless piece of wire. The orangutan pushed the boy out of the tree, and came angrily down.

We all, with the exception of the airplane pilot, ran for one of the bungalows. For the pilot the orangutan had developed a demonstrative and somewhat maudlin affection. When the pilot stood his ground and reached a hand out for the ruffled beast, the orang meekly took the hand and walked beside him with a sheepish expression on his face which seemed to say, "I just can't explain it, fellows! Love must be experienced to be understood."

The last thing I heard that night as I walked down the path from the dining house to the sleeping bungalow was Mr. Johnson calling after me, "Wait for the boy with the lantern! The hamadryads sometimes get out of their cages and sleep on the path at night."

Before the Johnsons moved the animals from Sandakan to Abai, the reptiles were kept in small cages. Word went around town that the Johnsons were buying rats to feed to the hamadryads. That night a feast was brought in, and an especially fine Borneo rat was placed in the cage of the largest hamadryad. The next morning the hamadryad was found dead with a hole eaten through his back, and the rat was alive and hearty. The cage had been so small that the reptile could not move freely enough to catch the rat.

The last afternoon the Johnsons were in Sandakan they came to our garden to try to make a sound record of the song of Anjibi, our large female ape. Martin said that he had had difficulty in obtaining a record of the song of the gibbon apes, as they will not sing in strange surroundings, or if they are terrified. Ordinarily with the coming of the first morning sun our Anjibi may be heard all over Sandakan. But that afternoon, with an opportunity to sing a song which would be heard all over the world, she sulked shyly and refused a note. I do not now know, as we have not seen Martin's film in Borneo, whether his sound track did ever produce that lovely jungle song which is so haunting and so wild.

Visitors

Osa was the most generous person I ever knew, and when she and Martin left Borneo our pantry was swollen with American delicacies of bottled watermelon pickle, maple syrup, popcorn, corn meal, California ripe olives, and Boston clam chowder, and my dressing table had Fifth Avenue beauty creams and lotions such as it had never seen before.

Martin's words were, "My time is money; I pay for speed," which is an iconoclastic idea in the tropics. Naturally they upset all Borneo standards for the treatment of servants and helpers. Martin would swear at them and threaten to beat them up at one moment, and write gift checks for them the next. When in Sandakan Osa showered clothing on the female servants; she let the amah iron in the living room and hang the washing on the front verandah; she wore a zebra-striped silk dress to Government House and stood in the middle of the drawing room there and brayed like a zebra, and everybody liked it.

The Johnsons' plane was the first to fly regularly in North Borneo. They were fearless in its use themselves, and generous in giving guest flights to the rest of us. Everything about the two of them was big, except Osa's physical stature.

They were two rare and real human beings; I think they would be recognized as such any place, and certainly they were so recognized in Sandakan.

When the word came by radio that Martin Johnson had been killed in an airplane accident his old servants came to us for verification of the news. No written tribute could have said more for him than their repeated words, "He was so good to us."

73

2

One Sunday shortly after we had received the broadcast of Martin Johnson's death I was engaged in the struggle with home mail when Arusap interrupted me to say that Saudin had returned from my country with news of its strange doings. We called him in, and Harry and I spent all morning listening to his comments about what he had seen.

Saudin is an aborigine of North Borneo, and a member of the Murut tribe of native hill people, one of the twenty-odd tribes of Borneo natives. He comes from Kampong Ambual, a Murut village in the interior which harbors about thirty of his people. Isolated from coastal contact with civilization, Kampong Ambual is self-supplying and self-sufficing. Saudin has lived most of his life in this small hamlet, where his experience of sophistication has been at worst a mild carousal induced by too much native-made rice beer during the harvest season.

A few years ago Saudin came to Sandakan, and, his reputation being excellent, he was here employed by the Johnsons to take care of the wild animals captured or purchased by them for their film. Saudin later accompanied the expedition on its return trip to the United States as a caretaker to the animals on the voyage, and remained in New York for three months in the Johnsons' charge.

When Saudin came up to our bungalow in Sandakan to tell us of his adventures in the outer world he had put away his store clothes and returned again to bare feet and singlet and brief cotton trunks. His manner retained its old native courtesy, and his attitude in presenting his tale of America

74

was that of a Marco Polo who scarcely expects his words to be believed. Saudin told us his story speaking in Malay, which is not the Murut tongue, but is the language most generally used in Borneo. For such words as "elevator" and "Central Park Zoo" we have no local equivalent, but Saudin had gathered the English words into his vocabulary with unconscious erudition.

I tell the story, as nearly as possible in translation, in Saudin's words.

Saudin Speaks

When I came to Sandakan from Kampong Ambual, I thought that Sandakan was a big place. But when I went from Sandakan to Singapore, I thought *that* was a very big place, probably the biggest place there was. At the great size of Singapore I was not surprised, because many Malays come to Borneo from there and tell much about it. Then we went from Singapore to Capetown, and that was even more mighty. So I asked men, was America as great as that? And men answered me that it was even greater. And now that I return to Borneo from America I think that Sandakan is only as big as the end of my little finger.

We left Singapore on a very big boat. White men did the work of natives on this boat, and spoke a language which was not English. We sailed to Colombo, a place I did not know of before, but a very fine place indeed, and I bought bananas and coconuts and ate them there. Then the boat sailed on again and we came to India. I did not see very much of India because the animals were sick and I was busy taking care of them. Sally, one of the orangutans, was very sick in her stomach and everything she ate came out like water, and she died. So I could not go into India, but I think it is only a small place, probably like Kudat, and that all the natives had come down to meet the boat.

After India we sailed on farther and farther, and the waves became very tall, and the captain said to tell men that a storm was coming. I saw black mountains ahead, and I said, "We are running into mountains!" But men said, "No, that is fog." And it was fog. In that fog we met a very cold climate, and taller and taller waves, and a stronger and stronger storm. The boat threw itself from side to side for many days. I was very sick, and the animals were very sick, and nine small monkeys died, and the orangutan from Kudat died, but I did not. But I was very glad when we arrived at Capetown, which is Africa.

In the distance I could see that Capetown was white and shining, and the only thing that I knew that was like that was the stone-water that white men use and call ice. So I said, "There is ice on everything there!" But men said, "No, that is the houses and the streets shining in the sun." And so it was.

Mr. Johnson took me to land at Capetown, and there the man said I could not land because I was Chinese. I said I was not Chinese, I was Malay. Then I could land. But always it was like this and men would think that I was Chinese. I never told men that I was a man of the Muruts because it seems that nobody knows about Muruts, but all people know about Chinese. So I said I was Malay because some people know about Malays.

In Capetown it was a very cold climate, and both the animals and I shivered. I had a shirt and trousers and this is a great deal for a Murut to wear, but it was not enough.

76

Visitors

Mr. Johnson asked me if I had any more clothes, and when I said no he took me to a store and bought me many clothes. He bought me shirts and trousers, and short coats, and a very long black coat which hung down to my feet and had big shoulders and was very handsome, and a hat and nine neckties. He told me that I must close my shirt and tie up my necktie around my neck when I was in Capetown, as this is the custom there. All my new clothes cost nineteen pounds, nine shillings, and sixpence.

We left Capetown and the ship sailed on until we came to Dakar, which is also Africa, but is very hot. So I said to men, "Why is it so cold in one place and so hot in another place?" And men said, "Well, because it just is that way." So I said, "Yes, probably that is just the way it is."

This time we were on the ship many days, and then we came to America. When we were going to land the customs man said to me, "You are Chinese; you cannot land." So Mr. Johnson said, "No, he is Malay, and I will send him back to Borneo in three months." The customs man said, "Can you speak English and read and write?" I said, "Yes, a little." He said, "Read this," and handed me my passport. I could not read it, but I remembered what was on it, because Mr. Johnson had told me, and so I said what was on it to the man. Then the man said, "O.K. Come into America!"

So we entered into America and went to a very great village with a thousand thousand lights. It was night when we arrived, but when I looked up at the sky above this village it was very bright and red and sparkling and there was light everywhere. And I said, "Is this morning?" And they said, "No, this is New York!"

Those Who Were Not Born There

I was so astonished by New York that I just wanted to look and look and look at it. I forgot all about feeding the animals and my work. Every night men had their names put in the sky with bright lights so that they would not be

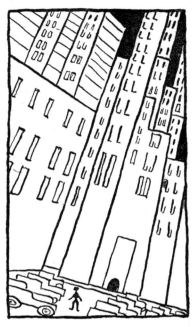

SAUDIN SEES NEW YORK

forgotten, because there are so many people in New York that it would be easy to forget some of them. All the time there was a great noise made by motorcars and buses and trains. There were trains above me on bridges, there were trains below me, and there were more trains that were below the trains that were below. Always the trains were very full of people. I think if the trains all stopped and the people got off them there would be no space in New York for all the people. So the people take turns living in the trains. I used to walk and walk because I was afraid to get on those trains to ride, as I did not know how to get off or where I should be when I did, or if I might have to live on one.

The streets were very clean. They washed and polished them every morning. I thought there could be no sickness there with everything so clean.

The buildings were very tall. Sometimes I had to go up and down in what men call an elevator. This is a little room that you get into, and very suddenly it goes up. And when it stops your stomach does not stop. But when it goes down you feel that everything has gone out of you. It is much worse than an airplane. I was always afraid in it, but said nothing, because I thought men would say, "He is just a jungle man!"

In winter there is a very cold climate in New York. Often I shivered and was cold although I wore many clothes and my handsome black coat. All men wore heavy clothes and coats like mine which hung down to their knees. But truly I was astonished at the women! They did not wear many clothes except around their necks, where they wore the skins of animals. They wore very little under this, because the wind would show me. Their stockings were just like nothing. Truly I was astonished that they did not feel cold.

In New York we put Mr. Johnson's animals in Central Park Zoo, and I went there every day to take care of them. At first Mr. Johnson went with me so that I would not be lost, and later I could go alone. But I was always afraid of the motorcars. I walked a great deal, up and down the same street and never far away, as I was afraid of being lost. At night I did not go away at all, because when lights were in the sky all things became different and I was confused.

One day he told me to go to a cinema. When I went in it was daylight, but when I came out it was dark. It was only five o'clock and in my country that is still daytime. But in New York in winter that is night time and the lights are on. When I looked up I could see nothing but very tall buildings and a red glow at the top of the buildings, and no sky. All men were hurrying from here to there, all trains made noises, all lights blinked, and I became confused. I walked and walked, but could not find the place where I lived. Mr. Johnson had written a letter for me telling who I was and where I lived in case I should be lost some day. And, as I was lost then, I looked in my coat, and was much astonished to find that the letter was lost also.

I went to a policeman and asked him how to go to Central Park Zoo, because if I could find that I could find my house, which was near it. The policeman said it was twelve blocks away, so I said, "Thank you very much," and walked on some more. Then I asked another policeman and he said nine blocks farther, and I walked some more. But the next policeman I asked said, "Here is Central Park Zoo!" And there I was at the Zoo, but I did not recognize it with the lights on. So then I found my house, which I think was very good fortune, because I had indeed been lost.

One day newspapermen came to talk to me, and they

said, "Do you like New York? What do you like the best?" And I said, "Yes, I like New York, and I like best the red electric light signs that run like streams of fire, and the lights that chase each other around like small animals."

One day I was out walking and I came to a large place with many horses in it. I said to a man with a uniform, "Can I enter?" And he said, "You must buy a ticket." I said, "I will buy a ticket. Now can I enter?" And he said, "Sure!" So I entered and I saw large and wonderful horses, and handsome men with beautiful colored uniforms. They played music and the horses danced to the music. I think the horses in New York are smarter than are the policemen in my country. So I struck my hands together the way people did, with astonishment and joy. When the playing was finished all the people wanted to leave at once in a great hurry, and everybody pushed everybody and I fell down. A man picked me up, and I said, "Thank you very much," and went home.

I went also to see boxing and wrestling. Boxing is all right, but wrestling is too rough. In my country we do not act like that unless we wish to kill men.

One day a man fell down in the streets and lay there wounded. Everybody just looked at him and walked on. So I looked at him and walked on too, because I was afraid if I stayed near him people would think that I had wounded him. Afterwards I told Mr. Johnson and he said, "People get killed here every day!"

I was out walking one day and met a man who was drunk, the same as a man is in Borneo when he drinks too much rice beer. The man said, "You are a Filipino like me!"

I said, "No, I am a Malay." He said, "No, you are a Filipino!" I said, "You are drunk. You had better go home.
Don't you know that people get killed here every day?"
But he didn't go home, and he wanted to fight me because
I wasn't a Filipino. So I ran and stood by an important man
in a uniform who stood at the door of a hotel. I stood very
close to this important man, and as he wouldn't let the
drunken Filipino come to the hotel he couldn't fight me.

Mr. Johnson took me to eat at a place where you put
money in a hole and take out a plate of food. The different
holes have names on them to tell you what foods are concealed within. We had vegetable and potato and meat all
cooked together in a flour wrapping which they call a pie.
I think this place was very cunning indeed, because the
hole to receive a ten-cent piece was so small that you could
not put in a five-cent piece, and the hole for the five-cent
piece did not answer if you put in a one-cent piece.

One time a man gave me some wine to drink. I drank a
little, and then I remembered about the many motorcars
and trains outside, the great noise and confusion, and the
people who got killed there every day. And I was afraid
I might be hit, lost, or killed if I drank any more, so I didn't
drink any more.

Mr. Johnson took me to a club where they were going
to talk to people about Borneo. When we arrived he told
me that I must stand up and talk to them in Malay. I said
that it was useless for me to do so, because they did not
understand Malay. But he said that I must speak in Malay
and then he would tell them in English what I said. I was
afraid and ashamed because there were many people there
and I am not practised in speaking to many people. But

although I shivered as with cold, I talked, and I told them about my village with only thirty people in it, which was so small that I was astonished that they wished to hear about it. And when I finished they struck their hands together to show that they were pleased, and I sat down and Mr. Johnson talked. He showed them a roll of his film about the bird's-nest caves at Gomantong, and the proboscis monkeys, and the walking fish. Afterwards people came up to me and said, "We liked what you said to-night. What did you say? Was that Chinese you were speaking? Are you Chinese?" So I said, "No, I am Malay. Thank you very much."

Mr. Jim, who used to drive the flying-ship in Borneo, was in New York too, but he did not live there. One day we flew from New York to his home in a very large flying-ship, much larger than Mr. Johnson's, with many people in it. I was not afraid because I was used to flying before, but it was very different from flying over Borneo. In my country I looked down on jungle trees and rivers of which I am not afraid, but here I looked down on buildings and trains which would be difficult to fall upon with comfort. In New York there were snow and ice on the wings of the flying-ship. It was very rough weather, the same as on our boat before coming to Capetown, and I was sick, but I did not vomit. We went many miles before coming to Mr. Jim's village, but I do not remember the name of this village. We went into his house and his people gave us food and drink. But I was ashamed to eat with them because I did not know how to eat the food cleverly as they did, because all my life in my country I was accustomed to eat with my fingers. It is difficult to carry the food with those small weapons to the mouth. I did not wish to be rude by not eating the food after their custom, so I pretended I was not very hungry, and I went to bed soon. The next day we returned to New York.

One day Mrs. Johnson came to the hotel to take me to talk to some women. I was following after her, but for one minute I looked away and when I looked back I couldn't see her. Then I saw her again and followed her until she turned upon me with anger. Then I saw it wasn't Mrs. Johnson, but a strange woman. So I feared I was lost again, but Mrs. Johnson ran after us and she said to me, "Why do you not follow me?" I said, "I thought I was following you, because this other woman looks just like you." And Mrs. Johnson looked at her and said, "Humph! I don't think so!"

For two weeks I was sick. They took me to the hospital, but I didn't stay there because I was afraid to, as people were dying there. So I got up from the bed and walked back to my house and was sick there. My bowels were like water, because I had dysentery. The doctor came to see me many times and after two weeks I was well.

One day Mr. Johnson said to me that in two days he must put me on a ship to return to Borneo. I was very sad to hear this because he was very good to me, and America was so astonishing. I cried like a child and I couldn't eat anything. First I thought that I would stay in America and work, but the next day I thought, "Well, never mind, if he says I must go, I will go."

This was the day before the New Year and he bought me a watch for a present. I went to Times Square that night to see the New York people make a holiday. There were so many people that I was frightened and wanted to return to my house. I could not return because we were like fish caught in a fish trap. Men blew things in my ears that made the noise of goats. I said to them, "Don't do that!" And they said, "Don't you like that? Don't you do this in your country?" And I said, "No!" I wanted to go home to bed, but I couldn't go home all that night, I couldn't go home until one o'clock in the morning, because it was New Year in New York and you can't go home on New Year in New York.

That was the first day of the first month, and I was sad because I had to sail for Borneo that day. Mr. Johnson took my hand and said *"Selamat belayar"* in Malay, and I said "Good-bye" in English, which I think was polite. Mrs. Johnson took me to the Dutch ship *Kota Djandi,* and I felt so sad to leave them that I forgot to take my two blankets, two pillows, and my rubber shoes, but I remembered my nine neckties and my big hat and my black coat.

So I sailed for home, and when the ship arrived at Singapore I took a letter to a man there from Mr. Johnson. The man took the letter, and after he read it he said, "Don't you know that this man is already dead? He fell in a flying-ship many days ago, and he is already dead."

And I just looked at him and I could not talk at all because I felt so sad and terrified. I could not believe that it was so. But I asked many men, and all men answered me that this was true. Then I cried like a child for two days and could not eat or sleep. And now I know my heart will always be sad for this man.

Those Who Were Not Born There

Now I will go back to my village and see my people. I will buy more buffaloes and plant more rice. When the harvest season comes I will harvest my rice, and I will drink rice beer and take a wife. But although I will live as all men do here, never will I forget America.

Part II

DIFFERENT FEET HAVE DIFFERENT WAYS

6. *A Son Is Born*

WHEN too many of Harry's stiff shirts have grown limp over tropical dinner tables, and too many polite phrases have melted from our lips over the port, we find a Spartan antidote. We remember then that the jungle is awaiting, that long rivers flow slowly down from forests where the pagans hunt, that green hills and wet valleys know only native feet, and inland plains hear only native voices. We pack our bedding, our bully beef and rice. And the only echo of words in our ears is the soft voice of Malay and Murut, and the only sound that follows us is the solid pad of the bare feet of our *kulis* behind us as we swing again onto a jungle trail.

For many years before I arrived in Borneo my husband was doing this.

Twelve years ago a strange white man crossed the Keningau plains and arrived at Kampong Pau, a small Murut village in the interior of North Borneo. Here he was received as an honored guest and made welcome in the longhouse, where he slept with the bachelors and young lads of the kampong, a sleep punctuated by the coughing and spitting of the old men about the fire and the restless scratching of the younger ones.

The white man spent several days in the hospitable atmosphere of the village. During this time he fished with some success, hunted with moderate ability, and drank rice beer with the headman with the best intentions. Invariably he was careful not to offend against Murut custom, seeming to be well informed of native taboos and conventions.

In the quiet hours over their own rice bowls the group of young khaki-uniformed natives who accompanied him were not slow in spreading stories of their master's authority. Gradually there formed itself in the mind of one of the village striplings a picture of the white man's life, a life of traveling happily from village to village, fishing, hunting, and drinking rice beer. When the white man left Kampong Pau to return to the coast, a journey of some days' walking, he did not know that in his wake followed the Murut youth, Arusap.

Arrived at the coast, Arusap presented himself to the man and explained that he had walked a hundred and fifty miles after him in order to enlist in his service. Not unnaturally touched by this homage, the white man engaged the lad as his personal boy. Thus, long before my time, began life for Arusap in my husband's household.

It must have been a disappointment to Arusap to discover that life with a European wasn't all fishing, hunting, and beer. There were long dull intervals in Sandakan when he washed dishes, flitted a feather duster gently about, and swept floors with lackadaisical strokes of the dried-grass broom. There were intervals when his pipe smoking in back was interrupted by shouts from the house for drinks and service. When Arusap finally appeared behind a tray of drinks after an interval in which he was engaged in putting on his shirt, trousers, turban, and sarong he still reeked with the strong fumes of native tobacco, but his dignity and beauty were unassailable.

Years later when I arrived these qualities of dignity and beauty were properly valued, and immediately endeared Arusap to me, and I learned not to expect too much from him in the line of energetic housework. Rather it was on our journeys through jungle and over plain that Arusap shone. Then he ceased to be just a Tuan's boy and assumed the status of a diplomat. He became an ambassador of good will to strange villages, a contact man between his master and worthy dignitaries, and a minister of the gospel of friendship and trust between the white man and the native.

He became efficient in dealing with the practical end of the journey. He was the only one in the household who could pack the camping kit without forgetting either the petrol for the lamps or the empty kerosene tins to be used to carry water. Such essentials to travel as the red-pepper sauce, the master's beer mug, and the gin were his first consideration. He ably marshaled all of the impedimenta, and then on the day of departure appeared himself dressed in a duplicate of his master's traveling costume. The year that the Tuan wore dark blue *kuli*-cloth shorts and shirts Arusap wore dark blue; the year that he switched to a khaki outfit Arusap appeared in a set of khaki topped with the Tuan's discarded Stetson hat. As I also wore shorts and shirt to match those of my husband the homogeneous appearance of our trio added to Arusap's prestige when we arrived in strange villages.

The combined firearms of the household went on these trips and Arusap usually managed to have one for his own use. As he was a better hunter than I we both realized that it was only reasonable that he should have first call upon my .22 rifle.

If the Sandakan interludes of domestic drudgery lasted too long for Arusap's patience he either asked for a vacation or resigned. Either action had the same result; he abandoned town for a few months and returned to his kampong. There he built up prestige for himself in tales of his Tuan's prowess, and drank rice beer steadily until his brown skin glowed a mahogany red. He drank rice beer through the weeks of the rice-harvesting season, and then spent the next few weeks recuperating and amassing a peace offering of gifts for us, before he returned to Sandakan.

Meanwhile Harry and I, still infuriated but no longer surprised at the faithless behavior of Arusap, would have promised each other not to take him back. But Arusap had a disarming way of returning to the house unconscious of having done anything except take a well-earned vacation. When met with splendid outbursts of vituperation from Harry, and the savage declaration that he should not enter our service again, Arusap sadly took counsel with himself. He agreed respectfully to all that was said, then unobtrusively retired to the back of the house, where the substitute boy recognized his superior claims and considered himself dismissed. The next time drinks were called for, Arusap would appear behind the tray, still reeking of strong tobacco, still dignified and beautiful, and life would resume its regular pace.

But if Harry's outburst had been very impressive Arusap went down to the town for a week or so. During this time he carried on negotiations by daily letters to the Tuan, written in the vernacular Malay which he had learned in Sandakan. These letters always stated Arusap's case reasonably. He assured the Tuan that he forgave him for his anger and that he held no hard feelings towards him. He remembered that he and the Tuan had been friends for many years and were very fond of each other. He, Arusap, was now ready and willing to resume work for the Tuan so that he might continue to serve him for many more years with the same affection and faithfulness.

The negotiations usually lasted about ten days, during which time we experienced many different states of emotion. After violent and then less violent anger, we finally arrived at recognition of the fact that, fools though we might be, we really did want Arusap back. Arrived at this conclusion it was only necessary to make Arusap the small advance in wages which enabled him to pay for his ten days' lodging in town and the household was again in running order. Or perhaps one should say walking order, as walking was more Arusap's gait.

2

On one of his vacations at home at Kampong Pau Arusap married Kuta. Of Arusap's age in years he was himself uncertain, but for several rice harvests then he had been "looking for tobacco," which is to say, seeking the company of girls. Kuta, although little more than a child, had given first evidence of womanhood, and was therefore considered to be of marriageable age.

That year the rice harvest had been large and the rice beer plentiful, and under the propitious dry skies and bright sunlight the gongs of the kampongs had boomed for days. Now the favorable half moon, which in its gentle swelling symbolized pregnancy, swung in the sky, and the month was ripe for the wedding.

The wedding gift, a generous one, for Arusap came of an honored family, was presented with suitable ceremony to the bride's father. Four ancient and valued jars, three heavy brass gongs, a blowpipe, a native dagger, a scarf with shell discs, and a buffalo were delivered to Kuta's parental home. This bride-price had come to Arusap intact, as it had been the price paid to his father by the bridegroom of Arusap's sister at her wedding. The gift had then been held prudently in charge for the benefit of Arusap when he should marry.

The ceremonial jars of rice beer for the wedding guests were filled, the fowls were killed and prepared, the preserved and rotted fish and meat were dug up and brought forth in little bamboo containers. The drinking teams, composed of the friends of the bride versus the friends of the groom, sucked thirstily upon the bamboo drinking-reeds placed in the beer jars until, from exhaustion and repletion, neither side was able to arise to its feet and declare a victory.

Then was the time for Kuta, with her twenty strings of beads about her throat, the gift of the bridegroom to his bride, to come forward and meet Arusap in the final rite which was to be symbolic of their union, the eating of rice from the same plate and the drinking of rice beer from the same great jar together. The pale bisque of her body shone in the orange light of the oil flames, and the brilliant beads swung on her bare, full breasts. The delicate moon-shaped face with the flat cheekbones was close to Arusap's as their heads met over the *tapai* jar. As her full-lipped mouth sucked on the bamboo reed she raised luminous eyes to his, then hastily, modestly, looked away. But those oblique eyes with the dark brown pupils liquid against a blue-white iris made Arusap turn a deeper red than did the rice beer.

Kuta had a small, perfectly formed body with sophisticated breasts, a bodily maturity made more entrancing by her facial childishness. She was as naturally luscious as a sun-ripe, golden-fleshed mango fruit, and as wild as the plump-chested pigeon that wings through the top of the jungle trees. And she was the only creature alive who could make Arusap hurry his dignified step.

Nevertheless in time Arusap was discontented with life at home in his village and desired to return again to Sandakan. Kuta, who had never covered her breasts in her life, who had never seen a white woman, who had never been away from her own kampong, refused to accompany him. So Arusap arrived back in Sandakan with only the memories of matrimony to solace his celibate hours.

For a number of months our household slumbered lazily in the easy tempo of Sandakan. During this time it was in the back of our minds that Arusap should have his wife with him, for a native seldom takes on that impersonality of bodiless service which in the mind of the master can emasculate a servant. Although we knew that there was probably more peace in the backquarters without an extra woman, our hearts persistently said Poor Old Arusap.

Then Harry told Arusap that the time had come to *pergi round* again. This phrase of Malay-English, literally "go around," is used by all native boys to describe their master's travels, and is accompanied by another word, *louse*, corrupted from "traveling allowance," and referring to the extra food money the boys receive. To *pergi round* and make *louse* was a delightful prospect for Arusap, and when in addition Harry told him that he would revisit Kampong Pau on his tour, our household awoke to action. I could not go this time as I was having fever, but my .22 rifle was going, and it adequately compensated for my absence.

Arusap supervised the preparation for four weeks' travel. All provisions, clothing, bedding, were packed in the tall native-made traveling baskets, and in the *bongons* of Harry's own design. Then Harry and Arusap, alike clad in khaki shorts, headed the *kuli* procession for the interior.

Traveling for two days by coast steamer to Jesselton, they then went by rail, the only rail in North Borneo, to Melalap. On horseback they followed the bridle path to Keningau, the District Station of the interior. From there they went on foot for two days, following the worn native track across the Keningau plain and through the jungle, to Kampong Pau.

The Murut villager always gives a hospitable greeting to old friends, and welcomes an excuse for a holiday interval. During the five days of their visit, Harry, Arusap, and the men of the kampong hunted wild cattle, wild pig, barking deer, and sambhur. Feasts were held daily and native dances

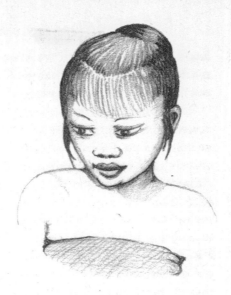

KUTA

ARUSAP

were performed. The village was in a perpetual state of celebration, everybody's belly was agreeably full, and a haze of good humor prevailed. Kuta alone of the village women remained in the background, shy and unapproachable.

Just before his party left for home Harry called together the headman, the elders, and Kuta's family, and summing up his knowledge of native custom and divorce laws he informed them that Kuta must accompany Arusap back to Sandakan. If she refused to return with him Arusap would divorce her, as he would have the right to do, for refusing to perform her conjugal duties. Furthermore, if Arusap divorced her under these circumstances, her purchase price would have to be returned to Arusap by her father. After taking counsel of itself the assembly agreed with the Tuan that this was custom, and Kuta must accompany Arusap back to Sandakan.

Although she had fought steadily against leaving the village, when the decision was once made Kuta accepted it with philosophical native resignation.

The party completed its preparations to leave. Arusap's blind old mother was led to Harry and bade him good-bye, begging him to be foster father and foster mother, brother, sister, and protector of her son. These duties Harry agreed should be his, and the party left Kampong Pau glowing with mutual esteem.

Arusap and Kuta lagged amiably in the rear together. Arusap's eyes were more dreamy than ever, his mind more abstract, his step more deliberate. When the party arrived at the first coastal town a *kebaya* was obtained for Kuta, whose clothing until then had consisted simply of a sarong wound around her waist and covering her legs. The *kebaya*, a short Malay blouse, was purchased, and Kuta strained it across her breasts and fastened it with one insecure brooch. From the prison of this brief garment important parts of Kuta seemed always to be escaping as if the small full body were struggling to be free.

Aside from the constant rebellion of her body against its clothing (which she removed at every opportunity) Kuta showed little antagonism to the civilized life of Sandakan. When an event did arouse her, however, she gave immediate and natural expression to her emotions.

From the beginning Kuta waged warfare with Ah Yin, Ah King, and Chan Yu, who was at that time our cook. The situation in the cookhouse was always complicated by racial, culinary, and hygienic differences of opinion as a result of the many persons who prepared food there. No matter how many new enamel pots and pans I purchased to be used only in the preparation of food for Harry and myself, these utensils could always be found harboring conglomerate assortments of other persons' food. Kuta's aboriginal color sense led her to appreciate the best blue enamelware, and these utensils she always used when cooking fish and rice for herself and Arusap. After they had consumed their portions for one meal Kuta left the remnants in the pot for the next meal. This habit of hers infuriated Chan Yu, whose duty it was to present clean cooking utensils for my inspection.

The feud between Kuta and Chan Yu had two stages. In the first stage Kuta paid no attention to his grumblings and mutterings. This phase might last for some time, depending on Kuta's humor. Then without warning the situation precipitated itself into the second phase, that in which

Kuta snatched up the carving knife and chased him from the kitchen. What might have happened if the cook had stood his ground and faced the violent little savage with the menacing blade was never determined because Chan Yu never did so.

During these engagements Arusap manoeuvred himself out of sight and call, as he had no desire to deal with either the cook or Kuta. After the excitement was over Arusap would be instructed to administer strong rebuke to Kuta, who by then would be in a disarming and doelike mood.

There were also occasions when Kuta retired early to bed in their small room in the backquarters down the hill. If Arusap was delayed until late to bring drinks for a party, he might find when he also retired that the door of the room was locked against him. On such occasions he silently climbed the hillside back to the cook shed and slept on the kitchen floor with the cats.

3

Above all things there were in Arusap's world to desire, he desired a son. Three times life had glowed in the womb of Kuta. And each time before the birth Kuta had prevailed upon Arusap to send her back to her village where pregnancy taboos and birth customs could be observed, and where her female relatives might administer the appropriate poundings of the abdomen and massage preliminary to childbirth.

The first time a six months' babe had been born dead. This, Kuta and Arusap reasoned, must have been owing to the fact that one night during the time of her pregnancy the fire had been allowed to die down under the house roof, and with the death of the flame the child had died in her womb.

The second time a babe was born who lived only two weeks. This death, thought Kuta, was probably due to Arusap's carelessness, for while out hunting with the Tuan he had forgotten one of the taboos which, as an expectant father, he ought to have observed — he had eaten the head of a deer. The disregard of this taboo had occasioned the baby's premature death.

The third child to whom Kuta gave birth had died after three days, and this in spite of the fact that the village midwife had cut the umbilical cord with a sharp piece of bamboo, the same piece of bamboo on which she had impaled the entrails of a buffalo, which should have given the child the strength of the animal. So Kuta and Arusap could only believe that there must have been witchcraft exercised against the child by some enemy.

Now for the fourth time Kuta was pregnant, and Arusap prayed for a son to carry the seed of his vanishing tribe. Again Kuta begged to go home to her village.

But Harry and I were determined this time, and insisted, that Arusap should forbid Kuta's return to the kampong so that the child might be born in Sandakan under a doctor's care. In his great desire for the child Arusap dared to oppose Kuta. After violent opposition Kuta once again showed a sudden philosophical acceptance of fate, and consented to remain.

Throughout her months of germination Kuta showed neither change nor maturity in her face. With her small body, her tiny wrists, her delicate little throat, and her immature face, she did not look like a pregnant woman, but rather like a beautiful child whose womb and breasts had swollen overnight into unexplainable fecundity. When she went up and down the stairs to the backquarters we all prayed silently that dogs, cats, and apes would stay out from under her feet, as her appearance threatened that the slightest jolt might precipitate the babe. But Kuta was oblivious of any worry. The larger she grew the less she moved about, the less work she did, the more time she had to lie on her mat and smoke.

Special morsels of food to which she as a pregnant woman took a fancy were brought faithfully by Arusap. Sometimes it was the sweet-sour pleasantness of a rambutan fruit, sometimes the rich, creamy kernel of a durian, and sometimes the roasted flesh of a jungle pig which Arusap must take the day off to shoot.

We were both very fond of Arusap and Kuta, and we felt bound to them by the ties of responsibility, and also by the even stronger bonds of the confidence which they placed in us. But it was not only our paternal affection which determined us that the coming child should have every opportunity for survival. We had both come to love the country in which we lived, and to cherish a dream of the preservation of its native races. Arusap and Kuta were both pure-blooded Muruts, members of a rapidly dwindling group of aboriginal Borneo pagans. There was something implicit in this coming babe, the flesh of two pagans and the blood of a dying race, something implicit that was greater than any individual.

As to the possible date of the baby's arrival Kuta and Arusap were vague. Kuta saw no importance in noting whether it was one, two, or three months since she had first evidenced pregnancy. Arusap tried to be helpful, but without Kuta's coöperation it was difficult, and his best guess was that the child was conceived at "the change of the monsoon." This guess was not borne out by her overwhelming size. But the doctor under whose care we placed Kuta from the time her condition first became noticeable said that she would in all likelihood present the household with a Christmas present.

Kuta was probably the first woman of her tribe to experience a medically supervised pregnancy and confinement. She was examined at weekly intervals by a nurse, instructed to take regular exercise, and told what to eat. Kuta was docile in the acceptance of this advice, but not in the observance of it. She continued to lie on her mat all day in a fog of cigarette smoke, and to eat only such morsels as she especially fancied from the hand of Arusap.

Her small room was cleaned and whitewashed, and a bed and mosquito net were purchased for the infant so that he need not sleep between his parents on the mat. A small tub for his bath, and a layette of diminutive bright calico *bajus* and sarongs, were supplied.

Christmas week arrived and Arusap was instructed to make no attempt at midwifery himself, but to call for help at Kuta's first moan, as the ordinary native birth is precipitate.

During the week there were a couple of false alarms occasioned by stomach-ache, the result of too much fried rice and pork. Then Christmas Eve, a dinner party, and Kuta's pains occurred simultaneously. The nurse was sent for and assured us that nothing would happen for some hours. The dinner party dawdled on over drinks. Arusap drifted about in a mental muddle. Shortly after midnight the guests left, and Harry and I and Arusap rushed to the backquarters to wait anxiously outside Kuta's room like three mutually responsible parents.

Kuta howled miserably. The light flooded out of the little room into the warm, dark night while the nurse stood in the doorway gossiping heartily. Kuta continued to howl, and the nurse continued to be cheerful, but at three o'clock she said it was time for the doctor. Despite the significant arrival of the doctor the infant took its time about actually entering a strange world, and it was almost dawn when the child emerged. But when the first tenuous thread of sound came from the lungs of the babe, and he proved upon inspection to be a son, everybody went to bed happy.

The small male form of Bayong bin Arusap was born beautiful and perfect. He sucked milk and slept, and slept and sucked milk, quite unconscious of the fact that a war was waging over his head, the war of hygiene against superstition and tradition.

During Kuta's pregnancy care had been taken to offend as little as need be against Murut customs and tribal taboos. After the birth of Bayong the doctor and nurse made small gifts to him in order to ward off possible danger incurred by their attentions, attentions which would attract the notice of an evil spirit who might harm the child.

But when it came to food and cleanliness we were determined that no compromise should be made between hygiene and tradition, *if* we could prevent it.

During the first forty-eight hours of Bayong's life the

milk did not flow to Kuta's breasts. Kuta was terrified that the child would starve, so she secretly fed him tinned milk from a long rubber feeding tube attached to an unwashed ginger-ale bottle. When we discovered this bottle lying on the floor under Bayong's bed Harry threw it out of the window into the bamboos, while I tried to explain to Kuta that Bayong wasn't really hungry yet. The next day I discovered the rehabilitated feeding apparatus again in use. This time I confiscated the bottle, tore up the tube, and warned Arusap and Kuta that if anything other than mother's milk was given to Bayong Harry would take the child away from them. Fortunately by then Kuta's milk was flowing. It was perpetually suspect, however, that morsels of a more "strength-giving" nature such as rice, pork, fish, and sweet potato crept into Bayong's diet.

In theory Bayong slept in his small bed, which stood by his mother's mat. But daily he could be found lying on the mat with Kuta, heavily shrouded under the mosquito net and almost invisible in the reeking haze of Dusun tobacco smoke. Kuta explained that Bayong would fall from the bed and injure himself, so the bed was banished and a wicker basket took its place. But Bayong still stayed with Kuta on the mat.

There was the problem of air, fresh versus fetid. Daily I went down and opened the window and door, removed the blanket from over Bayong's head, and lifted his mosquito net. I knew that this ventilation lasted only until I was out of sight, so I used to sit and talk with Kuta until Bayong had had a good breather.

When Bayong was a couple of weeks old we suggested that he should be placed outdoors daily in the early morning sun. Both parents were apprehensive about this. They feared the child would be stolen, or, if not stolen, strangers would gaze too closely upon him and attract the attention of an evil spirit who might harm him.

But Bayong continued healthy and hearty, either because of civilization or in spite of it, according to one's point of view. When only seven weeks old he was taken to the baby show at Government House. Among some three hundred infant entries of Chinese, Malays, Javanese, Indians, Filipinos, and natives, Bayong was the only Murut child. He received much attention and admiration, and a prize box of baby soap and a blue ribbon for being judged the finest native specimen in the competition. Arusap, Kuta, and Bayong remained dignified, agreeable, and impassive, accepting as their just due the plaudits of the multitude, but Harry and I were unable to hide our pride at the triumph of our joint production.

Three days later in the warm silence of the afternoon siesta hour my bedroom door flew open without warning, and Ah Yin burst in. Looking up from my book in surprise, I saw that her usually cheerful face was distorted with excitement and alarm, and she was crying as she struggled to command words in which to speak.

Ordinarily Ah Yin spoke passable English and Malay, but now in her agitation native Cantonese rushed to her lips and the chopped Chinese syllables poured out unintelligibly. Gradually into the excited Chinese flood crept Malay and English, and finally I made out the words "baby" and "sick."

Leaping from the rattan long-chair I snatched my kimono and thrust my bare toes into native sandals as I ran to the door. Down the slippery ironwood stairway and out through the food-scented cook shed, down the fifty sun-blazing steps which descended the hill to the servants' quarters, I ran.

Anguished wails guided me to Kuta's room. There in the stifling three-o'clock heat of the shanty I found Arusap and Kuta crouched on their mat over Bayong, almost covering the child with their bodies, while the tears rolled down upon his shielded form.

Shouting at them to be quiet I pulled them off the mat, and lifted Bayong, whose tiny body was swaddled in a hot damp towel. I listened for his heartbeat. A throb of heart and pulse seemed to be perceptible. His damp head lolled helplessly back and his eyes were glazed, but a warmth of breath still came from his open mouth.

Controlling the terror in my heart and forcing myself to be calm, I asked the despairing Arusap what had happened to the child. Miserable tears trickled hopelessly down his dark face as he sobbed his answer. Bayong had suddenly been taken ill at his stomach, the Chinese doctor had come and given him some medicine and then gone away, and then Bayong had stiffened out and become as I found him.

I waited to hear no more. With the child in my arms and the parents following I raced up the stairs in the torrid heat and ran through the cook shed and into the house to the telephone.

Before dialing the number I listened again for Bayong's heartbeat, but my own heart pounded so violently that I could not tell whether it was the baby's heart or mine which trembled through both bodies. Then with the child held against me and the cold sweat from my flesh bathing us both in a deathly chill I rapidly dialed the number for the doctor who had attended Bayong at his birth.

The telephone was answered by Dr. Lo Mat, his Chinese assistant, who explained that the doctor was away, but that he himself had attended Bayong that afternoon. There was nothing to be alarmed about, he declared. It was just another case of summer complaint.

"But, doctor, I tell you he's dying! He's dying in my arms!" I cried. "You must tell me something to do for him quickly!"

"Now don't excite yourself, madame," replied the cultivated voice soothingly. "It's just a stomach upset. All these native babies have summer complaint now. They will feed them improper things, you know. However, if you are worrying about the child let your boy bring him down to my office and I'll have another look. I assure you it's nothing to be alarmed about. . . ."

The soothing accents continued, but I no longer listened, for I now realized with despairing certainty that the child in my arms was dead. The little Murut's eyes, which had looked for so short a time on a friendly world, were open and sightless.

I dropped the receiver and turned to Arusap and Kuta. Wordlessly I looked into their submissive faces. In their resignation I saw what we had fought so hard to change, I saw conviction that the new world of white men and doctors was only as the old world of natives and midwives, helpless in the hands of destiny. Their son was dead. The lifeless body of the child spoke more loudly than anything I could say.

Arusap held out his arms for the child, and I laid Bayong in them.

There is little time for burial ceremony in the tropics. The damp heat with its powers of decomposition races the mourners for possession of the body.

Two Muruts, men of his own village, helped Arusap to construct a simple coffin for Bayong, and at sunset of the same day the small funeral procession struggled into the hills. On the top of a red clay ridge lay the patch of unconsecrated ground where the pagans buried their dead. Arusap and Umbul carried the coffin up the adobe hillside, and Kuta climbed after them, bringing Bayong's few possessions to lay on his grave.

As the sun went down and the distant thunder sounded, Bayong returned to the earth.

Knowing that outsiders are not welcome at a pagan burial, Harry and I watched the toiling group from another hill. When the mourners had departed we climbed the clay hillock to the grave.

Kuta's sarong was hung from poles to form a canopy over the grave, to shield Bayong's spirit from the rain on its journey to Mount Kinabalu. Bayong's small sarong was torn into strips and fluttered on poles about the mound. Thus mutilated it could not be used by antagonistic shades, but his own spirit would find the garment undamaged in the spirit world, and so make use of it.

Two small bowls of rice and water were placed near by to provide food for him on the trip. With his feet laid towards the east so that he should make no mistake in the direction of travel, Bayong was ready to set forth on his valiant journey to the kampong of departed spirits on the sacred mountain.

As I looked down silently at the bravely decorated mound, it seemed to me that here was buried not a child but a race.

All through the night Kuta wailed and moaned and wept, but Arusap had a duty before him. He must provide a funeral feast for the Muruts who had assisted him, and for anyone who approached the house in mourning. To omit the feast or to make it stingy would have been to disgrace Bayong, to bring harm to his body in the grave, and to endanger his spirit on its trip up the steep slopes of Kinabalu. All night Arusap served coffee and food, and the fires burned steadily to the sound of the pagan dirge.

Lying sleepless in bed that night with the voices of lament beating on my ears and in my heart, I pieced together into a sad sequence the events of the day. In the morning I myself had seen Bayong apparently bright and well, but after I had gone to my bedroom in the afternoon Bayong had been suddenly taken very ill in his stomach. Arusap was alarmed, but with the traditional Eastern respect for the afternoon siesta hour he did not wish to disturb me, but telephoned instead to Harry's office.

Harry then telephoned for the doctor who had attended at the baby's birth. The doctor was absent from Sandakan at the time, but his Chinese associate, Dr. Lo Mat, offered to attend Bayong in his place. Dr. Lo Mat then came to the backquarters, diagnosed Bayong's illness as summer complaint, left a bottle of medicine with Arusap, and departed without calling me.

Bayong became more violently ill, retching and vomiting.

Different Feet Have Different Ways

Arusap poured the medicine down his throat. The child gasped, and gasped again, his head rolled back, and he stiffened, and the medicine bubbled slowly out of his open mouth. Immediately Arusap and Kuta believed the child dead and squatted over him with flowing tears and Murut death wails, while the terrified Ah Yin ran for me.

Whether Bayong died in a spasm caused by gastric upset from contraband food, or whether he choked to death on medicine accidentally poured down his windpipe by Arusap, I could not decide. But I did believe that had Bayong been the child of a European the Chinese doctor would not have treated his "summer complaint" so lightly, nor would he have left the medicine in the hands of a person ignorant of the care necessary in its administration.

Arusap and Kuta had both taken oath that nothing but the mother's milk had passed the baby's lips. But I knew too much of the temptations of sweet potato, rice, and cucumber to feel certain that Kuta might not have succumbed to the native habit of popping these delicacies into an infant's mouth.

And in the minds of Arusap and Kuta the whole situation demonstrated the failure of hygiene and the white man's doctor in a battle with fate.

The following morning I called at the office of Dr. Lo Mat. As I was shown into his private office the little doctor arose to his feet with a slight bow and said quickly, "I was about to telephone you to ask how the child is to-day."

"The child is dead. He died in my arms while I was talking to you yesterday," I said abruptly.

"I am indeed very sorry, madame," the doctor answered. He did not show by his face whether the news was a surprise to him or whether, as I suspected, rumor had already informed him of the facts. "But babies die very suddenly, you know."

"So I have found out," I answered sadly. "But I cannot help feeling that if it had been a European baby he need not have died so suddenly. Doctor, do you assure me that everything possible was done to save that child?"

At the crude directness of the question the professional affability of Dr. Lo Mat's face set like a jelly pudding in a mold. The expression remained but the doctor seemed to have disowned it. "Madame," said he stiffly, "if he had been a European child he would not have been fed improper food and have become ill from it. All these natives feed their babies improper food. Every day babies are dying here with gastric enteritis. If the mother gives the infant tainted food the doctor cannot save him."

"I know they are hopeless about food," I admitted. "But no matter what caused the baby to be ill, you saw him only an hour before he died and he must have been seriously ill then. Why did you not call me? You know that Arusap and Kuta have lost three babies, and you know that we have tried to do everything possible to save this child. You know that natives are ignorant and irresponsible in the care of illness. How could you give medicine to Arusap to administer to the baby and then leave my house without any warning to me or to him of the baby's condition? Oh, I feel sure the child could have been saved with the proper care! How I hate this Eastern attitude which even you Chinese yourselves have that a European life is precious and an Asiatic life valueless!"

"Dear madame, why worry! Where three children have

been lost before why blame ourselves for the death of a fourth!"

I looked at him hopelessly.

"The natives are very shiftless, here. Perhaps it is better if they do die off and leave the country for more civilized people," suggested Dr. Lo Mat gently.

"Civilized!" I snorted. "Civilized! When all we civilized people have destroyed ourselves there will still be savages living happily in the hills of uncivilized countries!"

"That statement is not borne out by scientific facts, madame," said the little doctor urbanely.

I struggled with a desire to shout "To hell with scientific facts!" and left the office.

4

Some weeks later our household discovered itself in the second act of a polite drama of life in the tropics. The guest bedroom was temporarily occupied by the leader of a scientific expedition and his charming wife. The leader had come to study the behavior of tropical primates, and the wife was studying the behavior of other tropical primates known as lonesome bachelors.

The stage was set to demonstrate the traditional hospitality of the East, with gin and bitters and curry and quinine lending the proper atmosphere. I was giving an imitation of the efficient mistress of a well-ordered household of allegedly silent-footed Orientals. Harry tottered grimly under the white man's burden by keeping up a show of affability until long after his usual bedtime hour with a corresponding rise of bad temper in the morning.

A Son Is Born

Extra water carriers, wash amahs, and small-boys stumbled busily over each other behind the bungalow. English-speaking malcontents who had been unemployed since the last scientific expedition hung hopefully about. Shining-faced Indian peddlers who scented new blood stalked up the garden paths with their wares. The whole compound had been seething with industry, but this afternoon an ominous calm had fallen upon its erstwhile bustle.

Ever since the death of Bayong I had been watching Arusap closely, for I realized that his sorrow might formulate itself into a general resentment against the surroundings and circumstances which had to do with the baby's death. But in the excitement of new arrivals in the house I had temporarily forgotten to take note of his behavior. Watching him to-day, I saw that his broad-cheekboned face was a mask of tragedy and his shoulders were bowed with a world's sorrow. His conduct was as usual, but his being emanated tribulation, and in this aura of misery all of the compound moved apprehensively about. I recognized that a storm area engulfed us, but I hoped that the lightning would not strike until after the evening meal, for we were entertaining with a dinner party in honor of the visitors.

I was not surprised when the Sunday after-tiffin silence was broken by the amah's knock at the bedroom door. I groaned inwardly, for it sometimes seemed that the troubles of the day hoarded themselves up in order to descend upon me at this sweltering hour when my body was most loath to take action.

Ah Yin delivered a breathless and distressed message. Arusap and Kuta were leaving. They had rolled up their mats, packed a few clothes and a little food, and they were going home to Kampong Pau. Arusap was sullen and stern and even Kuta was subdued.

Ah Yin had begged them to stay. She had told them that to leave now with many people in the house was very bad. She had warned them that the master would be very angry. Arusap's answer was that fate was against him, there was witchcraft laid upon him, his child was dead of an evil curse, and he must go.

I relayed the message to my recumbent husband, who dealt with the situation by shouting loudly at Ah Yin, "Tell him to go to hell! And tell him if he goes this time he can never come back!" and then subsided philosophically into slumber.

I also realized the impotency of action. If the time had come for Arusap to return to his village, return he would.

Hidden by the curtains at the window I watched the truants descend the hill road. Arusap led the way with a bedding roll and a rattan carrying basket slung on his back. Kuta plodded at his heels with her best *kebaya* strained across her plump breasts and her brightest sarong wrapped smoothly about her little buttocks. In one hand she swung a blue enamelware kettle and in the other a basket containing Poor One, the kitten.

Some distance behind Kuta paced Ah Sim, the dog, with his tail down and dejection in every step. Close on the dog followed Usit, the Murut small-boy and fond companion of the dog.

All moved in silence. In silence they arrived at the end of the road. Here Usit and the dog stopped and Arusap continued on. The boy and the liver-colored hound stared after them in the sultry sunlight until they had disappeared. Then they turned towards home. Silently they entered the compound and silently vanished into the back-quarters.

Arusap and Kuta were journeying home. Smoking an old pipe of the Tuan's as he walked, Arusap held no rancor

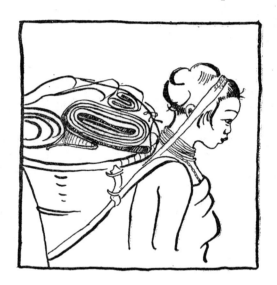

in his heart against him for his message about not returning. He knew he could leave that matter to take care of itself.

He puffed deeply on the pipe as he padded barefoot over the damp track, and his sad heart slowly began to find solace in the familiar sights. The friendly green trees about him, the occasional clearing with a palm-leaf hut, the crossing and recrossing of the river with the feel of the cool turbulent stream on his legs, the sound of wild pigeon rising startled from the trees, the crackling in the undergrowth of the timorous mouse deer, all these things which spoke of life brought life into his heart.

Until now the dead child had seemed to lie in his heart as heavily as does a dead child in a woman's womb. But in the feeling of life about him, in the beat of the sun and the smell of the warming earth, in the pad of his bare feet on the trail and of Kuta's bare feet behind him, in all these things was his heart quickening to life again.

He puffed on the pipe and he hummed a Murut chant. Soon he took the pipe from his teeth and his voice swung slowly into the drinking song of happy days of his people: —

> "As for these bodies of ours,
>   Truly we were great warriors in former days,
>   The heads lay scattered thick,
>   Have ye not heard how it was
>   In the days of old?" [1]

He puffed again on his pipe and hummed, and slowly, in his haze of tobacco smoke, sorrow, despair, and bitterness seemed to leave him. Slowly he came to know that all things adjust themselves in time, that when his village had finished the harvesting of the rice, when the men had finished the drinking of the *tapai*, when the sonorous-toned native gongs had become silent and the women had returned to work in the fields, Kuta might once more bear within her the seed of his vanishing tribe, and to him a son would again be born.

[1] Translation from Murut chant by Mr. G. C. Woolley.

7. *Sulu Sea*

Did you ever bathe in the hot blue water with your feet on a coral-reef strand, with starfish tickling the soles of your feet, with the bleached sand running beneath them, with the water melting into the sky in waves of sunshine, and your body melting into the water? Then your body has no burden, it wavers and washes in the moving of the sea, and your weightless feet, your water-washed thighs, your shadowed legs, your drifting hands, dissolve from you, and are born into the warmness and coolness and sweetness of the sea.

Every year in August we go by launch to the islands in the Sulu Sea. Off the east coast they lie — Selangan, Pababag, Penampangan, Timbun Mata, Omadal, Bod Gaya, Bakbak, Bamban, Punupunu, Mata Manuk, Sipidan, Pulau

Different Feet Have Different Ways

Babi — we go there to the islands of the Sulu Sea. Then again all words of beauty find a meaning. Then again all thought says, Men die; but these things live. And there, in the very perfection of nature, man also seems more what he ought to be.

Sometimes I dislike reading poetry — it has no sympathy with me, and says nothing to me, and I am distraught with it. Sometimes I am too crude and vulgar and bad-tempered for sweet-spoken words, and sometimes there is nothing in me that is, or ever can be, fine.

But there in the islands of the Sulu Sea I would have fine thoughts spoken with shapely words. Words that are cut and polished and set like precious stones, Tiffany words of rare workmanship used for flawless gems. There I would read an *Iliad*, and dream an *Odyssey*.

There in those islands the sun rises, and shines, and sets upon a tropical kingdom which belongs to us. There, lying on the deck of the launch, we divide the islands equally, Harry to have half and I half. Like rulers, we name our possessions.

"Bod Gaya mine. I want those tall three peaks, and the white orchids that bloom wild on the top, and the shallow hot bay where we swim."

"I'll take Omadal, with the native graves, and the phallic symbols, and the boats that are only half built, and the crescent of sand that you look across to see the sea on the other side."

"Timbun Mata mine. But it's large and you shall have half."

"You'd better have Bakbak, too, on account of the shiny blue crabs that you like so well."

Sulu Sea

All about us is the night-time blue. A yellow cantaloup moon perches upon one peak of Bod Gaya. Beneath it on the sleeping water spills a golden stream. The sky is very close and deep, and the stars are flung about most carelessly. The light flows from the stars into the water, and the ocean shimmers where the drops fall. The translucent depths of the sea are brilliant azure still above the clear coral sands. The shapes of sleepless fish are busy all the night, as may be seen by those of us who lie upon the deck and pry into the private life of tropic isles.

Thus we, two people here together, drift in the Sulu Sea.

2

Writing from Timbun Mata Island

Dumpas is waiting to lead the way. Dumpas is our river god. He arranges the tides that rise and fall in our island river. Only Dumpas can successfully navigate the *lipa-lipa* up the river from the sea to our jungle camp, and back again to the sea.

Si Budak stands behind. Si Budak does the dirty work. When nobody else will do it, Si Budak must. He is, perhaps, twelve years old, a wiry child, covered with sleek black skin and filled with iron springs and steel coils and metal organs.

Arusap is ready — Arusap, who has just been restored to our household after six weeks at Kampong Pau, and whose mood is momentarily that of the prodigal son. When Harry is not along Arusap is responsible for me, and he travels under oath not to allow me to use my own judgment.

Through the impenetrable jungle we go. Advisedly I

use the lurid word "impenetrable." I do not use it before the Accurate Mind, my husband. He would say, and rea-

sonably so, that if men penetrate the jungle it cannot be impenetrable. But when I am alone I allow myself these travel-book extravagances.

To-day Harry is away on another island exploring for a new forest reserve, so I go through the impenetrable jungle. The path leading from our camp to the river's head is a tunnel cut through primary forest growth. This tunnel is dark, low, damp, and hot, and it has every objectionable feature that a tunnel can have, except the whistle of a train behind one. Damp drops down overhead, and seeps up underfoot. I stoop often, but creepers catch my hair and clothes. *Nipah* palms cross above me, and I cannot see the sky.

We come to muddy meanderings which lead away from the river, and find that Dumpas has turned the trick again with the tide. The game is to arrive at the river before the path is under water, but not before the tidal flow will float the boat to the landing. To swim down the path in order to boat down the river is a doubtful pleasure.

On the other hand to wade through mud for three quarters of a mile before reaching the boat at low tide is even more depressing. That is so depressing, what with the stink of the mangrove mud as it sucks at my mosquito-bitten legs, and the loss of my sneakers, which are sure to remain in the mud, and the plunging of my hands into the horrid stuff when I lose my balance, that the thought of lurking crocodiles is as much a relief as a threat.

But to-day Dumpas has dealt craftily with the river tides, and we arrive at our *lipa-lipa* dry.

I lie in the bottom of the boat with bananas and dried fish, under the lovely bright sun. The lovely, lovely bright sun, I think, remembering the perpetual warm damp of our tree-buried forest camp. The beautiful, life-giving sun, I rhapsodize, expanding and stretching and drying to the very marrow, as I lie and look up at the clean early morning sky.

Si Budak, Dumpas, and I have our shirts off, I in a bathing suit and they bare-chested, and our feet are also bare. But Arusap sits with dignity on the sea, and cuddles the .22 on his knee, for Arusap is the trusted one.

"Pigeon!"

Dumpas stops paddling, Si Budak stops, and we drift. Everybody is attentive while Arusap aims at the treetops. I cannot even see what he is aiming at. He fires, and something drops from the brightness between treetops into the darkness of mangrove swamp. Dumpas paddles in the direction until Si Budak, who stands in the bow, yelps sharply and drops into the pool. He goes in like a plummet and disappears completely. Now he is up again, with the water pouring from his round black head, and the body of a wild pigeon in his hand. He squirms over the bow of the boat and plops back into it. Every little iron spring and steel coil inside his glistening body is working perfectly.

Honor is satisfied, and we need not return to camp empty-handed. Arusap continues to hold the .22, but I doubt if he uses it again. He loves to take the rifle, and taking it he must justify himself by shooting it, but only enough to justify himself into taking it again.

We reach the sea where the motorboat lies. The captain and crew, one Chinese, one Malay, have left the boat and gone to the shallows to fish with casting nets. Dumpas halloos them back, ropes the *lipa-lipa* to the stern of the boat, and throws out his fishing line. I tie my fishing line to the roof of the boat cabin. I only pretend to fish because the Bajau soul of Dumpas suffers if it sees an unused fishing line. Then I stretch out on the top of the cabin in my bathing suit. I lie on my back and look up above me. Clouds are in the sky and islands are in the sea, and islands are in the sky and clouds are in the sea, and sea and sky are one inseparable iridescence of reflections.

Never in all the aeons of time has there been such a day as this. Never in all of the lives of men has there been such a day, such an hour, such a moment, as this, I think. I am a cloud in the sky, an island in the sea, a breeze on the water, a freshness in the air. I am a girl in love, I am a woman well-wedded, I am a man adventuring, and I am a child enchanted.

I am thinking extravagantly, I rebuke myself. But this is an extravagant day.

And then a cloud above me, and suddenly comes the rain, as excessive in its violence as the day has been in its beauty. We haul the mattress into the tiny cabin. The rain beats and blows and drives on us. Dumpas and Si Budak sit in their *lipa-lipa* holding mats of *nipah* palm over their heads for umbrellas. The water pours from the black-tar head of Si Budak and shoots off his nose like a waterspout. Si Budak sheds water perfectly; he is always dripping but never wet. It must be a waterproof quality in his skin inherited from generations of Bajau ancestors who have lived on the water.

The motor put-puts back a horrid petrol odor which smells fine to-day because it is part of Robinson Crusoe's equipment. I sit and grin at my bare toes, and think how surprised Man Friday would be to see toenail paint on his island.

The rain bounces brusquely off the sea. At the stern of

the boat the Malay captain has made a bed of coals in a large iron basin. Two pots are cooking over this. One has rice — that I know without looking; the other has boiling octopus.

The rain stops. It doesn't grow less and then abate; it just turns off and the sun turns on. We anchor over the shallow coral strand where I may bathe. The water is transparent over the clean white reef. Dumpas stands at the stern and Arusap takes the bow to watch from the boat for sharks, octopus, or river-mouth crocodiles. The sandy bottom is daintily crusted with starfish, and these alone look up to see what I am doing.

In the little cabin again, I put on very short shorts and a shirt with the tail out. The tail being out marks the low point in sartorial imperfection, but it gives coolness to the stomach.

The others gather at the stern for food. Everybody eats, putting the rice in individual white shells that look like blanc de chine, and dipping into the common pot for the fish. It smells good and I am hungry. I should like to eat with them, but I distinctly hear my husband describing various possible diseases to be encountered in that common kettle. I open my hygienic tin of bully beef.

Now we are going down to the little island with the Bajau village on it that I saw the other day. How thrilling it is actually to see a little island in the distance, and then to be able to go to it! Other people go by islands and say, "How quaint! We must go there sometime." But they never do go there. And now I am going there.

We are at my little island and the motorboat anchors. There is my toy matchstick village under the coconut palms.

BAJAU KAMPONG, SULU SEA

Dumpas is going to take me ashore in the *lipa-lipa*. Dumpas takes us all ashore, the captain and crew happily abandoning the motorboat. We all have our fish to catch, our food to wangle, our evening kettles to fill, and we are full of business.

Several families of Bajau women are wading over the coral-reef shallows, in water up to their thighs. They stand silently to watch us in our *lipa-lipa*, and for a moment they are figures painted in burnt sienna on a jade, water-color sea. Then they wade on through the water and become groups of women doing their marketing on the ocean bottom.

I climb out of the boat and follow behind them. After that first interested look they do not stare. They are not surprised at me, and they are too unfamiliar with European women to see anything astonishing in the costume I am wearing, shorts and a flying-tailed shirt. It is natural to them that I should wish to follow in the shallow waters and search with them for the wealth of the sea. There is plenty there, plenty for all, and to-morrow the tide will leave more.

Their henna-red and indigo-blue sarongs are twisted tightly above their breasts, and hauled high between their legs. Occasionally a woman untwists her whole sarong, slips it loose, and then retwists it snugly.

Naked babies are tied to their backs and naked children wade with them. The children are little burnt almonds. The young women are firm-bodied, with conical breasts and nipples like young round ginger roots. The plum blush of their cheeks glows through the brown sienna. The old women have stringy arms and faces like walnuts.

Different Feet Have Different Ways

I follow the emblazoned path they are leaving behind them on the sea bottom, a ghoulish path strewn with the dead bodies of black sea slugs, black *bêches-de-mer*. A vermilion rosette of floating velvet ribbon blossoms from the middle of each dead slug. The rosette streams out in the water over the white sand bottom. I follow the ribbon-budded funeral path, and come closer to my Bajau market-women to see what they are doing.

I watch one old mother. She slides her arm down into the water and picks up a slug, rips him down the belly with her knife, and probes for a piece of sweetmeat while his crimson internals gush out. Then she tosses the embow-eled black bladder back into the sea, and the red guts trail from it, in the salt water. The black bulb lies like a beautiful, empty, ribbon-tied package.

I walk with the women now, and try to tread warily as they do among the starfish, tiny squid, and jellyfish. When a jellyfish is sighted mamma warns the children, and I take heed too, standing quite still until I locate it.

Sea snakes we find also. This is a travel-book exaggeration, for they are sea snakes only as long as they are under water. They are of all sizes, from a couple of inches to six feet in length, and they are usually a pale, best-quality jade green with opalescent rings about them. They are terrifying under water, but lift them carefully out of water on the crook of a stick and all the terror drains from them as the water flows away, and they become nothing but twisted, empty snakeskin stockings. I drop them quickly in the water again so they may recover their self-respect.

Enchanted coral gardens grow under the sea. They bloom with bright perennials, miniature herbaceous borders, blazing balsam beds, bright blue salvias, and periwinkle *petreas*. Surely the best seed of the Empire is here; surely it was catalogue-ordered long ago and Sutton himself has gardened diligently over it; surely, surely it doesn't just grow!

The occupants of these gardens are little darting fish, little blown-glass fish from art-shop windows, little fish too fragile and beautiful to be real, little fish of every hue. Watching them flash is seeing a prism turn in the sun, is looking into a spectroscope. They are enchanted and belong in these gardens; they bedizen, delight, and adorn them. I move carefully, apologetically, among them.

The Bajau women at their marketing give little attention to the unedible side of our surroundings. Old mother and I have arrived at an unspoken agreement. I am collecting sweetmeat from sea-slug rosettes for her, and she is saving the largest, clearest, and thinnest clamshells for me. This is good, this is very good indeed, we all agree.

The Bajau baskets are filling quickly. It is a good market day.

(And what have you to-day, Mr. Ocean? A nice mess of clams for Papa Lamug? Some little sweet mussels for Baby Bagat? And a bit of sea-slug sweetmeat, please — we do all like that so much! Oh, no, Mr. Ocean, not that one, nor that one, nor that one. . . . You know those are not your very best-quality sea slugs, and I am not satisfied. I shall just keep on opening them — *yes, I will pinch the fruit* — until I find the ones I want with the delicious little piece of sweetmeat down the centre. And a couple of twists of that tender, slimy seaweed for old Grandmother. She does fancy a chew of that. And just throw in a couple of squid for that lazy dog of ours. *A soup bone for Fido, please.* If it wasn't for the children I'd put him in the pot too.)

The sun comes and the rain comes, and the rain comes and the sun. The sea is clear blue glass in the sun, and then the sea is frosted green glass in the rain. The rain dries on my face and hair, and the salt dries on my legs, and my clothes dry to my body. The clouds swim over us, the sun beats on us, the brown babies cling to us, the naked children follow us, the spun-glass fish play about us.

Oh, life, this is very good of you! Oh, little girl that I used to be, what more can I ask than I have!

Dumpas comes after me with the *lipa-lipa*. Arusap says it is time to go home, and home we must go. Back on board the motorboat I return to my mattress on the roof. It is sunset now, and there is nothing left in the world but beauty. I am too small for such beauty. I only know that I give thanks to the blazing, clouded sky, the tossed-up black tropical islands, the oily, resting sea, for existing until I could see them. There is nothing in me great enough for this, but all of me that is gives thanks.

The boat bangs over an uncharted coral reef and bumps to a stop. I nearly shoot off the roof. Everybody stands up and poles and shouts and we move again. Full speed forward goes our Malay captain. Bang onto a coral reef again we go. This is like riding over a rough road on a tire-less wheel rim. Again we pole forward, again we shout, again we move, and again we bump. I think that this must be very unseamanlike navigation, but nobody seems to care.

Now we are off the reef and moving smoothly. Arusap

shoots at jellyfish which burst obligingly on the surface of the water. I hope that jellyfish aren't very sensitive to pain.

We arrive at the river's mouth, where the high tide is faithfully awaiting us. River God Dumpas has made his usual infallible arrangements. Dumpas, Si Budak, Arusap, and I cast loose in the *lipa-lipa*. In the dusk of the river's mouth they paddle very carefully among the flooded mangrove roots. Here every night near the muddy banks Dumpas sees Grandfather Crocodile. To-night he will not even let us joke about him lest he should show himself. Until we are well up the river we keep a respectful silence, not daring to mention his name.

Where the river goes dry and the path goes wet, Puasa meets us with flashlights. It is stumbling business to follow our tunnel through the jungle back to the camp by flashlight. A large monitor lizard out for an evening debauch flops off the path in disgust. A wild pig grunts in the undergrowth, and barking deer call. Si Budak slithers into a pool and is again in his native state of drippingness. Old Father River has become impatient about his delayed business, and sometimes now we wade on a flooded path. But Robinson Crusoe doesn't mind wet feet on his way home.

Through the black bars of trees the campfire greets us. Harry shouts "Ho-Ha," cookie asks if we brought something for the pot, and I ask if a new forest is now reserved.

"Was it a good day?" says Harry.

I am lying flat on my cot now, with my shoes off and my muddy feet dangling. A hot bath is cooking in the petrol tin. I smell pigeon curry. When I have the energy to stretch my arm out I can reach the cigarette tin, and if I stretch further I can reach the whiskey flask and have my little drink.

Extravagant phrases come to my mouth, and travel-book exaggerations are on my tongue.

Then I sigh happily and say, "Every day in the life of Robinson Crusoe was fun."

3

But not every night!

Our camp on Timbun Mata was cut in primary jungle, where the wild pigs had wallowed unto the third and fourth generation of them that had pig ticks.

I awoke in the middle of the restless night, scratching. Every pin point of my body crawled, the hairs of my flesh stood on end, and even my mind itched. In this condition it was maddening to listen to the regular breathing which told of Harry's sleep. He had as many pig ticks as I had, as many sand flies, and more leech bites, and it wasn't interfering any with his night's rest. He didn't even have the decency to wake up and sympathize with what I was enduring.

I grip my hysterical thoughts and say, I do not itch, I do not itch. I am very comfortable. What a nice cot I have to lie upon. Now I am going to sleep. Now I am going to sleep. Now I am going to sleep. Now I am going to sleep.

I jump out of bed and disentangle the mosquito net, feel on the floor for the alcohol bottle, pull off my nightgown and douse myself with spirits, then crawl back in bed, tuck in the mosquito net, and start counting sheep. I herd them up to the fence, and boost a couple over, and then recall having read an article which exploded the somnolent theory of sheep-counting.

Now the mosquitoes which bit me while I was out of bed are producing their own itches, and the pig ticks are burrowing again in jealous exasperation. I give up mental soothing syrup and indulge in a thorough, complete, and satisfying scratch. But scratching is only good if you are prepared to keep it up until you tear yourself to pieces, throw the pieces to the pigs, mop up the skin and hair, and call yourself a melancholy memory. To stop short of this is torture, and I am not a stoic.

I think about two possible courses. One is to be a hysterical wife, wake Harry with screams, and tell him he must get me out of this. Women do do things like that — why not I? But Harry would be such an unresponsive audience. An imagined glimpse of his face at such a performance shrivels the idea. He dislikes being awakened rudely under any circumstances, and I feel sure that his wife's sobs while she scratched pig-tick bites would not call forth the best in him at two o'clock in the morning.

I will take the other possible course and get out of this to-morrow. I will quietly and sensibly ask Harry to send me back to the mainland, and from there I can catch the steamer to Sandakan. But this is Tuesday and I have missed this week's steamer, and that means a week as uninvited guest some place, inconveniencing men who have more business here than I, being another woman who thought she could take it and couldn't. Oh, dear, why did I ever come!

But I can't stand this — hard days in the jungle and then sleepless nights. If Harry sleeps I can too. I will sleep.

I do not itch. I am very comfortable. What a nice cot to lie on. The *kulis* have no cots. And I have a nice little cot mattress, too. Damn, I'll bet the ticks are in that mattress! I'll douse it with petrol to-morrow, and the blankets too. If I can get rid of the ticks I can stand the other bites.

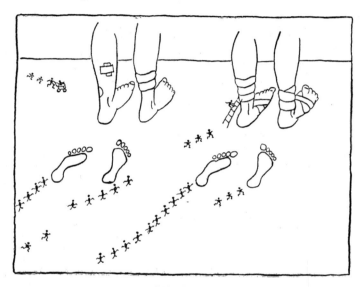

PIG TICKS

But the ticks have no respect for decency — under the arms, around the middle, up the legs, over the stomach.

I get out of bed and get a cigarette. The flame of the match is comforting. The clock face shows me three o'clock.

Harry turns over and grunts, "Time to get up? Anything the matter?"

But this is not the time to tell him.

"No, it's not time to get up."

My bites are leaking now and will probably get infected. I cannot continue with this performance night after night. I shall ask to go home to-morrow even if it hurts my pride. And once I am home I will never come in the jungle again. So that's settled, to-morrow I go home. . . .

Can it be that I have slept?

I smell coffee. Life-giving, humanizing, sent by Heaven to put hair on the chests of heroes — coffee!

"Ringgggggg!" I shout across at Harry's cot. But he already has his cigarette lighted and his socks on and is searching for his always lost garters.

I pull shorts and shirt from under the mattress where I keep them out of the night-time damp. I disentangle myself from the mosquito net. We both sit on the steps of the *sulap* [1] drinking coffee.

The jungle morning opens, and the heaviness of the night pours away into the freshness of the dawn. The weight of my sore and sleepless body lifts from me in the vigor of the coming day.

It is light enough now to see to comb my hair, and I put on a little rouge, and Harry is whistling.

"Have a good night?"

"Lousy."

"What's the matter?"

(Now is the time to say I want to go home.)

"It's those damnable pig ticks. I itch so. I think I'll not go in the jungle to-day with you."

"Tell you what, we'll both take a holiday. We'll go off on the motorboat and look for a shallow beach to bathe

[1] *Sulap* — small native-made hut, usually constructed from matting strips of screw-pine leaves, and roofed with strips of *nipah*-palm leaf.

from. The salt water will do our bites good. And there's a plot of teak on the other end of the island I want to look at, too. Come on, hustle up."

(Now is the time to say I want to go home.)

(*Eeeah!* If you go home now you're gonna miss a lotta fun. *Eeeah!*)

"Ready?" Harry calls.

"Just a moment." (There is a funeral being held for one hysterical wife.)

"Coming," I answer.

For all I know better men than I may have wanted to go home — in the middle of the night.

4

Writing from Selangan Island

And now, in one short but extravagant section I recall the ridiculous behavior of the leaves, the crabs, the sails, and the *sulaps* on Selangan Island.

As soon as Arusap lighted the petrol lamp we heard stealthy movement and persistent rustling in the fallen leaves upon the ground. I climbed down from the *sulap* and stood with the flashlight focused on the clearing. The dead leaves at the edge of the jungle were moving toward the *sulap*, undulating with a whispering voice, and surrounding us like a creeping carpet. I watched very carefully to be sure it wasn't the effect of my second gin.

"Harry, come here. If you don't see what I see I'll give up my gin forever!"

Harry, shocked perhaps by this proposal, joined me quickly on the ground, while the dead leaves crawled in on us. And then, by the simple expedient of lifting the leaves and looking, we found crabs and crabs and crabs and crabs.

They were moving curiously in toward the circle of our lamplight, probably the first bright light in their lives.

Within the hour they had all been up to see us and gone away again. Looking for them later, we saw nothing.

That night we ate too much. There were turtle eggs with sunken shells, tapioca root baked crisp like long French rolls, boiled heart of wild palm with a flavor like oysters and artichokes, *durian merah* roasted to a magnificent scarlet and tasting like chestnuts, and a roast of barking deer, and rice.

After that there was little left that we could do, or wished to do, except admire our great content and tightened stomach skins. Lying on our backs under the mosquito nets, with nothing itching for the moment, with Timbun Mata jungle camp and pig ticks left behind us, with the breeze blowing from the sea through our *sulap*, we were in luxury. The only other thing to make that luxury complete was a book. The sole remaining unread volume of the books that we had brought was Somerset Maugham's *Traveller's Library*. Harry had possession of it.

"But I want half," I said. "It's my book, too."

Harry took a razor and cut the back binding through the middle. "Here's your half," he said.

My half began with Arnold Bennett's *Old Wives' Tale*, and was a very satisfactory half.

Like that we lay under the mosquito net. And Harry quickly fell asleep, and I was nearly so, when suddenly the breeze became a wind, the wind a gale, and I looked up to see the roof blow off. The stars were there above me, and nothing else.

Again I blamed that second gin, again I called for Harry, and then, I in a nightgown holding onto the vanishing sides of the *sulap*, Harry in a sarong hanging onto the last piece of palm-leaf roofing, we cried for Arusap, Dumpas, Puasa, and the *kulis*.

More quickly than it seems such things can happen the supports of the *sulap* were swarming with the bare brown legs of rescuers. Lashing down with strips of *rotan* such *kajangs*[1] as remained as house walls, and running to the jungle after the fleeing *atap* roof, they reassembled certain pieces of the house.

Meanwhile the gale blew harder, I rescued Harry's glasses, the Leica, our garters, and any small luxuries that still remained, and crawled into my bed with them, trying to stifle my laughter and remember that this was a situation which might be serious. Above me in the *sulap* wove a network of human legs. Never have I seen so many, such good-looking, such brown and shining and active legs, in such unconventional and unstudied and innocently risqué poses. Such a beautiful tangle of masculine legs would surely save us from anything.

But fast as the men worked to get the house together, struggling to have us sheltered before the rain, that quickly the wind puffed the house apart again.

Then Dumpas the Bajau, who lived in his boat, climbed down the cliff to the shore, took the great bronze sail from off his *lipa-lipa*, climbed up the cliff again, and wrapped our little house up inside that great bronze sail.

---

[1] *Kajang* — strip of matting made from *nipah*-palm leaves.

THE SULAP THAT BLEW AWAY
SELANGAN ISLAND

A. N

Harry and I were left inside. The men crawled out, and bound the sail about the house with *rotan* strips, twisting and knotting and making all secure. With the house bound about thus in the sail, no wind could get inside; our *sulap* rocked and swayed, but held together.

"Do you think she'll blow to the Philippines, Captain?" I asked. Just then my eye fell on the gin bottle, tipped over on its side. "And don't you think, Captain, that a storm like this calls for a tot of grog?"

The Captain made no answer, but the First Mate knew what she thought. And so then the Captain, just to be matey, joined her in one.

And the gale blew, and the sail billowed, and the vessel swayed and creaked, and the next morning we awoke in Manila Bay.

So I should like to say.

But we didn't. With sails furled close, with anchor dragging and wheel lashed fast, with the Captain and the First Mate drunk in the hold, the ship rode safe through the storm and awoke to another dawn on Selangan.

A month later Harry and I board the coast steamer together. We are very brown and very thin and very healthy, and our legs are embossed with adhesive patches.

"Good morning, Mrs. Keith," says the Captain. "Did you have a good time out there on your tropical islands?"

"Wonderful. Don't we look well?"

"That you do. I always thought those little islands would be nice to go to for a holiday. I'd like to send the wife and kiddies off to one for a couple of weeks. They could have a good rest."

"Yes, indeed, Captain, just the place for the wife and kiddies. Air conditioning, modern sanitation, vacuum cleaner, sewing machine, and a circulating library being installed next year."

The Captain looked a bit confused, as well he might, and said, Well, well, he hadn't heard. And then the steamer stopped at Lahad Datu and Mrs. Tuxford came on, and she said, What fun it must be on the islands, she must go there some time. And then Miss Sawyer came along and she said, too, she must go there some time. And then the steamer sailed again and we went by more islands, and people said they would all go there some time.

But we go there.

8. *A Man of the River Goes Home*

OUR return trip from the islands usually leaves us at Semporna for a night. After the green and blue of jungle and sea, the glaring white strand of Semporna seems to strike out at me like a violent hand across the cheek, painful almost in its heat. But there is one time there, after the sun has first gone, when the scene becomes unbelievably beautiful. And perhaps because that darkening coast holds the memory of the *amok* of 1935, that sunset beauty is also sad.

The story of the *amok* of Abanawas was my first experience with the fury of the Far East. All the week-end in which Semporna was besieged by one crazed native, the news was tapped out for us in Sandakan over the grapevine telegraph system. The Timber Company launch brought word of it, the police captain wired reports from Lahad Datu, the Semporna Bajaus spread news by native boats, and the coast steamer *Kinabalu* brought back report that she dared not touch at the Semporna wharf, where her decks would be under fire. While we waited in safety in Sandakan, with the hungry gossip on our lips, the *amok* took its course.

Many times since then I have slept in that small fort, in the mosquito house which is still rusty and dark with the blood of Abanawas.

The baked Semporna strand was still hot from the vanishing sun at five o'clock that evening. The air in the small fort on the coral-reef sands was heavy and scented. The sweet

odor of buffalo, the sharp stench of drying fish, and the sick beauty of night-blooming trees hung in the motionless air like musk.

Inside the area of the blockhouse compound the prisoner Abanawas looked longingly into the Corporal's kitchen. Jijah, Corporal Dullah's wife, stood by the coals of the open fire preparing the evening fish, rice, and coffee. She lifted the lids, stirred inside the pots, and sniffed at the steaming aromas. The painted bun of her black hair shone, her bare feet made soft noises on the floor, her thin blouse showed pleasantly the shadows of her bosom.

Abanawas breathed in the seasoned tang of frying coconut oil and squid. He bent carefully and swung the tins of water which hung from his yoke to stand on the earth. The lightened yoke still fitted into the dented groove of his naked shoulder.

He stood at the door, and the ever-slumbering heart sickness awoke in him. He looked into a world where a man had a home, and the joy of food shared, where a man had the comfort and warmth of a wife.

As the water in the tins slopped into quietness Jijah turned to the door and saw him and called out to him to bring in the water at once for her cooking. The prisoner stood immovable on the threshold of Paradise, lost in the longing of a dream.

From the blockhouse behind the prisoner Corporal Dullah appeared, stepping rapidly towards his kitchen. His plaid sarong worked energetically in and out between his long legs. He saw Abanawas standing motionless in the twilight, staring at his wife.

The Corporal came closer. Still Abanawas did not move. The Corporal saw the longing on his face. The Corporal was indignant. Here was insolence and he resented it! He could afford to resent it, for he was Police Corporal Dullah! He was supreme in this fort, in Semporna! He was the white man's law! The Corporal became more indignant.

"Animal," he shouted, "do not look at my woman with dirty eyes! Empty the water and go!"

Abanawas stood stupid before him.

"Pig! Insulting swine! Empty your water and go!"

The mind of Abanawas struggled dreamily back to a swaggering Corporal.

"I do not insult the Corporal's wife," he said gently. "But I see inside the Corporal's house all that a man desires. And my heart is sick for it."

"So your heart is sick! Then here's medicine for it!" The Corporal struck the prisoner on the cheek with his open hand, and entered his kitchen to Jijah.

Abanawas stood motionless. The blow became part of his misery. Then submissively the shoulders of Abanawas bowed with the yoke, the hands picked up the tins of water and emptied them in the Corporal's water jars and returned the empty tins to the water cart. Submissively the body of Abanawas went to the barracks, entered the sleeping quarters, and sat on a cot. Here at last the mind of Abanawas took note of what had happened.

He sat on his cot in the hot close shadows with the Corporal's blow stinging his face. He thought back on his life, and in the sweet sick dusk he saw the years move clearly.

2

He saw the slow-flowing, deep-forested Kinabatangan River. He saw the hidden upper villages of its penetrating course, where native superstition had slept uneasily with the teachings of Mohammed. He saw the isolated kampongs. He saw Abanawas, man of the Orang Sungei, man of this river people.

Even the child Abanawas, running naked as at birth,

had been master of the jungle and pirate of the river. Later, when of an age to search for tobacco, to wind his loincloth and look for a woman, he wooed a wife of his own village. In all of the tenderness and violence of love he took his dark bride to their wedding mat.

By day he went to the river to fish and trap, to steal from its plenty his livelihood. By day he entered the jungle to hunt; sambhur, wild cattle, barking deer, elephant, rhinoceros — with daring and skill all might be his. And by dusk when the rays of the sun were long through the trees he turned back content. He turned back content to his home and his woman, and fierce joy and possessive pride were his in that palm-leaf shelter.

One evening in gentle dusk he padded quietly out of the trees with a fresh-killed deer slung over his shoulders. A last shaft of sunlight struck through the doorway of his hut to illumine the interior. In its pale glow Abanawas saw what he would not have believed to be true, had another man told him of it.

The shame entered his heart like the poison dart from a blowpipe, and ·Abanawas stood in the long shadows of the trees in terrible humiliation. The stiffened deer slid from his shoulders. He turned stealthily and went down to the river.

In the noisy darkness of the jungle night he sat by the river and thought. In only one way could the shame be lifted from himself and his wife. He, Abanawas, a man of the river people, had no choice in the deed which he must do. He must do what his ancestors had done, what his conscience told him to do, what his native law gave him the right to do.

He arose from beside the river, picked up his spear from the muddy bank, and unsheathed his heavy hunting knife. Then he returned soundlessly to his palm-leaf hut.

When the shame had been lifted by blood Abanawas looked down on the twisted, once lovely body of his adulterous wife transfixed to the ground by his spear. The bleeding torso and severed head of her lover lay near her. As Abanawas looked sadly down on them he knew that his action was just.

A report of the killing was made by Abanawas to the headman, whose word in the tribe was law. The headman recognized the justice of the deed, but he remembered also that any death of violence must be reported to the white men who held authority over the district. So Abanawas took his small hand-hollowed boat and paddled for two days down the Kinabatangan River until he arrived at the palm-leaf station of the native clerk.

Here he explained his deed, and prepared to go back to his village. But the native clerk told him that he must report to the District Officer. Obediently Abanawas embarked again in his slender dugout, and for two days more he paddled down the river towards the sea.

He passed unfamiliar villages drowsing on storklike legs in the mud. As the water became brackish he slid through the shadows of great *nipah* palms, and along the black-silted shore of mangrove swamps. Finally his boat slid with the river into the pale, motionless water of Sandakan Harbor, and Abanawas placed himself in the presence of the District Officer.

He explained his deed of justice; he explained that in their sin the lives of wife and lover had become a debt to fate, and that he, Abanawas, had paid this debt, and that now he waited to return to his people. But the District Officer said that the act must be judged by the white men, and that Abanawas must remain in custody until the magistrate spoke justice.

Abanawas waited many days in the unfamiliar sanitation of Sandakan jail while the magistrate studied his books. Then the voice of white law spoke. Adultery, it said, could not be punished with death. The prisoner, because he had enforced a law of his own people, had broken a law of the white people by killing.

The magistrate asked Abanawas if he had done the deed in the madness of anger. Abanawas explained that he had done this thing in sadness and sorrow, and only after thinking about it by the river's bank. The magistrate said this was a greater offense than if he had killed in anger. This was so mystifying to Abanawas that he gave up trying to understand, and just waited patiently till they should tell him that he might return to his village.

Then the law spoke its final word. Abanawas could never return to his village. He must spend the rest of his life in the custody of prison.

But Abanawas did not believe this could be true. His imagination could not envision unending captivity. Mercifully his mind never embraced the extremity of his penalty.

Season slipped into season, and back into season again, while the prisoner Abanawas stayed on in his cell. The monsoon of the north shifted into the monsoon of the south, the morning rains drifted into the evening rains, the evening rains vanished into the droughts, and the droughts vanished into the rains again. Always with the shifting of each season, with the coming of each change, with the veering of old winds, Abanawas told himself that perhaps by the next season he would be paddling up the Kinabatangan River to his kampong.

In his dreams he paddled once more his slender *gobang* against the sluggish river water. He saw again the black mangrove-shaded banks slip by, and the sharp-sworded *nipah* palms cut boldly into the sky above him. He saw again the shadow of Grandfather Crocodile slide warily onto a sunny mudbank, he saw the glittering blue mangrove crabs sprawl in the mud and the tiny land fish jump after them. And then — then it was only a dream.

And thus from dream to dream, from season to season, never quite understanding that a succession of these would make up his lifetime, Abanawas spent ten years in the prison quarters of Sandakan.

Those ten years made the body of the man of the Orang Sungei into that of the prisoner Abanawas. The beauty of glowing skin and supple muscle was gone, his feet were set in a narrow way, but his mind still lived with his people.

And then because of continued good conduct a prison board judged that he should be given the privileges of a long-term good-conduct prisoner. He was moved to Semporna, where he lived in the constabulary barracks, virtually a paroled prisoner. Here he was allotted menial jobs to do for the Indian policemen, in return for his limited freedom.

3

As Abanawas sat on his cot in the close dusk with the Corporal's slap hot on his face, the nostalgia of ten years

146

swept over him in a terrible nausea, and he leaned forward over the edge of his cot and vomited onto the floor. The nausea of spirit and body shook him with its violence, and his thoughts pounded in his head.

He was sick . . . sick of being a good-conduct prisoner, sick of being good old Abanawas, sick of getting a little handout of tobacco when he worked hard, and an extra bowl of rice because he carried water and cleaned latrines for filthy Indians. He was sick of sleeping in a bug-ridden barracks, sick of getting an occasional night free to lie with a Bajau wench in the deep grave grass under the coconut trees, only to slink back to the barracks at dawn.

All his life he had only wanted what all men want — his woman, and a home. For ten years they had forbidden these to him. And now the Corporal beat him, beat him for having a dream, beat him and called him swine. He heard again the Corporal's voice . . . "Pig! Animal! Swine!"

Slowly the illness passed from his body, but not from his brain. Physical weakness left him and was followed by strength, and with the strength came purpose.

He got up from his cot, naked except for thin cotton prison drawers, and pulled himself erect. His dark body became vital and his loosened muscles tensed. He felt no more the water carrier's yoke furrowed across his shoulders. He became again a man of the Orang Sungei, a man of the river people, a man with ten years of heart sickness behind him to wipe out.

His eyes traveled across the room and stopped at the locker door; it was there the ammunition was kept. In the rack near by stood the rifles. He unconsciously counted them and took note that all were there. True to the slackness of custom not even the sentry on duty who guarded three Javanese prisoners was armed.

Abanawas well knew that the policemen who were off duty would be gossiping over their coffee cups in the bazaar, or lolling by the football field. And Corporal Dullah was doubtless deep in his rice bowl, shoveling down fluffy kernels with his fingers, while he reminded Jijah what a fine fellow he had shown himself in smiting an insolent prisoner.

Abanawas's eye glowed with appreciative pleasure as he realized that Corporal Dullah himself, in a lazy avoidance of the nuisance of issuing and reissuing ammunition, had turned the fort over to the hands of his prisoner.

Quickly Abanawas moved towards the ammunition locker with a prisoner's heavy gardening hoe in his hands.

4

Corporal Dullah and Police Constables Hernam Singh and P. Sherzaman sat in the popular shop of Ali Merdan, the ex-policeman, and leisurely drank their coffee. Corporal Dullah uncrossed his skinny shanks inside his sarong, and scratched the annoying insect bites which kept his slender fingers always moving. P. Sherzaman, who also enjoyed the pleasant freedom of a sarong, waved one hand gently to dissipate the flies from a small yellow cake before pushing it into his mouth.

"It is good fortune indeed that men may see the approaching boat of Tuan D. O. from a distance," remarked P. Sherzaman with his mouth full. "Otherwise a man must always bear the discomforts of a heavy uniform."

A Man of the River Goes Home

"Good fortune, indeed," agreed Corporal Dullah. "When men see the launch in the distance it is then the hour to put on uniform and distribute rifles and ammunition."

"Long days before, when I was in the Sandakan police, it was not like this," continued old Ali Merdan, the shop proprietor. "Long days before we were proud to wear uniform. We were clever with the rifle and not afraid to bear its weight. And as regards a sentry without a rifle . . . *Cheh* . . . such a thing would be disgrace. But it is not now as it was, long before when there was pride in men. *Cheh!*"

"*Cheh* indeed, old man. If the old days were good, what of it! Wear uniform, carry rifles, and what now? Now you are an old package of dried bones crawling about a shop and bringing coffee for better men. *Cheh* to you, old man!" And Corporal Dullah redoubled his attack on his itching shanks.

"Nevertheless, it is not good that men should not have pride," soberly reiterated Ali Merdan.

"Never mind, old man, you yourself shall defend Semporna in time of trouble!" suggested P. Sherzaman, popping a final saffron cake into his curving-lipped mouth. "Now let us return to the barracks, Hernam Singh."

Hernam Singh, who had been amiably and fruitfully picking his teeth during the discussion, gathered his long body together, adjusted his sarong, and arose to accompany his friend.

"I linger here," said the Corporal idly, "to let this old man instruct me in the proper conduct of policemen while I drink another cup of his coffee."

Five minutes later the lazy discourse of the coffee shop

was interrupted by two sharp reports coming from the direction of the barracks.

"There is confusion in the street," spoke Ali Merdan, looking out. And even as he spoke Constable Saga Singh burst through the doorway.

"Abanawas runs amok!" he shouted. "He has killed Constable Sherzaman and Hernam Singh. He hides in the fort! He shoots at all who come!"

"By the Holy Prophet of Allah!" Corporal Dullah jumped to his feet. "The rifles and ammunition are in the fort! I must get this Abanawas!"

"But you have no rifle," protested Saga Singh; "he will shoot you also."

But the Corporal was already out of the door with his sarong scuttling about his ankles. As he ran he called back, "If my constables are dead I may as well be dead also."

"A brave man, even though a lazy one," said old Ali Merdan. "And you, Saga Singh, you are a constable. Why do you not return to get that Abanawas?"

"I am unarmed. Of what virtue is it to allow myself to be shot, old man?"

"Take action, then. I myself, Ali Merdan, only an old man and a keeper of a coffee shop, will get gun and ammunition and assist." And the old man ran from the shop.

5

Abanawas bent and squinted through the blockhouse loophole. His eyes traveled serenely beyond the sarong-clad bodies of constables Hernam Singh and P. Sherzaman which lay on the ground near the blockhouse entrance. They had been the first to appear upon the horizon of the disordered world in which he now moved. They had been a part of that ten years of heart sickness which he must erase, and in the moment when they had fallen before his rifle he seemed to find his strength.

Six loaded rifles lay beside him and four hundred rounds of ammunition. His loophole overlooked the town and shops and the approach to the barracks. The loophole on the other side of the barracks commanded the range of the customs shed and the pier. Under this lookout lay four more rifles and four hundred rounds of ammunition. Thus the blockhouse could not be approached without coming into the range of Abanawas's fire. The prisoner himself was invisible from without, while in a stooping position near the loophole. But if he straightened himself to move, his head and shoulders became visible above the half wall of the upper story of the blockhouse.

A tall racing figure sprang into Abanawas's view. Rapidly it approached, and Abanawas waited.

Jijah, who was crouching in terror in the doorway of her kitchen a chain distant from the barracks, recognized her husband. She screamed at him to take care. But the Corporal came on with his sarong flapping in and out between his running legs.

As he entered the fort compound and ran towards the door of the blockhouse he cried out to the invisible prisoner. "Put away the gun, Abanawas! If you have anger for any here it is for me alone. If I did wrong to strike you I ask your pardon for it. Do not avenge this blow on other men, or on me, for I ask your pardon for it!"

Abanawas's rifle gave answer. The Corporal screamed, clapped his hands to his stomach, and fell to the ground. Jijah shrieked and started to run from the kitchen towards him. Abanawas fired two shots above her head, and Jijah ran screaming back to the kitchen to enter and bar the door. Abanawas looked dispassionately down on the three fallen figures in the dark courtyard.

Distant patches of light shone from the shops into the main street of the town. Abanawas could see people running confusedly about. He subdued activity there with a couple of shots. He went to the loophole overlooking the customs, and cleared wanderers from the wharf with another volley of fire.

He climbed to the top of the fifteen-foot-square mosquito house which was built in the second story of the barracks for the accommodation of the District Officer during inspection tours. Lying on top of the wire house, Abanawas was concealed from the outside by the eaves of the barracks roof. He himself, peering under the eaves, was able to see the territory surrounding the fort. Here, with two loaded rifles and a number of rounds of ammunition, he decided to spend the night.

In scrambling to his position on top of the wire roof Abanawas shook a shower of rust and dirt onto the bed beneath. As he looked down at the dirtied bed he imagined the indignation of the District Officer if he could see the desecration of his sleeping quarters. Abanawas smiled to himself to think what a surprise he would have if he were in that bed now.

Lying there through the stuffy night, with his mouth dry and his stomach empty, Abanawas felt neither curi osity nor anxiety as to the resolution of his fate. He accepted without question the inevitability of his actions.

6

Ex-policeman Ali Merdan was busy all night. After the first report of Abanawas's *amok* reached him he ran to Abubakar's house and borrowed a gun with fifty rounds of ammunition.

He approached the fort, and seeing Abanawas's head move above the second-story verandah railing he took careful aim. The gun refused to fire, being of a mechanism with which he was unfamiliar, and the discomfited Ali retreated hastily.

He ran to the home of Penglima Abdullah, where he borrowed a rifle with ten rounds of ammunition. He returned to his coffee shop and climbed the stairs to the second story. Here he stationed himself at a window which was within sight and range of the blockhouse.

All night he kept an unrewarded vigil, but in the first light of coming dawn he saw a figure move above the open verandah rail of his target. He fired, and the figure dropped from sight. As the sun rose, Ali Merdan descended from his vigil to bathe and pray, and to ask the blessing of Allah on the well-placed shot of his disciple.

Inside the blockhouse Abanawas limped to his loophole and watched the sun gradually illumine the glaring expanse of blue bay water. He had placed a crude tourniquet above the wound in his upper leg which Ali Merdan's shot had inflicted. He was less annoyed by the pain than by the weakness from loss of blood.

Different Feet Have Different Ways

He limped back to the other side of the blockhouse and looked towards the town. The shop windows remained shuttered and the street was uninhabited. Already the heat of the day was settling down, and in the clearing by the barracks the swelling bodies of Hernam Singh and P. Sherzaman gave off a faint sweet stench.

With difficulty the prisoner crawled back on top of the mosquito house again.

Throughout the delirious heat of the day the scene in which he himself was the central actor became less and less real to Abanawas. There was a wounded creature who descended at intervals from the mosquito-house roof to sprinkle the town and pier with rifle fire. There was a mad-eyed apparition who took note of the approach of a Government launch in the distant glare of the noonday sun, and of the renewed activity in the town thereafter. There was a deranged, water-thirsty, suffering being who dragged himself regularly from loophole to loophole and then back to the vantage of the mosquito-house roof. This was the central figure in the Semporna *amok*, and Abanawas watched him play his part through to the end. But already the real Abanawas was beginning to move in a dream which had never known the shadeless sun of Semporna.

7

It was dusk and the shops swarmed, but always cautiously, with the police constables from Sandakan and the Police Captain himself, with the Resident and the District Officer and the doctor, with Chinese merchants and Semporna Bajaus, with almond-eyed children and with curious women.

A Man of the River Goes Home

Even the Resident and the District Officer found it not too undignified to enter and depart by the rear doors of shops, thus avoiding the risk of the open street.

The not distasteful stimulation of it all drew everyone to frequent cups of coffee and anticipatory speculations. The shop of Abubakar was hospitable to all, the shop of Ali Merdan was a rallying point, and the timber office of Imam Mohammed buzzed with excitement.

Snatches of talk were here, snatches of talk were there. Snatches of talk in Hindustani, in the staccato cadence of Bajau, in loose-voweled Dusun, and lisping Murut, and vociferous mongrel Chinese-Malay. The prisoner Abanawas had had relations with Jijah. The prisoner Abanawas had never been near Jijah. Corporal Dullah had beaten Abanawas. Corporal Dullah had not beaten Abanawas because the Corporal was too lazy to beat anyone. There was sufficient food and water in the fort to last a week. There was neither food nor water in the fort. Why had the sentry on guard not carried a rifle? Where had the Javanese prisoners disappeared to?

Snatches of talk in English. Bad show this, difficult to explain. Slack, very slack. Unarmed guards, nobody in uniform! Bloody fool of a Corporal Dullah. Where's his wife now? Crying, eh? Well, she ought to be, she's probably at the bottom of it. Take it from me, there's usually a woman behind trouble. She's a Membakut Dusun and they're a bad lot. Ah well, two bloody fools, Dullah and Abanawas! And together they are going to make a nasty mess for Somebody out of this.

Snatches of talk in the field behind Imam Mohammed's shop where the Police Captain superintends operations.

Machine-gun fire to-morrow morning. Get four-inch iron-wood logs — that's the thickness of the blockhouse — and see if the ammunition penetrates. Stand the logs against that coconut tree. Now, fire. My God, look at that log! Machine-gun fire will go through the blockhouse like a dose of salts. Look what it's done to that tree. Now we've

got Abanawas for sure. To-night, under cover of darkness, we'll place the machine gun near the compound, and at daylight to-morrow we'll tear into it. All right, men, turn in now for a couple of hours' sleep. Cheerio!

It is six o'clock in the morning and five drums from the Lewis machine gun beat into the top story of the block-house. It is seven o'clock and two drums more blaze from the Lewis gun through the heavy walls.

The dark lifeless body of the prisoner Abanawas is insensible to the tumult. Rifle and gun fire blaze again. Bullets mushroom through the walls and mutilate the quiet flesh of the huddled body above the rusty mosquito house. Now the only sound within the fort is the measured drip of blood trickling along the wooden rafters to splash on the floor below.

The prisoner Abanawas lies here.

A man of the Orang Sungei, a man of the river people, paddles slowly up the Kinabatangan River. The fresh color of dawn is on everything. The fragrance of life is in the air. A chorus of tenuous sound comes into being as the sun gives birth to the jungle morning. The mangrove-shaded banks give greeting, the *nipah* palms bow gravely overhead, the cool river waters open tenderly to the canoe, and sun and shadow, river and jungle, all things give welcome, as the man of the Orang Sungei goes home at last to his kampong.

9. Small-Boy

HERE it was the season when the heavy rains stopped; in other lands they called it springtime. After the lights were lit at night the emperor moths embroidered themselves on our walls with the profusion of fantasy, the black rhinoceros beetles bumped at the lamps, emerald cicadas snapped their joints in corners, and lizards stalked on the ceilings. And in those long, pensive evenings I seemed still to hear the small voice of Usit reading his lesson aloud in the back.

It was just one full moon since Usit had gone down the hill from our house, and had not looked back. It was four full moons since he had wept in the garden, and the *wah wahs* had sung him to peace. It was twelve full moons, and the feast days of a year, Puasa, Hari Raya Haji, Christmas, Chinese New Year, and Easter, had passed over us since that morning when Usit first stood on our verandah and stared at me with bright eyes.

I remember now how the long soul-lock of black hair

fell down on his brow that day, and how jauntily the black velvet Mohammedan cap sat on his little head. His eyes stared bravely into mine. They were as bright and dark as fresh drops of tar. His underlip stuck pugnaciously forward, and seemed to say that he was a man and he would not run, while his eyes said he was a baby and frightened.

All that week of the Coronation celebration the natives had poured into Sandakan. Barefoot they had traveled over the native tracks, by dugouts they had journeyed down the rivers, with their inky-sailed *perahus* leaning before the southwest monsoon they had cruised up the coast, coming at last to Sandakan to honor the day of the new white chief. Muruts, Dusuns, and Kwijaus, native chiefs, headmen, and elders, they had come, the pagans of North Borneo and the subjects of a king.

In Sandakan they had spread their sleeping mats wherever they found a friend. The backquarters of every house with a native boy had hosteled unbidden guests. Coffee, tea, and milk flowed direct from the housewife's shelves down the thirsty throats of the visitors.

Six brother Muruts had spread their mats in Arusap's room. The day of their arrival I had gone down to the backquarters. While a solemn, small child sat cross-legged in the corner and stared, the men arose before me. They were naked except for loincloths, and their bodies were lean and sleek. The wound black buns of their long hair shone, polished and molded with strong coconut oil. Their bright sloe eyes were inquisitive, but not rude. They spoke with dignity. They asked to know of the new white chief, speaking to Arusap in Murut, which Arusap translated to me.

"Is he greater than Tuan District Officer?"

"Is he greater than Tuan Resident?"

"Is he greater than Tuan Governor, then?"

"In many lands men honor him," I answered. "Villages in all the world make feast to-day, and drink rice beer for him. Rivers, and mountains, and valleys, and great countries, are like small villages to him."

"Then indeed this white chief is great. He is greater than we men can understand," Arusap translated.

It was one of these Muruts, the one called Rantai, who stood before us on the verandah that morning at the close of Coronation week. With him was the child who had squatted in the corner. Rantai addressed my husband.

"I ask to leave the small child Usit with the Tuan."

The small child Usit squirmed a bare foot from which one toe was missing. A wispy loincloth hid little of him, and I saw that he was thin with the thinness of an animal. There were marks of ringworm down his legs and pale patches in the mocha color of his skin.

"The child has neither father nor mother. I go to seek work and I cannot take the child. If he may live here he will work for the Tuan."

"What father and mother had the child?" Harry asked.

"His father was an Iban Dyak, Tuan, and a man of Islam faith. His mother was a Murut of my own village. Long ago the spirits of both have joined the spirits on Mount Kinabalu. In our village Usit was as a son to me. When the white men made this new chief King I left my village and came many miles to Sandakan to honor this chief. Now the great days of celebration have passed. I have

DUSUN GRANDMOTHER

DUSUN MADONNA

no money. I must go now and seek work. Will the **Tuan** keep the child?"

"What age has the child?"

"As the Englishman reckons I know not. But he is not yet of an age to carry a blowpipe, nor old enough to seek for a woman."

"I will keep the child, Rantai. I will feed him, clothe him, and care for him. He shall learn to be a Tuan's boy."

Rantai left and Usit stood alone. He stared at us for a moment longer, then he turned and padded down the verandah. I liked the way he put his bare feet down, quickly and firmly. I saw that he had the situation better in hand than we did.

Harry spoke first. "He can help Arusap bring in the drinks."

"The last thing we need is more servants to bring in more drinks."

"He can help Arusap with the housework. He can take care of the animals. And we'll take him with us when we travel, and he can learn to pack my things."

I saw that Harry's pleasure was not to be hampered by practical details. My own enthusiasm was clouded with a vision of one more dependent to whom I would feed cod-liver oil, calomel, quinine, and salts.

2

"He'll never get rid of that *kurap*[1] if he doesn't bathe. I've told him and told him he must take a bath every day.

[1] *Kurap* — a scaly skin disease.

Look at his neck, it's filthy. You'll have to do something about it, Harry."

"How many days since Usit took a bath, Arusap?"

"Twenty-three days, Tuan."

"*Mana boleh!*"

"Truly it is so, Tuan. That Usit will not bathe. Other men of his village are not dirty. I never saw any man of our village like Usit, Tuan."

Usit stood in the background, listening unabashed.

"I'll give him a bath myself this afternoon, Arusap. I want a tub full of hot water, soap, and a coconut husk to scrub him with."

Usit stood naked in the washtub and we scrubbed him with Lifebuoy soap. He was so busy trying to hide his poor little mauve penis which was hardly big enough to see that he made no resistance.

"That's Sandakan, Harry! They run naked in the villages and don't care whether it's a front or a behind. You bring them in here and they go shabby genteel."

Usit dried the dishes for Arusap. At regular intervals he appeared before me with broken pieces of china or glass in his hand. The explanation went like this: —

"I was holding very tightly to this bowl, Mem, and wiping it dry so carefully. Suddenly dog [cat, monkey, *wah wah*, squirrel, man, or amah] came running, running, and knocked into me. Immediately bowl jumped from my care and fell upon the floor. And now, see, it has broken itself!"

The explanation had a variant.

"The cat broke it."

Harry suggested that I should dock Usit's pocket money each month for breakage. I figured out that it would take two and a half years to pay for one hand-signed, emerald-green glass goblet. The only way to cover the cost of breakage was to raise the scale of Usit's pocket money. This I did on paper, and by owing him a tremendous wage for one month, and writing off the cost of the goblet against the wage, we came out even except that we did not have the goblet.

3

Through the wild grass of the gully, under the whispering bamboos, between the fiery canna beds — thus ran the trail that led from the jungle growth up to our cook shed. And there in the sun by our kitchen stood the chipped, various-sized bowls of fish, rice, and meat that fed the animals. At any hour of the day the bowls stood there, and some animal stood nosing in them. Those bowls were known from the garden's edge deep into the shade of the jungle. By a shake of the tail, by a nod of the head, by a snap of the jaws, the word had passed. Rice and fish for all, a soft corner in the godown to sleep in, and the next thing you knew you were one of the family. A soft life, and freedom to leave when bored.

Only they seldom did leave. Perhaps with animals, as with people, easy living dulled the desire for freedom. We were always glad when they came and happy when they stayed.

There was Herman, the baby gibbon ape, whose beaming eyes and ecstatic body tempted us to baby talk.

Herman lived in a friendly world of soft words, admiring glances, and loving caresses. There was Anjibi, the large female gibbon, beautiful, fey, and frightening. People did not attempt to embrace her, they stood back and asked if she would bite. And she didn't bite her friends. And there was Dishface, the orangutan, with the heartbreaking eyes and the insatiable appetite, who, like an idiot child, could never be kept in the background.

There were Niffles and Sniffles, the otters, who didn't swim when all other otters did. There was the ginger-plush loris who lived at the end of the garden and clung to her limb like a mechanical toy, and the yellow-plush "Missing Link" that the scientists called *Tarsius spectrum borneanus,* and the white moon rat with the terrible smell.

And there was the pink baby's-bottom pig that had its bath every day, and Ah Sim, the hybrid, liver-colored hound, whose escutcheon was all blots. There was the royal family of semi-Siamese cats — Thomas the libertine, Mary the indefatigable mother, and Wimbush the china-eyed trollop, and behind them, for as far as the eye could see, uncountable offspring.

All these were Usit's playmates. Through sultry afternoons when I lay unclothed upstairs in siesta and wondered when the heat would break, Usit and the animals ran in the garden. Leaping over the yellowed grass in the heat, boy stalking dog, dog stalking cat, stalking *wah wah,* stalking monkey, stalking boy, they howled for glee. Their joy never wilted in the sun, their spirits needed no siesta.

Every household, I thought as I lay and sweltered, should have something unreasonably happy in it.

4

I was aroused one afternoon by angry screams from the back garden. I knew there was only one person other than Dishface who would dare to make such a noise. I looked down from the top verandah on boy turned into satyr. The tears streamed down Usit's face so copiously that he looked like a bronze gargoyle spouting in a fountain.

"Stop that noise!" I shouted.

"I think he is crazy, Mem," said Arusap.

"Stop that noise immediately, Usit, and tell me what is the matter."

"Arusap struck me!"

"What is the matter, Arusap?"

"That Usit is a bad one! Every day he makes trouble. To-day he throws away the polish cloth, he hides the shoe-shine, he carries away the dish-wipe cloth. Many times I run after him to bring them back and he laughs and laughs. Then I sit down to clean brass and he throws rotten man-goes at me. So I catch him and strike him on the behind here. Not very hard, but the way the Tuans do their chil-dren. And he opens his mouth and makes a great noise. I think that Usit is crazy."

Arusap looked at Usit with the expression he wore when he squashed a cockroach. Usit, who had paused to listen to the explanation, then bellowed more loudly.

The amahs stood in the cook-shed door. Ah King had forgotten to throw away the cigarette she had borrowed from the silver cigarette box after tiffin. Her uncut pigtail was still wound around her waist to keep it out of the wash-tub. Ah Yin had taken off her long Chinese trousers to scrub the kitchen floor, and was in thin cotton undershorts with her round legs bare to the thigh. She looked like the good little girl who gazes with righteous disapproval at the bad little boy. Arusap stood back under the blue morning-glory trellis and washed his hands of the whole affair. Their smug looks suggested that now I would see my beamish boy for what he was. Only the immutable Husin scythed on in the garden unmoved. Nothing disturbed Husin except to be short of cow-manure soup for his orchids.

"Stop that noise before the Tuan comes home," I commanded.

I was still fastening my culottes, into which I had hastily jumped when I heard Usit. Between shouting and buttoning I got Usit quiet and myself clothed. But when I disappeared to get my shoes Usit began again. Everybody on the hill would hear him. I saw the story beating its way from door to door about the Keiths' small-boy that they just couldn't do anything with! Usit was still in the garden spouting tears when Harry arrived for tea.

"Leave it to me. I'll deal with him. This is a tantrum."

With relief I continued my dressing. I remembered guiltily some tantrums of my own childhood, and hoped Harry wouldn't be too severe. Anyway, the howls were stopping.

Some minutes later I went to the tea table at the end of the garden. The *wah wahs* lived there in a wire house built around two trees. The squirrels lived in the trees above them and raced in and out of their cages, and stole the papayas and cucumbers, and rebuked the *wah wahs* when they sang too passionately in the early morning sun. The ginger-plush loris lived there too, on a branch of the little tree under the *wah wahs.* Her baby lived in her fur, and looked like nothing at all but an extra pair of eyes. They slept all day; Arusap said it was so they could stay awake at night and play with the spirits.

There was such excitement there now that even they were awake, and the mother loris had eaten her evening egg and blubbered it down her chest. Harry and Usit stood inside the cage, hand in hand. Usit's nose needed blowing and his chest still heaved.

Herman was brachiating recklessly from trapeze to trapeze; his timing was perfect and his dives were death-defying. Anjibi swung in long, jealous horizontal arcs, trying to distract attention from Herman. Mother loris did a series of ringside acrobatics, while baby loris squeaked with excitement as she gyrated beneath her. The squirrels who had come in to rebuke the debauchery stayed on for the fun. I waited to see the little dog laugh and a cat run away with a spoon.

And then Herman, who has the soul of Pagliacci, executed the *coup de grace;* he dropped on Usit's shoulder, put loving arms about his head, and sang. My husband left them then, and came out to me for his tea.

All very touching, I thought, but it gets us no place with the question of discipline.

"I think the best thing we can do is to send Usit to the Malay vernacular school. That will keep him out of the way in the mornings at least, and save a little of the glassware from being broken."

There was a pensive child pictured on the cover of the Malay School Reader, Story Number One. The child sat cross-legged in his sarong, and wore a figured *baju* which fell naïvely from his slender shoulders. The black velvet of his Malay cap bound his young forehead, and his eyes looked up to wisdom. This pensive child was not Usit.

I dressed him up like that the first morning, but when he came home from school at tiffin time he wore blue shorts and a football jersey. He had traded his sarong and *baju* for them.

"Why did you change your own clothes for these?"

"At school all boys dress like this, Mem. A boy must dress as other boys do."

"Do you like school?"

"No, Mem."

"Why not?"

"At school a boy must sit too much. Also all boys there have friends. I have no friends."

"What do you do beside sit?"

"The schoolmaster gives us tin milk to drink. Also a man sells papayas and bananas. To-morrow I must take three cents and buy fruit as other boys do."

Usit learned very quickly. Every night he sat on the table in the cook shed, reading aloud his lessons from the Malay reader.

"The father chicken crows and struts about;
The mother chicken sings and lays an egg."

Usit had noticed that himself.

"The man from Java sells *sati*,
The man from Bengal sells bread."

True enough! The man that wrote that lesson evidently knew.

"This boy Buyong likes very much to play football;
Every day he goes down to the *padang*."

This lesson was Usit's favorite. Did not all boys like
to play football?

"*Si-Bu-yong sa-ngat su-ka ma-in bo-la* . . ." His voice
sang it out while he tapped with his heels the rhythm. The
Malay *keronchong* record crooned with him, the gongs
throbbed it faintly across the bay, and the frogs in the
garden barked it back. "*Si-Bu-yong sa-ngat su-ka ma-in
bo-la*."

Shortly after Usit commenced going to school a new
small-boy appeared in the background.

"Who is that, Arusap?"

"This small-boy has come to do Usit's work."

"Cannot three men do the work here?"

"It is good to have small-boy for some kinds of work.
Small-boy can bring bundles from the market, and clean
the shoes and the brass, and do whatever the Mem desires."

It was obvious that the household was to continue to
support one leisure member in the person of Arusap.

"Who pays this small-boy?"

"Ah Yin and Ah King and I."

I understood that I was here supposed to be conscience-
stricken at the thought of my overworked household, and
offer to pay the salary of the second small-boy.

"Very well, if Arusap and Ah Yin and Ah King want
small-boy they must pay him."

I heard loud jubilee in the garden that afternoon. Usit
and number two small-boy were playing football. They

had a fine afternoon. The next day number two was discharged by the backquarters.

Ah Yin, Ah King, and Arusap shook their heads sadly over the problem of ourselves and Usit. Why we were keeping a small-boy and not making him work they did not understand. They could only put it down to an inherent simple-mindedness they had suspected in us before.

In an effort to spare my glassware I had removed dish wiping from Usit's sphere of activity. After several Bristol-Milk-Sherry tragedies I also said he was not to be sent on errands which involved breakables. Finally as an apologetic gesture toward neatness I emancipated him from housecleaning.

5

Four full moons passed, and it was not a time of perfect peace.

"Where is the Shrimp to-night?" Harry asked one evening at dinner.

"He disappeared after tiffin, and he hasn't been home all afternoon. He spends most of his time in the town now," I answered.

"Little devil! He'll get into trouble down there."

"Yes, but I don't blame him for going. We would have gone too, at his age, if our mothers and fathers had let us."

"Well, I'll not have him staying out all night. It's nine-thirty now. Arusap, what does Usit do in Sandakan after he finishes school?"

"Sometimes he goes to the pictures, Tuan. Sometimes he

goes to the Chinese theatre. Sometimes he goes to the boxing."

"Where does he get the money to do this?"

"He goes to Government House in the afternoons to run after balls from the game of tennis. The Tuans give him fifteen cents."

"Didn't he come home to-night for his food?"

"That Usit no longer eats here. Day by day he gets his share of the food money from Ah Yin, and when he finishes school he goes to the coffee shop and buys his food there. Then he goes with his friends to play on the *padang*. He only returns to the Tuan's house to carry in the Tuan's dinner for him, and later on to sleep."

"Apparently he doesn't even do that any more. I'll attend to him to-morrow."

Then I said something I had been thinking over for some time.

"We can't keep Usit like a pet any longer."

"But I thought you liked having him!"

"I do. But not this way. We must either give him time and attention and discipline, and make a good job of it, or send him back to village life. Sandakan is bad for him. And I'm afraid I'm too lazy to take on the job of being a parent again."

For a long time then we sat looking into the flaming flower bouquet in the middle of the table, while the ants came out of the crimson canna lips of the flowers and crawled down their stems till they met the water in the bowl, and then turned around and crawled back up again.

Finally my husband said, "Yes . . . yes, I suppose so. With your own kid it's different, you've got no choice.

. . . I'll find out where Rantai is and send Usit back to him."

All the next week it hung over me. Always I reasoned it through. Life in Sandakan wasn't doing him any good. Vernacular school education at best could only offer a minor clerical job. Better for him to go back to his village again and be just a Murut boy. I reasoned it through. But I felt it through differently.

Harry ascertained that Rantai was working as head *kuli* for our own Swiss friend, Dr. Wenk, known to us as Wee Winki, the Oil Company geologist. He was at Winki's jungle camp, sixty miles up the Kinabatangan River, and well away from the night life of Sandakan. Harry sent a message by boat to Rantai that he wished to send Usit back to him.

When Wee Winki came into town once a fortnight for supplies he used to come up and talk about Switzerland with us, and try to forget that he was lonely. He told us that he always had the Swiss flag flying at his camp. It wasn't a militant patriotism. It was a simple feeling like the one that makes you take the same old hat whenever you travel. Winki had young blue eyes, and his skin was blond-suntan, and he was a very fine ambassador for the Swiss nation.

We were sitting eating waffles, with the hot, black sugar-palm syrup irrigating the little squares, and sometimes seeping through and dripping down our chins.

"Winki, will you take the Shrimp out to Rantai at Tambisan with you this trip?"

"You do not want the Shrimp any more?"

"He's ahead of us, Winki. Spends all his time in the

dives of Sandakan. I'm expecting him to bring home his wife and child any time. The town is not good for him. I want to get him out of it."

"Yes, I take the Shrimp."

"And Winki, will you take a kitten too? A distinguished Siamese, by Thomas out of Wimbush, best features of both parents inherited?"

"Yes, I take a kitten."

"Do you really like kittens, Winki, or are you just being amiable?"

"I like kittens. They make the jungle more like home."

The last morning Usit stood before us. He was plumper now, but still small, still of a patchy mocha color, and there was still ringworm on his legs. His underlip stuck boldly forward. I thought that it trembled, then I thought it didn't. His very beautiful black eyes looked at me, for that moment as pensive as the child on the Malay reader.

His worldly goods had increased. He had a pocket now in his meagre pants, and money in his pocket. He had a plate, a cup, a cooking pot, and rice, a tin trolley car, a slate, books, and his football, a sleeping mat, mosquito net, and blankets. It was a lot for a Murut child to possess.

"Do you wish to go out to the jungle to Rantai? . . . Or do you wish to stay with us?" my husband asked him.

"It is as the Tuan wishes," he answered. And again it was Usit and not ourselves who had the situation in hand.

I followed Usit's figure down the hill with my eyes. I watched until he was only a swaggering shape. He didn't turn to look back. I knew that he wouldn't, but I wished that he had.

173

Different Feet Have Different Ways

A picture stood on the table by us of our little girl at home in her party dress. She took piano lessons, and had a wrist watch and a stamp collection. Her round face smiled, and her underlip was sweet and quiet. She also liked to go to the pictures. When my eyes ceased following Usit they came home to her picture. But I could not see it very clearly for the salt in my eyes.

10. *Their Private Lives*

WHEN I left home one bright autumn day and traveled across the waters for six weeks to a land on the other side of the world, I cut loose from many affections. At first I dwelt on returning to those affections, but after living in the new land for four years I came to know that some of the dearest of those attachments would not be there to return to, and that nothing returned to is ever the same. And in the new land I learned also that the bones of affection are slow to form, and, in any case, human attachments are numbered.

Perhaps the reason that our animals have never been kept in their place is because their place in our lives has ceased to be that of animals. For true it is that every living thing that has wandered up to our hilltop has come in time to be joined by almost consanguine ties to the kindred life of our household.

The capture of gibbon apes is forbidden by law in North Borneo, as the mother is usually killed in the capture of the baby, and the possession of such apes in captivity must be licensed by Government. When apes are illegally captured they are confiscated by Government and sometimes placed in the custody of my husband, who is a game warden. These baby apes, when once separated from their mothers, cannot be turned back to the jungle until grown to a size to take care of themselves, and when ours are grown they will not leave us. For apes who live with people come to show an intense craving for human affection and companionship, and seem quite happy in captivity when they receive these.

2

Jojo

That love may only be experienced between human beings was once my pedantic conviction. Jojo changed my mind about this.

He was my first ape in Borneo. Whether it was love or lust with which his being thrilled, I never challenged, for it created in him some great rapturous sensation which made the world a very desirable place in which to live, and one peopled by extraordinarily pleasant creatures who were, in his mind, all there to make him happy. Jojo's capacity for affection was such that not to have given it to him would have been as brutal as to have beaten him.

He lived in freedom in and out of our house, spending his lesser moments in the tops of mango trees, but always ready to come when I called. When I stood on the top verandah and called "Oooooh? Oooooh?" he would come from far trees, swinging and dropping from mango to jack fruit to *chiku,* and then through the burning crest of the flame-of-the-forest, his black face pushing through the crimson flowers like a Golliwogg lost in the garden of Proserpine. As he neared me he would make small answering noises of infinite delight until, in that last moment be-

JOJO

fore he flung himself into my arms, he was the very soul of ecstasy embodied in the fur coat of an ape.

When I would read upstairs in the afternoon he would lie for hours on the bed with me, taking his ease. Jojo taking his ease was the easiest ease that is taken. He would lie on his back with one leg cocked over the other, and one arm tucked under his head, and the other reaching out and plucking gently at my hand if I stopped stroking him.

As he was my first ape, our wedding presents were still intact. With a human curiosity Jojo would surreptitiously pick them up and look on the bottom for the price marks, and if what he found was not to his satisfaction, as apparently it frequently was not, he dropped the gifts scornfully, thus clearing the house of surplus ornamentation. Table lamps with trailing cords were his idea of indoor trapezes. Jojo would swing his way through the house on the artistic effects, and the indirect lighting system which I had installed suffered in consequence.

There were other things he could not learn in one ape's lifetime, and one day he had a very sad experience. He tore up some of Harry's Murut vocabulary. It was the sort of thing that might have happened to him, or to me, new as we both were to the sanctity of scraps of paper, but an ape can be thrown out of the window, and a wife cannot. While Jojo was describing that graceful sweeping arc in the air from the library window to the garden below, Ah Yin and I were racing to catch him. While in the air he nipped his little tongue between his teeth, and when he lit in Ah Yin's arms one small drop of blood came on his lip. We wiped this blood away on Ah Yin's blouse, and then we three mutually indignant creatures retired from the esoteric sight of learning to grumble at intolerant man. At teatime that day, when Jojo would take his cake from my hand only, it was cutting rebuke to all angry writers of Murut vocabularies.

There was also the sad case of the lipstick, a new one,

poppy-red, ordered from the United States and waited three months for, and expected to make of me what nature failed to make. I left it uncapped in my open drawer while I went down to answer the telephone. That lipstick could not possibly have been to Jojo's stomach what it was to have been to me. And when he ran to meet me with the lipstick clotted in his fur and oozing thickly from his lips, facetious comment on the well-groomed woman, I almost beat him. But of the many mean, unkind, and unjust actions that there are in my life to be ashamed of, that, I am glad to say, was not one of them.

When I studied Jawi, which is Malay written in Arabic characters, with old Ismail, Jojo always sat on the arm of my chair with his arms wound around my neck like a feather boa. Ismail, who did not like our animals and thought them unseemly in the household of a European, dropped many hints which we all disregarded. But Jojo knew that Ismail did not like him, and at intervals Jojo would arise and stand on the desk with his back to Ismail, then bend over with his bottom in the air towards him, twist his head and catch his eye and say "Oooh! Oooh!" and then sit down again.

This was known among *wah wahs* as the Retort Discourteous, a Borneo edition of the Bronx cheer, and was reserved by them as a sign of disapproval. Like two black mushrooms side by side, shiny and always very neat — such was the bottom of our Jojo. That Ismail should have been pleased by the sight of such a well-finished bottom, much superior doubtless to his own, was our opinion, but not, judging from the uneasy actions of Ismail, his.

At that time we were keeping four apes for Martin

179

Johnson in a wire house in the garden, and Jojo would sit on the lawn outside their cage and tell them the household gossip. His attitude was that of the eldest son who owns the manor, but is being condescendingly gracious to transient guests of uncertain status.

One of the visiting apes wore a threadbare flaxen union suit of fur, from which his long black hands and wrists came reaching out as from the shrunken sleeves of winter underwoolens. His black elbows protruded through the light fur as if they needed patching, and his black neck and face above the fuzzy underwear had the vulnerable look of a man without his collar. He was impressed with Jojo and sat close to the wire to listen, but the two rose-beige male Siamese apes known as Wilde-and-Friend were interested only in themselves, and sat all day entwined in each other's arms, picking at each other's fur and other less mentionable things. The smallest, blackest, youngest, and wisest ape pretended that he didn't give a damn for anyone, and would swing and swing and swing, then suddenly drop down by the flaxen one and make a blasphemous comment on the situation which would tell you that he had been listening to the whole conversation.

Although Jojo took food from a basin in the kitchen, he always sat on the arm of my chair at mealtimes, and accepted selected dainties. He was careful in his manners and took tiny bites with a discriminating air, and if I gave him quickly what he was eyeing he would not snatch for it. The quietest mealtime solution was to involve him with a chewy caramel at the beginning of the meal.

Once a day we fed him cod-liver oil, and combed his silky fur, and bathed him in warm-water suds. And as his belly grew round, his actions grew precocious, and his body throbbed with love and well-being, and we all came to recognize that he was indeed the young scion of the household.

And then most embarrassingly one day he developed diarrhoea. Of all ailments for a house-proud ape to have, that is the most humiliating. For three days we dieted him, fed him castor oil, tried to assist nature in every way we knew, while Jojo grew weaker and weaker. All he could do was to lie on a chair with a rubber sheet under him and ask us to Please Excuse.

He could retain nothing in his stomach. I tried him with milk, Ovaltine, Bovril, beef tea, chicken broth, and the gruel from rice which Arusap made, and then brandy to help his heart, which scarcely seemed to throb. At first he opened his mouth for my tiny spoon; and then he could not swallow and the liquid ran from his mouth onto his silky fur; then he could no longer open his mouth, and his round potbelly was shrunken in, and his black hands fell on his chest, and his shiny face was cold, and his eyes said Don't Bother Please. And Jojo was dead.

I had not known, before having Jojo, that people felt like that about animals. I had not known that the tissue-paper relationships of society were transparent and thin, but the feeling of man for animal was body and bone and pain.

I did not go out to the visiting *wah wahs* for some time after Jojo died. When I went again he of the threadbare flaxen union suit still needed an elbow patching, the rose-beige Wilde-and-Friend still twined in each other's arms, were still doing nasty things in a nice way, and the smallest, blackest, youngest, and wisest *wah wah* continued to swing and swing and swing.

But there was a subtle change. Gone was the air of polite subservience. The scion of the house was dead. Had Jojo worn shoes and left them behind him, the visiting *wah wahs* now seemed to say that there was no reason for waiting longer before they stepped into them.

3

Anjibi

Anjibi and I have not much longer now to be dear friends, for an ape walks alone when humans begin to fear her.

For a long time now in her increasing power and wildness she has been too much for everyone except myself, but she and I have always had an understanding which allows us to see only virtue and comeliness in each other. We bring out such fine qualities in one another that the deviltry that may be found in either of us with unwise treatment is a surprise even to ourselves.

Three years ago when I first saw her she had no friend in all the world, or so she thought. She was cowering in the corner of our room and waiting for the blows to fall. As I approached her there she made herself smaller and smaller as one who would by very will power disappear before my eyes, and when at last I gently stroked her, she bared her teeth in a soundless extremity of terror.

Slowly I touched her, slowly I picked her up, and slowly I made her know that whatever the terror was that she had known, it was no longer there. I kept her with me all that day, carrying her about, letting her sit with me, bathing her, combing her fur, and talking to her of the things we seemed to understand. I did that several days, and that was all I did, but ever after that she knew me as her friend. It was as if she had found just one thing in the world in which she could believe.

The sores of her body were many when she first came to us, and it was obvious that she had been badly treated by the Chinese *kulis*, in her former captivity in a timber camp. The fur was rubbed off her neck from the tight rope that had chafed it and the skin was raw and bleeding, her hands were cut and sore, the fur of her body was patchy and sparse, and her emaciated stomach caved in beneath her ribs. For all of this we knew what to do, and the ills of her body we happily remedied. But the scars of her mind, and the memories that whispered to her of fear and of flight, she could never forget. She never knew the ecstasies of our Jojo, or any tender affection for persons other than myself. She knew instead that she was woman and born to weep and cry. She snatched her favors hurriedly and never looked for more.

She would have nothing to do with any man, or with the Chinese amahs in their trousers. Harry wooed her most assiduously, but her flight in terror from him to me was a slap in the face of the suitor who pleaded for a smile. To me she came for everything — to protect her from the cruelty there was not, to understand her for the female that she was.

It was flattering to me to have Anjibi thus, but it entailed responsibility as she grew up. I was the only one who could keep her off the dinner table spread for guests, who could

lead her to the godown where she slept, who could entice
her away from our shelves of Sung celadon, who could
remove her from the guest's bathroom, who could distract
her from the new bougainvillea shoots, who could keep
her from tearing the amahs' trousers and biting their legs
when they worked. Anjibi and I could have had a full

ANJIBI

life together, had I been ready to give up my husband and
friends.

Finally we built a large wire-covered enclosure at the
foot of the garden around the great mango tree, and there
Anjibi went to live with the tree squirrels. At first she expected that I was going to live with her in the cage, and
every time I left her there and disappeared into the house it
was a new betrayal. And then she came to know that the
wire house was hers against the outside world, and she grew
tempestuous and vehement and deliriously active, and

wilder every day. I would go out to her each morning, and some days she would pull open her door and come out to me, and the longer she lived in the wire house the wilder she was when she went free. She would not leave our premises and go back to the jungle, but neither would she be one of our family and bow to conventions that make for peaceful community living.

When Anjibi got loose from her house Arusap would not touch her, Husin let her pass him by, and little Usit ran from her. Straight for the house she would come, tiptoeing silently up the stairs, and then like a gray simian shadow she would drift through my bedroom door. I would look up and see her, our eyes meeting, and hers so melancholy. It was a proud moment for me when she came softly in and put her great arms about me, placed her brooding face gently by mine and touched her lips to my cheek, and sang the yearning jungle *wah wah* song. The haunting cry would echo so deeply that it seemed to come from the lungs of us both. It was our song, the only one either of us could sing, and when the clear strong notes ceased she was ready to go.

I would take her hand and lead her back to the garden. She was tall, and moved beside me like a mortal married to the grace of winds. Under the *chempaka* tree at the gate of the wire house, where the subtle sunlight fragrance welcomed her musky female scent, we would stop. I would thank her then for coming, tell her she should come again soon, and tell her that her song was the loveliest in all the jungle world. Then slowly I would turn to go, while she pressed her satin black face against the wire in a submissive but eternal melancholy.

Different Feet Have Different Ways

That is the way that it used to be, when I was the benevolent mistress, and she the suppliant one.

But Anjibi got out of her wire house this morning, and she did not come to me.

Perhaps if it had not been for the two small new apes who arrived last week, she might have come. But they have been living innocently enough on the verandah among bananas, basins of water, and small piles of ordure. Anjibi came to the house looking for me, and she found them. Their only offense was being there on the verandah, which in Anjibi's mind is either mine or hers, but never in any case is it the verandah of two small, strange, interloping, upstart apes. She swept upon them in a sudden crazy rage, and battered them on the floor, hooting and screaming and crying, and in the excitement, the heartburn and blood lust and shrieking, she forgot that she had ever been tame.

I chased her away from the babies, but she would not come to me or let me catch her. I tried all my wiles on her, — I called to her like a lovesick ape, I crouched on the lawn and wept, I sat and squinted my eyes shut and pretended I didn't see her, I lay on the grass and waited for her to examine me, I used all those pretty artifices which she has in the past given me to understand are pleasing to her, — but she would not come.

I would have left her alone then to follow her own pleasure, except for the baby apes, but with them exposed to her anger I did not dare to do so. I called to Arusap, and together we played a game which alternated strategy with pursuit, with Anjibi outwitting us at both of them.

A strange chase that. The running, leaping ape going

from bush to bush and snatching a flower, an orchid, a frangipani bloom, a crimson hibiscus, and carrying it in her mouth like a Carmen, almost waiting for Arusap, and then flying before him like the shadow of a bird; the rushing barefoot Murut boy, now running, now crouching in ambush, pouncing and missing and running again — and before them the cats scattering in flight, the baby apes trembling and hooting in the rafters, Ah Yin running from the kitchen, Husin coming from the valley, two hawks crying and swooping above, the Hakka women staring up from the road, and all the time Anjibi knowing more and more her strength and her swiftness, Anjibi knowing that she need not ask favors again.

And all the time I thinking, "Oh, God, what beauty! What glory of movement and form! If this is animal, why can't we all be so! If this grace is only mortal, who asks to be immortal!"

But none could catch her. So I told them to go away and to let quietness come, while I sat down on the verandah at the far end from the baby apes, and waited.

Some time I waited, and then Anjibi went up the mango tree. I called to Arusap quietly, and he climbed up it after her, and she went out a small high limb till it bent over with her weight, and then dropped down from limb to limb until I could reach up from the ground and grasp hold of her arm. She would not come, she held tightly to the limb; I pulled with all my weight, and still I pulled; and then she came away with her teeth bared, and a leap upon me, and a savage bitter cry, and she turned on me and put her teeth on my arm to bite.

When I had pulled at her against her will I had been frightened to do so, and when she leaped on me I knew that she would bite. The teeth were sinking into my arm, the jaw was closing, and she was desperate fighting me, and then — she was Anjibi, my dear friend. She did not bite. Her jaw relaxed, she rested in my arms, she shook her fluffy fur, she put her face near mine, her cheek against my cheek, and waited, and remembered.

I called to Arusap then to go away. I put her down and held her hand, and we walked quietly back to the wire house. She entered compliantly. But we both knew that she had come with me by the grace of Anjibi, that she had spared me from harm by her generous will, and that she and not I was now the gracious lady.

4

Herman

Herman was to be Anjibi's husband.

To match her growing passions, her changing female whims, her frustrated desires, and her moody despairs, the Great Ape Herman was coming. And a new chapter of jungle history was to be written in the welcoming garden and under the fascinated eyes of one who had never lived out of the cities before. In my mind Black Beauty and Beautiful Jo, and Mowgli and Kaa, and little furred brothers and four-footed friends, and Tarzan of the Apes and Rin-Tin-Tin, and all the animal heroes of book and of screen, were already making place for the legend of Herman the Bridegroom.

We felt so certain, when we heard that there was a new

male ape coming to us from Keningau, that he was going to be Anjibi's mate, that we enlarged the *wah wah* house into two connubial compartments, and installed a double sleeping house, double trapezes, double rope swings, and double perches, in preparation for the nuptials.

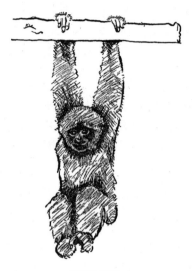

HERMAN

And then came Herman! Herman, who was of a size which allowed him to arrive in the orderly's pocket with a banana, and if the pocket had been smaller and Herman had had two bananas, there would still have been space in the pocket. Herman was obviously not of the age of consent, and although he showed himself from the first anxious to oblige, anxiety alone was not sufficient.

Oh well, we thought, he'll grow; meanwhile he shall be the beloved son. But Anjibi's maternal instinct was as undeveloped as Herman's sex appeal. When Herman was placed in the connubial apartment she chased him from corner to corner, nipping, biting, smacking, pommeling him until he was a teeth-bared spectre of his former care-free self. We thought that in a day or two they would become accustomed to each other, but after twenty-four hours Herman's tender black hands and feet were raw from climbing on the wire in an effort to escape the re-jected bride.

So we took him out to live with us as all the new pets do: a few days of clinging to us, a few nights in the bed-room, then downstairs to the godown, then the whole house for a circus, while there follows for me the picking up and feeling sad about, the becoming resigned to and sadly throwing away of, the broken remnants of more lamps and bowls and vases.

But Herman was worth it. My husband has always been as severe upon the subject of my talking baby talk to the animals as if he did not do so himself. But Herman's lov-ing personality pleaded for an affectionate diminutive, so we called him the Little Lamb Chop. We could say Little Lamb, and then change it hastily to Lamp Chop if the other of us was listening.

And sometimes we called him Herman the Vermin. One day a young doctor of science from Harvard who had come to Borneo to study the behavior of apes was fondling Herman on his lap. When the doctor arose he had received his first lesson in the behavior of apes. Herman and Usit, who was with us then, always aroused the same emotions in visitors, who wanted either to cuddle them or to send them to Hollywood.

Usit had a red box with a rope fastened to it, and in this he used to drag Herman about the garden. Herman would hang on to the sides of the box for dear life, his eyes popping in fascinated terror as his vehicle rocked and reeled over the turf. Exactly that expression must have been in the eyes of the first people who rode in automobiles. Scared to death, but they loved it! Vowed they'd never get in another one if they got home safe this time, but the next day there they'd be tearing down the road again! Herman would emit tiny terrified squeaks, and when the chariot slowed down for a corner, or perhaps tipped over, he would leap out and scuttle away. But in a few minutes he would be back again, hopping about the overturned vehicle, twitching at Usit's sarong, pleading for more attention, and begging for another ride.

One morning when Herman came in for his coffee he was dragging his leg behind him. We had it X-rayed and found it was broken, and the doctor set it in splints. Herman took the splints off, and the doctor set it again, and Herman took the splints off, and the doctor . . . and Herman . . . with Herman always having the last word.

So then I trussed the leg up in a shiny leather appliance made from my best red patent-leather belt, which was lightweight and pliable. Hermie got about admirably with this, and would swing himself along using his two long arms like crutches, with the little red leg sticking out stiffly behind. The leg knitted quickly, but long after it was well Herman still insisted on going on crutches with the leg out stiff behind.

Meanwhile the bride tarried while the bridegroom grew.

He grew until we thought he would no longer be ridiculous in the sight of Anjibi. Then we built a further addition to the wire house, this time leaving the screen in to separate the new compartment, and we sent Herman to live in the extension. At first he and Anjibi were antagonistic and would leap at the wire with their teeth bared. Then in time both came to cling to the wire, one on each side, and when they slept each sought his corner shelf and there, knees humped up to chins and silver arms folded on somnolent chests, their gray fur mingled through the wire.

Then section by section one day Harry took out the wire that separated them, and they were together. It was a big moment for Harry and me, but Herman and Anjibi were less sentimental. Herman, making the circle from wall to wall, found that the fourth wall was not there, and flew through onto Anjibi's trapeze, while Anjibi swung across to his basin of water and flung it to the ground. Then both swung together to the top trapeze, and there, with the excitement of apes which causes an illustration of the Biblical reference to bowels that turn to water, they made it unsafe for Harry to remain longer in the cage below them pulling out nails. So we left them then to what we hoped would be marital bliss.

Now if I go into the wire house I can no longer pet Herman because Anjibi becomes furious, and when I embrace Anjibi he does his amiable best to be indignant. Anjibi grows steadily wilder, more vigorous, more beautiful, and the Little Lamb Chop is now most anxious to please her. Whatever Anjibi desires from Herman he will give her, I know, if he can.

5

Lili

Our *simpalili*, better known to us as Lili the Simp, was the best endurance flagpole sitter in all of North Borneo. He was brought in to us from the jungle clinging to a long stick, and his expression of strained affability, and his determination not to leave his stick, always reminded me of the expressions and actions of the human contestants in American endurance contests.

Scientifically speaking this tarsier, or *simpalili*, as the natives call him, is an important link between lemur and monkey, and is popularly considered to be an ancestor and close relative of man. Our first *simpalili* was twelve inches long including his tail, and he would have been a pretty surprise to find in the top of a Christmas stocking. He had soft buff fur of the best-quality plush, and a hairless tail which was longer than his body. The tail extended stiffly below him along his stick, and he sat on top of it as the flagpole sitter rests on the top of his flagpole. The hairless underside of his tail helped him to cling to his stick and maintain this upright position.

He had attenuated fingers and toes, with diminutive nails like a human's, but with small adhesive pads at the ends of the fingers which he used like suckers to cling with. His head was large, with two round popping eyes and a perpetually surprised expression, an expression perhaps accounted for by the fact that in Simpalili each eye received a different picture, although his nerve cells very nearly provided for the stereoscopic vision of man. His capacity for vocal expression was limited, and Simpalili would open his mouth in terror while only a thin squeak came, like the cry of one in a nightmare who calls for help but finds his voice paralyzed.

Our Lili could do just one thing well — he could sit indefinitely on his flagpole. We cut a stick for him five

SIMPALILI

feet tall and leaned it against our wall, and then moved it from place to place, — into the dining room for dinner, onto the verandah for tea, up to the bedroom for sleeping, — with Lili always clinging to it.

We liked Lili, but he didn't have a responsive nature. His eyes were night-seeing, and his ways nocturnal, and his only warm interest in life was cockroaches. As soon as dark came we would hear a soft thud which was Lili jumping a yard or so from his flagpole to capture a cockroach. He ate them with epicurean relish, first quieting the victim with a crunch of his jaw, then holding it in padded fingers and daintily nibbling around its wings and then mangling its vitals.

Lili lived with us contentedly until one night his perch was left outside on the verandah, and the next day there was no Lili. Well and good, we thought, the wilds have received again the wild, and other appropriate sentiments. Then the telephone rang, and a neighbor said, "Our cat has just brought a peculiar animal into the house. Does it belong to you?"

So we brought Simpalili home uninjured, as the cat had been too surprised at his appearance to do him violence. Then we took him down to the jungle growth at the foot of the valley and bade him return to the freedom of the mammals of Borneo, out in the great outdoors. But the next day Lili had returned to our verandah and seemed to be searching for his flagpole.

The following day we took Lili and his flagpole in a motorcar to Mile Fifteen, where the deep jungle begins, and there we planted his flagpole and left him, still intent on establishing the endurance record for flagpole sitting.

6

Niffles and Sniffles

During the summer months in Sandakan we are companioned by the southwest monsoon, a wind of great precipitancy which arrives at our back doors like an invading army, and bangs its way through the house with inconsiderate tread. It leaves by the front door, proudly, and in the sudden silence that follows I look about at the marks of its arrogant boots.

But with the change of the monsoon in November the troops of more ruthless soldiery form in the glowering bay, and in the distance I can watch them come. Savagely they ride the black clouds up from the harbor, with the guns of their artillery detonating behind them and the flames from their rifles leaping in the sky. Before they leave they will deluge us with liquid bullets of rain and lash at the garden with wind whips until the house animals cower in corners and the garden kind cry in the trees. The morning after such an attack we emerge cautiously to count our losses, and inspect broken telephone wires and cracked electric-light transformers.

It was just at the beginning of this riotous monsoon season that Niffles and Sniffles came to live in our drains, and it was as innocent victims of the militant army of wind and rain that they finally came to die there.

Niffles and Sniffles were created in the image of otters, with one important difference — they didn't swim when all other otters did. Apparently they realized that this was their only claim to distinction, and when we tried to encourage them in aquatics by dropping them in the goldfish pond they immediately demonstrated that they would drown sooner than lose their individuality by swimming.

In appearance they were inconspicuous, being built so close to the ground that every time you lifted a foot they slid silently under it, and were there waiting to be stepped upon when you put the foot down again. They collected dirt on their white shirt fronts and wore their food on their chins and collars. They had rapacious appetites, but never learned to feed themselves, and always required to be fed with a medicine dropper at inconvenient times.

Harry and I, who frequently debated the perversities of the English pronunciation, named them Niagara Falls and Saint Niagara Falls in tribute to my country, and pronounced them Niffles and Sniffles in tribute to his.

NIFFLES AND SNIFFLES

Our house was surrounded by a cement gutter which in the dry season was irresistible to animals, but in the wet season was good only for aquatics, as it joined a larger drain whose waters spurted down the hill like a millstream. Niffles and Sniffles proved to have a natural aptitude for life in the gutter, and spent most of their time niffling and sniffling up and down ours.

Then precipitantly one day in November the northwest monsoon fell upon us, and in the downpour that followed, the drain rose almost instantly to flood tide. It was typical of Niffles that he should fall in. Sniffles stood on the brink and waved warnings, as if shouting last-minute instructions for breast stroke and crawl. But for too long Niffles had neglected his normal function of swimming, and the last ever seen of him he was pouring helplessly down the drain on the crest of a foaming wave. Not even his small mouse-smelling body was ever recovered.

Sniffles, alone, was inconsolable. During the ensuing week of mourning he attempted suicide repeatedly, prostrating himself beneath people's feet like a sacrificial offering under a Juggernaut. But we had developed such agility at jumping over otters that Sniffles was unsuccessful. At the end of the week he gave up more sensational methods of suicide and quietly laid himself down in the gutter on the spot where Niffles had last been seen, and died, with no more apparent cause for demise than a broken heart.

7

Georgie the Musang

Georgie the Musang was a very fine fellow even when four inches long. Although in the end he was outlawed from domestic living as a dangerous desperado, we knew in our hearts that it was never in Georgie's desire to be other than a loving friend.

Georgie came before I was accustomed to undomesticated animals, and when the forest ranger first sent him to us he was so bright-eyed, so infinitesimally perfect, with such a pounding heart and throbbing pulse of life in tiny body, that when I held him it was like feeling the heart of the jungle beat in the palm of my hand. To hold Georgie thus was to hear the story of creation, "And every living thing that moveth upon the earth."

Georgie was a dark fawn color with darker markings down his back, and on his forehead in the pompadour of his hair there were bright streaks which made him look like one who has turned white too young. He had a winning expression on his catlike face, and a vigorous, not unpleasant scent of mouse-shampooed-with-fish-oil. When he moved he rubbed his bottom on the floor to leave this Georgie smell. His tail was almost prehensile, long and strong, and in the use of it he was adroit. Favorite position

GEORGIE THE MUSANG

of Georgie in play was being held up by the end of his tail while he arched his body upward almost, but never quite, to form a circle.

Small desk drawers and behind the books on shelves were Georgie's habitats in daytime. There he would sleep the sunlight out, emerging with the dark, the coolness, and the evening drinks, to have a bowl of milk, a raw egg, and a wee-wee. That was the time for play and he was good at it, though it was difficult to guess whether we were giving Georgie a good time or he was giving us one.

When my red toenails charged across the floor like a platoon of dragons Georgie attacked them like a Giant Killer. His teeth were piercing sharp, but the tiny bulk of his jaw behind them could only tickle me. When I would dress for dinner at night, sitting barefoot at my dressing table, Georgie would rush madly back and forth from my bare feet to Harry's, nibbling and tickling and biting until we were frantic. He moved with lightning speed, and the only way to catch him if he didn't wish to be caught was to lie on the bed and pretend to be asleep, when Georgie would bite us awake again.

One night when we were going out and did not wish to leave him in the screened room, I lay enticingly on the bed pretending slumber, while Georgie bit hysterics into me and then eluded me, and we were late for dinner and Georgie was not caught.

He made a little noise in the back of his throat which sounded to me like "neh-neh-neh-neh," and if I made a noise like that at Georgie he always had the courtesy to answer me, for he was a most obliging fellow in the little things that count.

When he was so little, held in my hand, he had seemed like the heart of the jungle. And growing and strengthening and lengthening out he became truly the heart of the jungle, and no longer suited to hold in our hands.

During one monsoon season Georgie grew so fast that when he stretched along the rafters where he lived he measured full three feet from nose to tail. He no longer wanted milk or egg when he came down at dark, but lived on insects and cockroaches, and snakes and small prey which he stalked in the jungle at night. He no longer wanted anything that we could give him, but dutifully, like a grown son who humors his parents, he still came with our evening drinks to give us a little play. But the bulk behind Georgie's sharp teeth then, and the clamp of his jaw, were too innocently destructive to allow for our bare feet, and well-slippered we would sit while Georgie led the game.

He would whisk about us in a perfunctorily light mood for a moment, his mind on something else, then suddenly retreat under the stair from where his eyes burned sternly, while he looked at us as if to say, "That's enough for to-night. I, at least, am no longer a child."

As our bungalow could be entered or retired from by animals via the ventilation space between the roof and walls, Georgie had free run of the house, the garden, and the bamboos and jungle at the foot of the valley. Harry and I were away for some weeks, and when we returned Ah Yin had cleaned house extensively, not even sparing Georgie's rafters where he hoarded cockroaches, and Georgie had not been seen for some time.

I hoped then that when the lights came on he might return again, but he did not. I thought when we went up to bed that night he might be in the rafters there above us; I hoped to see his footprints on the verandah roof, or the tip of his long tail hanging over the bathroom partition, or the shining globes of his eyes in the dark, but there was nothing.

Some weeks passed, and still no Georgie. Then one night I smelled the familiar mouse-shampooed-with-fish-oil scent. There above the centre beam of the ceiling I saw Georgie's night eyes glowing, while his body and tail spread lengthily along the beam, a full three feet.

I shouted joyfully, "It's Georgie!" jumped up, stood on my chair, and reached my hand up for him. Georgie recoiled with a bristling defiance, spat out and clawed at me, just as Harry called, "Don't touch him! He's dangerous!"

Georgie crouched on his beam then with his teeth bared, like a fugitive defending his life. I stood uncertainly below, rebuffed and disappointed, while slowly my scent went up to him. Then I think he began to remember, for he relaxed and lay out easily again, but would not come to me. Perhaps if I had waited before making my first move we might have met again. But now it was too late. With Harry's words, "He's dangerous!" Georgie the Musang was branded, and joined forever the society of outlaws from men.

He came often after that to look down at us from the rafters, and I knew again that he liked us, but we never attempted to touch each other. Beautiful, swift, wild thing that Georgie was now become, powerful and dangerous, he would look down with glowing eyes that seemed to say, "Not that I ask anything of you now, you understand. But I want you to know that I think of you sometimes."

Part III

WE EAT THE WIND

"To eat the wind" (in Malay, *makan angin*) means "to walk for pleasure."

If I am met on the road by some old mother or some young man, when out for a morning walk, we greet each other thus: —

"And where are you going so early, Mem? Are you out to eat the wind?"

"Greetings, Old Woman, it is so. I am out to eat the wind."

11. *A Pioneer Prepares*

ADVENTURE for me has three stages. There is the first un-shackled interval before starting when my dreams are bounded by nothing, north, south, east, or west. There is the second interval when, footsore and insect-bitten, aching-backed and broken-spirited, I wish that I had never come. And then comes the third interval — and in *this* interval I know that such adventures are the caviar of my existence compared to which other events in my life are *Schwarzbrot*. In this interval the fantastic, the unreal, the magnificent, and the unimaginable, which might have occurred only to other people, are occurring really to me. And then I know that it is right that such things must be paid for in discomfort, discouragement, and weariness; I know it is right that they are not free.

Stout-hearted people seem to escape the second interval

of discouragement, and rush valiantly into a third interval of endurance and resolution which makes them thrive on hardships. They become like lions, exultantly licking their own wounds back to health again. I admire them and envy them, but I cannot emulate them. Compared to them I have only the lamb's place in adventure, which is in the stomach of the lion.

From the time my husband said to me last June, "Are you coming to Ulu Kwamut [1] with me?", and I answered him "Yes," I was both hot with expectation and cold with premonition. I wasn't afraid of possible dangers on the trip, for if I were as dependent as an incubator baby my husband would still bring me back alive. But I knew that there was nothing which could insure me against the discomforts of jungle travel with which I was so familiar. And my spirit which was bold at home in the library was a craven, with wet feet in the rain.

Thus when I looked up at the books on the shelves about me on the day that we were to start, my eyes rested with especial pleasure on the title *Everyday Life among the Head Hunters*. It was a reassuring idea that the head-hunters had everyday lives.

The other titles that I saw on that shelf led my mind on to where it wanted to go: *Home Life of the Borneo Head Hunters; Head Hunters Black, White, and Brown; Head Hunters of Borneo; Primitive Peoples of Borneo; Pagan Tribes of Borneo; Pagans of North Borneo.*

And on another shelf: *Men of the Inner Jungle; Where the Strange Trails Go Down; The Pirate Wind; Borneo,*

[1] Ulu Kwamut — upper waters of the Kwamut River.

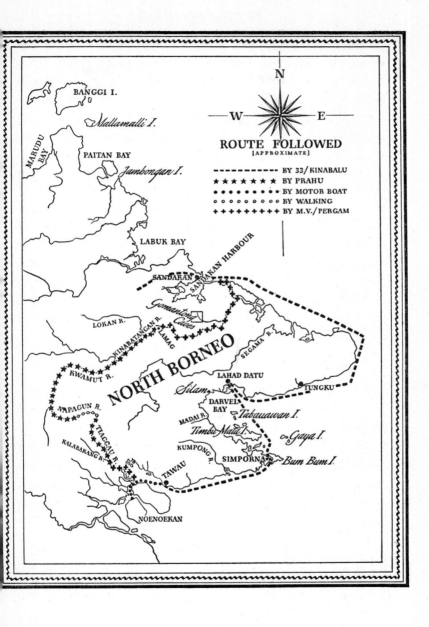

Stealer of Hearts. I saw that the pioneers of Borneo had dreamed long years before me.

Then I turned to my typewriter, and wrote a last letter home: —

We are leaving Sandakan to-day for a trip into the interior of North Borneo, through territory that is the last stronghold of the head-hunters. Although I have been on a number of trips with Harry before, and I have met many interesting and amusing natives, they have never seemed to be the same wild men of Borneo that people have written about. They always turned out to be the brothers of Arusap's friends, or cousins of Saudin's wife, or old men who asked after Governor Humphreys, or young men who asked about flying machines. But now we shall be going through a district where there has been almost no European travel. The natives who live there are the head-hunters of North Borneo, and are still reputed to take heads. There, if any place, we should meet the wild men of Borneo.

I sealed the letter, and sat for a minute wondering if other people ever felt as skittish as I did when they were looking bold. Then I left the room and closed the library door behind me. Vicarious Borneo adventure lay there; I was going out now to a real one.

The Chinese women *kulis* were carrying our *barang* [1] out to the bus.

"Have you forgotten anything?" Harry asked.

"Probably, but even if I remember it I can't get anything more into the *bongons.*" [2] We watched the bedding

[1] *Barang* — luggage.
[2] *Bongon* — a lightweight carrying box which is measured to fit the back of a native *kuli*.

rolls go down the garden path; we watched the camp beds, the medicine box, the carrying baskets. . . .

"There's too much luggage!" Harry said.

Before we were married my husband lived on rice and game when he traveled. He didn't use a mattress, he didn't take a tent, and he didn't take a wife.

"Yes, I know there is, but what can we leave out?" I always felt apologetic at this stage. "Here is the list of the pieces and what is in them." I read the list aloud: —

6 *bongons* — food, cooking and eating utensils, bedding and towels. Mutual use Harry and Agnes and Arusap.

2 *sikutans*,[1] holding camp beds and mattress rolls. Mutual use H. and A.

1 tent fly — H. and A.

1 medicine box — Harry. Equipped for every emergency except childbirth, and could probably assist with that.

1 .22 rifle — Harry.

1 shotgun — Harry.

1 rucksack — films, camera, cartridges, pipe and tobacco, fishing lines, pickling bottle for insects — Harry.

10 flower presses for collecting specimens — Harry.

1 *sikutan* — Arusap, personal.

1 *bongon* — Harry, personal.

1 *bongon* — Agnes, personal, and a miracle of compact packing!

"That's the list. Is there anything we can leave behind?" I asked.

"Nothing except you," said my husband, and this was too near the truth to be laughed at.

Arusap followed the *barang* down the path to the bus.

[1]*Sikutan* — native rattan carrying basket.

He was carrying one basket full of eggs, and another basket full of vegetables, and Ah Yin was following him with the blue cotton umbrella which she was telling him not to forget on my account. Harry looked after them protestingly, but the will to resist was broken. And then we also went down the path to the motor. I knew that when next we should come up that garden path there would be jungle mud in my toenails and campfire smoke in my hair, strange scents in my nostrils, and the memory of the things that I wanted to know in my heart.

"Good-bye, Ah Yin."

"Good-bye, Missee. You take much care. I one man alone now, I very lonely. Good-bye, Master. Good-bye, Arusap. Peace go with you!"

"Peace remain!"

I looked back at our sheltering home. I was intensely anxious to go, but I guessed that I should probably be intensely grateful to get back home again.

2

This was a trip which we had tried for several years to make. We had set the date three times before, bought the provisions and packed the *barang*, and then been prevented from going — once by an emergency call on my husband for other work, and twice by floods on the rivers we planned to travel on, which in time of heavy rainfall were not navigable.

Our plan was to go by coast steamer to Tawau on the east coast of North Borneo, and then to travel overland from Tawau back to Sandakan, a trip through an inaccessible part of the country. As there were neither tracks nor trails in this section of the jungle there was no European travel there, and part of the interest of the trip lay in the fact that the natives of the area had no contact with, and little experience of, white men. The river travel would be accomplished in small native canoes known as *perahus*, and the jungle travel would be on foot.

My husband believed that there were good forest areas and desirable agricultural lands along these rivers and covering the watersheds between. If there were, as he hoped, good forests, it was important that the areas should be protected and preserved. He also expected to find certain rare and hitherto uncollected trees peculiar to Borneo.

Twenty-five years ago the headwaters of these rivers had supported flourishing native kampongs; now these villages were buried in secondary forest growth, and the natives had vanished. A wish to know more about their disappearance was also in our minds.

The lurid memory of the tragic story of the Flint brothers, Walter and Raffles, had been largely responsible for the journalistic reference, among Europeans of North Borneo, to this part of the country as the last stronghold of the head-hunters. For the story of the sanguinary Flint expedition of 1890 up the rivers which we now planned to travel was one of the most hair-raising of the half-told stories of North Borneo. In my mind there had always been the desire to hear the other half of the story from the lips of the natives themselves. I hoped that now I might be going to do so.

The trip could only be attempted in one of the so-called dry months, June, July, or August. The rivers involved were in the hydrographic centre of the east coast, and were subject to flood to such an extreme degree that you could not tell from hour to hour whether you could continue your travel on them. Borneo river travel is always uncertain, for when the rivers flood you cannot travel, and when they do not flood they fall too low for travel, and a loaded *perahu* dragged by natives through the boulders of a dry rapids is slow motion, even for Borneo.

But there comes a brief fluxing interval between spate and low water. Then your *perahu* takes wings, your boatmen sing, your body glows with enterprise, and you forget the hours of waiting, and remember only that the water is cool and the sun is hot and the day is clear, and the whole long river belongs to you.

So we were going in June. At home it was the month for brides and trousseaus, for graduations and summer vacations. But in North Borneo it was the dry month.

I was bothered by only one thing. All winter I had been having spells of fever which did not by blood test show to be malaria, but which resisted every treatment. I did not mind in Sandakan as Ah Yin ran the house better than I did, and I could lie in bed and read until the fever relaxed its grip. But I knew that I could not take my bed, book, and fever with me up the Borneo rivers.

When we decided on the date of the trip I made a hasty visit to the doctor, who recommended an anti-infection serum. The Dispensary was out of the serum as a party of American gold prospectors had bought the entire local supply, and the new serum which had to be ordered from Singapore would not arrive for three weeks.

This meant that I should have to take all of my injections the last week before our trip commenced, which would leave no margin for unfavorable reaction.

The serum arrived. I took seven armfuls in two thin arms, and went about in a state of spiritual vigor and physical decay. Would I be able to start? said Harry. That had nothing to do with it. I knew that I was going to start.

I did my packing in a feverish state. Fortunately there was not much demand on me in the line of packing. Ah Yin allowed me to pack my own personal possessions, but not those of my husband. Arusap did the food, bedding, tent, and camping equipment. Harry did the medicine kit, the armory, the photographic supplies, and the contributing influences to culture, which always included *Blackwood's Magazine*, an omnibus volume of stories, a family cycle novel, and his pipes. Everybody appeared to have more packing responsibilities than I did, but the paradox was that if anything was missing from what anyone packed I was the one to blame. This prevented my accepting with a carefree spirit the back seat which was offered to me.

So I made lists. I made Arusap a list, written in Malay, of the food, camping equipment, et cetera, for which he was supposed to be responsible. I gave Ah Yin a list of things to pack for my husband. She checked off all items immediately with a red pencil, and hung the list in the kitchen with the dinner menus. She then packed what she thought best for him to have. This was all right for Ah Yin, who was not present to hear his language when he unpacked.

On this trip I had been successful for the first time in

packing everything for myself into just one *bongon.*
Harry always said that I could only travel with him if
I could go as he did, with the same light luggage as he
used, and traveling at the same rate. Although I did not
really travel at the same rate, at least I traveled as far by
nightfall of each day as the *kulis* and the luggage could
travel, and measuring by that rate of speed I was not holding up the party. Harry's edict I knew was right, as the
trips were Government expeditions, and not conducted
for my edification.

And so I had one *bongon.* It took me three days to pack
it. In the end I had created a perfect design out of many-
sized articles and vari-shaped pieces, and had formed an
analogous whole from liquids and solids.

I needed a greater variety of clothes than Harry, who
used only shorts and jerseys. I took shorts for active jungle
travel, long trousers for appearing in native villages, and
culottes to wear when traveling in native boats. The
culottes were anticipated to protect me from too violent
sunburn, and from *kurap,* an infectious skin disease which
many natives have. I always took culottes, I always expected to wear them, and I seldom did. Shorts were better. On a hard trip freedom of action and escape from the
horrible hindrance of clothing was the only thing worth
while. Skin diseases, sunburn, and lost beauty did not
enter into the reflections of a tired body, and I discovered
that the briefer the trouser the lighter the foot.

I had also in my *bongon* six jerseys, six pair of rubber-
soled canvas shoes, a dozen pair of socks, a negligible bulk
of underwear, a leather coat, a kimono, four nightgowns,
journal, ink bottle, nose spray, sewing kit, drawing paper

and pencils, and a pillow, a luxury for which our bedding rolls did not allow.

All of this was contained in an oblong *bongon* of light three-ply wood, one foot by one foot by two feet. This was Harry's own design of carrying pack for jungle tours. The box was measured to be narrower than a *kuli's* back, so that it would not catch on trees. It was fitted with carrying straps, and it must not weigh when filled more than thirty-five pounds, as it was designed to be one man's burden. Unless the sliding lid slipped, the contents of such a *bongon* were almost secure from water.

3

Small Borneo steamers affect people violently; they either like them or hate them. Those who hate them support their cause by complaining of the cockroaches which frolic in the tiny cabins, by fretting at the single bath which is to accommodate all, by professing inconvenience at the indefinite arrivals and departures from ports, and by complaining at the boisterous motion with which the boat wallows through the sea.

People such as myself, who like them, are sometimes put to it to tell why. Perhaps the real reason for liking a Borneo steamer is in the generous proportions of the captain's heart, which organ always seems to be enlarged to an alarming degree. The captains of these coast steamers carry personal messages, books, magazines, news, dogs, servants, children, radios, and flower gardens from one isolated outstation to another. This time our captain had been entrusted with a bouquet of orchids from the garden of the Resident's wife, to be carried for a two days' trip to the District Officer's wife, for her dinner party.

Our cabin was small, but the door stood open and let in the horizon of the Sulu Sea, than which I think there is no sweeter, softer, bluer stretch of water in the world. I lay in my kimono on the bunk with the breeze spraying over me like a tepid shower, when Harry came down to get his tobacco.

"Are there any other passengers on board?" I asked.

"Only Goldie. He thinks they've found gold up the Segama River."

"Does it make any difference to anybody if they have?"

"Not unless it's in sufficient quantities to make mining it worth while. They've been finding gold on the Segama River for years. Back in 1898 the London report of the Chartered Company said that they were waiting daily for a telegram about the discovery of gold in Borneo, from which discovery enormous profits would accrue. They are waiting still."

"Ask Goldie what those serum shots did to him," I said. "I have more fever to-day, and my arm is very swollen." Goldie was one of the American prospectors who had been responsible for the Sandakan sell-out of my serum.

"Do you think you are going to be all right to make the trip?"

"Yes. We have one day more on the steamer, and one day upriver by launch, before the real travel starts. The re-action will be over by then. Where does Winki meet us?"

"In Tawau, and then we spend the night at his camp on Sebatik Island."

Dr. Wenk, the oil geologist, was at that time engaged

in making a geological survey of North Borneo, and when he and Harry discovered that they were both projecting a trip through the same district they had decided to go at the same time and take advantage of a single organization of native boats and boatmen, and launch.

"I wonder how we will all get on together," I ruminated. "I suppose that Winki and you and I will know a lot more about each other by the time we come back from this trip."

Winki met us at Tawau and we sailed back to Sebatik Island with him behind the black and yellow sail of a pirate *bagong*, with our city shoes piled in the bottom, and our socks wadded into them, and our feet bare and comfortable. Harry said the boat was a *bagong* such as the old Borneo pirates used to use. Winki said it was a *gobang*, and Arusap said it was a *pakarangan*. In arguments like that it was well to have one person such as myself along who knew nothing about it.

Winki's camp on Sebatik Island had a strong Swiss personality. It was a compound of Winki and of Dr. Schneeberger, the Swiss geologist who had been in charge before him. I could see Dr. Schneeberger in the perfect handicraft of the little *sulap*, the camp bungalow which he had moved with him from camp to camp, taking it beam from beam, and then carefully putting it together again on each new site. I could see Dr. Schneeberger, and his two years of loving care of the little house, in the smooth hand-worn polish of the white wood, in the carefully fitted shelves, and the convenient recesses for tinned goods. And Dr. Schneeberger's large blond bulk was obviously intended for the double-sized camp bed which Winki now slept on, but which was still known to everyone in camp as "Tuan Schneeberger's bed," although he had abandoned its use two years before.

I could see Winki in the folding camp chair, one of his few luxuries, in the meagreness of the tinned food supplies, one of his frugalities, in the shelfful of books on Iceland and the Arctic Circle, one of his few enthusiasms, and in the neatness of the camp, one of his hobbies.

I could see Swiss hotel efficiency in the way in which the rainfall was caught in handmade gutters which were tied to the palm-leaf roof of the *sulap*. The water was then carried overhead through a handmade pipe from the *sulap* to a small bathhouse fifty feet away, where it emptied into a huge native jar and was used for bath water.

We pitched the borrowed African safari tent for the first time that night. Harry had borrowed it from the Medical Department because it was small, and lighter than our own old tent, and would be an easy one man's burden. He had borrowed the fly alone, which was intended to be used only over the main tent. When it was up I looked without enthusiasm at the manner in which both ends of our beds came flush with the open ends of the tent.

"It's nice and small, isn't it!" said Harry approvingly.

Unggib, a Forest Department *kuli* with a face like a baked potato, was helping us pitch the tent. I didn't know many of the men yet, but Unggib immediately became outstanding among them because he couldn't get an idea. New ideas came to life in him after long suffering. When he laughed it was a rumbling in his intestines, where apparently he did his thinking, but the laugh never went with the event which caused it. It came like a Christmas card on New Year's Day, with a sentiment that was inappropriate to the festival.

We all ate dinner in Winki's *sulap* with him. There was rice for everybody; boiled cucumber and pineapple and

snake gourd for Winki and me, who like vegetables; stewed chicken for Harry, who hates vegetables; sardines and cheese for Winki, who doesn't like chicken; and tinned peaches to lighten our luggage. I could see that the menus of Winki and ourselves were not going to be compatible.

Winki showed us many of his air-survey photographs, which to the naked eye looked like squares of caviar with worms crawling across them. Looked at through the stereoscope they showed a deep mass of jungle. The treetops pushed up towards you from great depths of hiding jungle, and the worm that seemed to be crawling through the caviar of the jungle was the Kalabakang River which we were about to travel on.

We went to bed then, Harry and I sleeping for the first time under our African safari tent fly. My fever was better, but I was glad to know that we were going to have an extra day on Sebatik, as Winki wanted to dig more oil test holes and Harry was collecting tree specimens.

"Make coffee for us yourself in the morning, Arusap," Harry warned him before he went to sleep. "Don't let Tuan Winki's cook make it. I like my coffee strong. Good night, Banana Legs."

That was to me, because I already had black and blue bruises on my legs.

4

I was pleased the next afternoon when Winki said that we would sail down to Noenoekan, across the Dutch Borneo border, and say good-bye to his Swedish friend, who managed the timber camp there, and his sister. I had heard the story before of the little Swedish woman who lived on Noenoekan with her brother, and of her daughter, Anita, the small fair-haired child. The child had become almost a legend among the Dyaks of Dutch Borneo. They who were swarthy and sturdy and squat, who were ferocious and adventurous, who had no equals in daring either in battles with rivers or in battles with enemies — they had never seen the like before of the Swedish child's tow-silk hair and china-blue eyes. They would gather admiringly about the Noenoekan house and stand for hours to watch her at play.

A Pioneer Prepares

We left Sebatik Island with a good breeze behind us, and swept down the coast behind our black and yellow sail. Then the wind weakened and a following rain caught up and deluged us. We furled the empty sail and found to our pleasure that the outboard motor would work, but by the time we made Noenoekan Landing our clothes were soaked through. We waded through the red mud, and found Mr. Lindquist, the manager of the timber camp, and stood in the rain and tried to look amiable, while my fever came back and my teeth chattered. I was thankful when he asked us up to his house for tea.

When we arrived his sister and the little girl were sitting on the verandah in the warm rain, both dressed alike in straight gingham dresses, and both with bare feet. Mother and daughter had pointed faces, and soft, streaked childish yellow hair, and blue eyes and fragile bodies. They were both very tanned, but shockingly yellow and unwell-looking.

The mother told me that they had had repeated attacks of malaria, and that they were not well owing to the deficiencies of their diet. She said they could get no meat at Noenoekan except what they shot, and that once a month her brother went out all night after game. And then, quite ravenous for the flesh, and unable to keep it long without ice, they would feed like the Dyaks, eating nothing but meat for several days, until it was all gone.

She told me also, and this I had already heard by rumor, that she had annoyed the wives of the several Dutch timbermen who lived on Noenoekan because she went about barefoot, and dressed in shorts, and did not change for dinner. While she was telling me this she was serving us tea on the rainy verandah in her simple dress with the same pleasant courtesy and quiet poise that she might have shown as hostess at an Embassy "at home."

We sat and drank a great deal of tea, and watched a great deal of rain falling, and even the Chinese *wonk* dog slunk under the verandah, while the Swedish woman and Anita and I shivered gently in the grip of our fever and chills. When we finally left the house and walked back to our boat I looked back at the three Scandinavians waving after us through the rain. I looked back and thought that the lure of the East demanded much from women.

5

What a turmoil there was in Winki's Swiss hamlet! The whole encampment, including men and houses, was being shifted to the other oil camp at Tambisan, there to await Winki's return. Mimi and Kiau-Kiau, the kittens, were placed in a basket; the chickens which Dr. Schneeberger had bought and become too fond of to eat, but which Winki discovered to be competent egg layers, were rounded up out of the jungle; the *sulap* was dismembered, the beams piled together, the *atap* roof stacked in bundles, the overhead pipe line telescoped into an armful, and Winki's bed collapsed into a travesty of its former amplitude. Amongst all this excitement the quiet withdrawal of Winki, Harry, and myself, with our men, for the first lap of our journey up the river seemed hardly worth noticing.

We were going up the Kalabakang River by launch to the village where we expected to get our native boats and boatmen. As I still had fever, I slept all day on the deck,

only opening my eyes at intervals to watch the long swaying line of river that trailed behind us, and the imperative
arrogance of the *nipah* palms which flung their sword-like
shadows across us. When Harry awoke me at noontime to
move me into the shade the *nipah* palm outline had softened
into the featheriness of forest tops. The colorless shine of
midday was about us. Air, water, insects, and even the life
within ourselves, seemed to have become stagnant in it.

The next time I awoke it was to be rescued from the rain,
which plunged through the bridge-house windows and
beat on the decks. But before we had time to finish a pot
of tea in the cabin the rain had passed, and the decks were
sweating and the trees were steaming and the air was as
still, as thick, as hot, as before, and even less breathable.

That night Harry and Winki put their cots up on the
bridge, and I stayed in the cabin, as the deck space was
limited. The cabin was in the exact centre of the boat,
with doors on two sides and windows on four sides, the
engine room to the back of it, the sleeping deck for the
boatmen to the front, and passages along both sides. It made
me think of a Paris *pissoir* — one saw legs below the partition and head above, and there was no need to wonder
what the owner was doing.

There was a wooden grating in the cabin on which we
stood while we bathed, and during the bath the water
poured generously over the luggage. There was a commode
which stood high on a stand like a throne, and was flood-
lighted by shafts of light from all the windows. The bunk
had two portholes opening over it which were level with
the deck outside, where the ship's crew slept. I could think
of nothing to make the cabin less convenient, unless it was

to take the bunk out and replace it with the Diesel engine.

We anchored up the river that night. Degrees of heat when one is completely uncomfortable are difficult to judge, but a long time after it was so hot that I thought it couldn't be hotter, it still continued to be hotter. When I finally slept I dreamed that I was in a kettle stewing over a slow fire, while the fat on my body clarified into grease and the flesh fell from my bones.

6

I have decided now that all native headmen look respectable. For a long time I used to hope otherwise, but now I know that you can't get away from that look of eminent probity.

And thus it was with the Orang Tua [1] of Kampong Kalabakang who came to meet us in his *perahu*. His naked brown chest, and the tattooed designs on each shoulder which indicated that he had to his credit the taking of human heads, in no way interfered with that look of respectability.

Here was a good old man, his face said, who had lived an honest life, had gone to church every Sunday and given dimes to his grandchildren, who had never known violence except to condemn it or sex except to apologize for it, an old man eminently respectable.

Or, here was a Murut headman in only a loincloth, private and sex life unknown, violence suspected. Respectable?

Nevertheless, that's the way he looked.

[1] *Orang Tua* — literally *old man*, but it is the term of address used for the headman of a native village.

His *perahu* was surrounded in the water by smaller *perahus* that darted about like startled fish. These boats were manned by the Old Man's children. The relationship was as complicated as that in the verse: —

> Brothers and sisters have I none,
> That man's father is my father's son.

For convenience' sake they were all known as the Old Man's children, and it is not my intention to suggest

promiscuity in a character whom I have just established as respectable.

Small men these natives were, of that rich polished-wood color which goes so well with the out-of-doors. Most of them were naked except for their rust-colored loincloths. These natives, who are known as the Tengara Muruts, made me think of the men of Arusap's tribe, the Bokun Muruts, and this association made their Mongoloid features seem familiar and pleasant to me. Their loose buns of long black hair, their mouths crimsoned by *sireh* juice, their well-muscled legs with the unkind sores and ulcers, all these I recognized with a feeling of amity.

Arusap called to them in Murut. It was the first arrow to start the verbal onslaught. The air sang with greetings, laughter, and jokes. Amidst this atmosphere of jovial fellowship the Orang Tua mounted our launch and stood on the deck before us. While Harry and Winki gave him cigarettes the business began.

"What is the news, Old Man?"

"The news is good, Tuan." A pleasant smile embroidered itself in red scallops on his lips with the oozing *sireh* juice from his betel chewing.

"Did you receive word from the District Officer to tell you that we wish men and boats?" Harry asked.

"Yes, Tuan. Five of our boats and eighteen of our men are prepared to go up the river with you."

"We wish strong men and strong boats, for the trip will be hard."

"It is so, Tuan. The men and the boats are strong, and I myself will accompany them to guide you."

"Whatever wage is fair I will pay to the men. They should take enough rice for at least two weeks with them."

"It is so, Tuan."

Business being over then, the Old Man turned his attention to me. Natives can stare and yet not be rude. I do not know whether this contradiction is in the quality of the stare or in my interpretation of it, but the result is that the stares are not discomfiting to me. The Old Man employed his best occult powers to the edification of both of us. His black eyes were bright and never wavering, yet what he saw might well have made him blink.

He was seeing a person who was as tall as either of the Tuans, as thin and as brown as they, with shorts and jersey and sneakers and native knife like theirs. On this person's head was bound a bandana such as the Tuans also wore. Three men in the jungle, perhaps? And yet — was it in the shape of the hands? in the different turn to the calf of the legs? the smaller features of the face? the tone of the voice? Or was it that this person alone of the three seemed to have nothing important on his mind? Certain it is that the Old Man turned to Harry and said with conviction, "This is the Tuan's wife."

Harry admitted that it was.

"Does the Tuan's wife go with him all the way?"

"She goes all the way."

"In jungle also?"

"In jungle also."

The Old Man thought about it. Then he looked at me and shook his head and said cryptically, "I hope the Tuan's wife has good luck!"

I felt that I was introduced then, and thought I would be about my own business, on this expedition, of collecting information. "Greeting, Old Man. I see by your tattoos that you have taken heads," I said.

"Probably I have, Tuan, but perhaps I have not," he answered me diplomatically, being familiar with the fact that the Government has forbidden the taking of heads. He called me Tuan because, like most upcountry natives, he did not know the term "Mem" as it is applied on the coast to white women.

"Do you remember, Old Man," I asked, "the great trouble fifty years ago when two white men with many police and guns came across the jungle and down the river, to punish the Tengara Muruts for the murder of Walter Flint?"

"All men on the Kalabakang River remember that, Tuan." The Old Man's eyes turned away from me as if to look back fifty years.

"How many Muruts were killed that time?"

"Some say one hundred, and some say two hundred. The story is very bad, Tuan."

"Tell me, Old Man," I said. I wanted the story of Walter Flint; I wanted it the way the natives told it. I wanted it here on the Kalabakang River beside the rice fields and under the coconut palms which grew so peacefully to-day in the long shadows cast by events of fifty years before.

"Tell me, Old Man," I said. And then I listened carefully.

12. *A Hundred Teeth and a Hundred Eyes*

THIS is the story of Walter Flint as it lives to-day on the lips of the people of the Kalabakang. The Orang Tua told his part of the story as if it had happened yesterday, for the Tengara Muruts are of the same tribe as were the natives who took Flint's head.

The version current in Sandakan, which everyone interested in "wildest Borneo" repeats, is based on reports to the Government of an expedition of inquiry. The story current amongst the natives is as it passes from mouth to mouth. Both reports are perhaps prejudiced by the sympathies of the narrators, but the native's story has not before been told.

Its truth — its falsity — each listener decides for himself.

229

We Eat the Wind

The rains were long on the Kwamut River, and between the rains the sun was hot, and the air steamed up from the mudbanks and the jungle to hang like an exterminating vapor over the dank mouth of the river. The sand flies and mosquitoes were energetic, and nothing else was. The wild pigs died of starvation, the crocodiles moved only when they had to, the natives waited for the crocodiles to move, and the traders waited for the next boat. And so it was in 1890.

The little shop of Flint and Company on the mudbanks of the river carried sardines, sauces, biscuits, sausages, tongues, chocolate assorted, and soap. The shop was hot, and the tins were dusty, and the labels were no longer bright, and they came off some of the tins entirely, so that you could not tell the oxtail soup from the greengages in syrup. But this didn't make any difference to the customers, because they were the natives of North Borneo.

There was a great deal of sitting to be done in that little shop. The natives sat, and Walter Flint sat. Flint sat very comfortably now, because he had discovered that although trousers become a man who walks on city streets, a sarong is of better use for purposes of sitting.

And as Flint sat he found that there was nothing to look forward to in the morning except the first drink at night, and there was nothing to look forward to at night. He found that it was dull to go from a dusty shop to an empty house, and an immaculate bed was a poor companion.

But there was the little Tengara Murut girl, Lingud. Her eyes were a shining blackness set in such clear whiteness as Flint had never seen amongst his own women, and her admiration of his magnificence was also unequaled in his experience of women. Her body had vigor and warmth and roundness, her simplicity of mind was pleasant, and her streak of wild savagery was amusing.

But she was the daughter of Semporna Numpal, the head of the tribe of Tengara Muruts, and not to be had for nothing. Like a good trader, Flint was willing to pay for what he wanted. He paid Semporna Numpal one hundred and twenty-five dollars as the bride-price of his daughter. Then, in accordance with Murut marriage ceremonies, with dancing, feasting, and rice-beer drinking, Lingud became Flint's wife.

And Flint became the son-in-law of Semporna Numpal, and it was in that relationship that the difficulty arose. For Semporna Numpal was a primitive savage. Not he, nor his father, nor his grandfather, nor any ancestor, had ever lived by law other than Murut law. Such was the man whose son-in-law Flint became.

A Murut house has a flexible body and a communal soul and it always has room for one more. The native shares his mat and his rice till his mat is worn and his rice is gone, and then he shares his friend's mat and rice until these are gone, and then together they look for another friend.

But to Flint, communal living was not as simple as that, and when father-in-law Semporna Numpal and mother-in-law Masian settled themselves in the house with Lingud, Flint was not pleased. Certainly there were brothers and sisters who came too, and cousins who took things home with them in carrying baskets, and friends who collected the swill for their pigs and the scraps for their snarling dogs. And Lingud liked to sit with them all, and gossip and talk, and neglect her work, and spit betel juice into the corners, and be a little hellion when she was angry. And the once empty house of the white man became gradually much too full.

It was a problem which grew on Flint for two years, and then he dealt with it like a white man. He promoted the idea to his father-in-law that the Tengara tribe needed a change of air, needed to get away from the damps and dews of Kuala Kwamut and the commercial atmosphere of Flint and Company, and go up the Nasan River to the fine long stretch of virgin jungle which lay high above the river's mouth. There they could make a new clearing where the land was still fertile from a never-felled forest, and grow better *padi*, and more tapioca root, and have bigger pigs to nuzzle under a better longhouse than the Tengara Muruts had ever had before.

Numpal agreed with Flint that the idea was promising, for by then he was heavily indebted to Flint and not in a position to disagree. When the time came to go, Flint said that Lingud should take their two babies and go also with Numpal to Nasan, while he, Flint, went down to Sandakan for a holiday. They all parted on friendly terms, and if each one suspected the sincerity of the other's motives at least he didn't say so.

But Flint went only a short distance down the Kinabatangan River to Lamag. Then, like the suspicious husband of stories, he returned unexpectedly to Kwamut, and went up the Nasan River to visit the new Tengara settlement which father Numpal was clearing on the nice strip of virgin land which Flint had suggested to him.

But father Numpal was not clearing the virgin land, nor building the longhouse, nor planting the *padi*, or tapioca, or coffee, nor doing any of the things that Flint had planned. Part of the Tengara tribe was there sitting, sitting and waiting an omen from fate. But Numpal himself had left, with his wife and Lingud, and disappeared through the jungle and over the watershed, headed for the Kalabakang River. Numpal had reckoned that that fifty-five miles of jungle was a journey that would delay a white man for some time. Numpal was thus free of the imminency of his debt to Flint, and he had his daughter back, who was again worth a bride-price to him from someone else.

But by Numpal's move Flint had lost both his debtor and his wife. Considered on either a cash basis or an amorous one it was annoying, and Flint found it so. Accompanied only by two native boys he followed Numpal's steps through the jungle and over the stormy watershed of the rivers, to Numpal's stopping place at Linidis on the Kalabakang River. Events of the family reunion which must have occurred there remained for a time obscure.

2

Soon, however, the story began to pass down the river from mouth to mouth of a misfortune which had occurred to Flint after that reunion. The journey, the story said, had been too much for the white man, and he had been taken ill of a strange disease, and had died a few days after arriving at the house of his father-in-law. And the making of his coffin had taken seven days, and the digging of his grave had taken three days, and great had been the mourning at his burial.

Slowly the story passed down the rivers, from the lips

of the Muruts to the lips of a Dyak trader, to the lips of a Dyak policeman in Sandakan, and thence to Raffles Flint, brother of Walter.

Raffles, it seems, had never trusted his brother's household at Kuala Kwamut. Now when he heard the news of his brother's death he remembered the glut of native life which had finally cloyed his brother's digestion, and he remembered it with suspicion. He went to the Government and requested that an expedition be organized to accompany him to the Kalabakang River to inquire into the causes of the death of his brother. The request was granted, and the expedition left Sandakan with a personnel of the Sandakan Resident and Raffles Flint and thirteen Dyak policemen. The expedition was not organized as a punitive expedition with an object of avenging Flint's head, if the head should be found to be detached from the body. The expedition was sent out from Sandakan to be an expedition of inquiry only.

Slowly the men of the expedition moved, slowly; everything had to be waited for. There was waiting for boats, waiting for boatmen, waiting for floods to recede, waiting for rivers to rise, and the rain to be watched while they waited. Slowly the men moved up the rivers, up the Kinabatangan, up the Kwamut, up the Nasan, then through the jungle, and over at last to the Kalabakang side.

Always as they moved they asked for the story of Walter Flint. Every native knew it. Walter Flint had died of an illness, he had died of a great cough, he had died of a sick stomach, he had died of passing blood, he had died a sick man's death in the house of friends, and great was the mourning thereat.

A Hundred Teeth and a Hundred Eyes

As the Muruts of Kalabakang River were known to be a shy tribe, and a group that shunned contact with white men, the expedition had employed as a go-between a Dyak trader who had married into the Murut tribe and was trusted implicitly by the natives. They sent this confidant on ahead of them when they traveled, to assure the people of the Kalabakang of the good faith of the expedition, and that it came to bring them no harm, but only to make inquiries into the death of Walter Flint.

Six weeks after the expedition had left Sandakan it arrived at Linidis on the Kalabakang River. The Dyak trader had been able to persuade most of the Linidis Muruts not to retreat to the jungle, but Semporna Numpal himself, with his wife and daughter, had vanished. Of those who remained at Linidis, Raffles Flint interviewed many witnesses. Old women described again to him the extreme degree of the illness of Flint, young women told of the affection of Lingud for her husband, old men told of the affection of Semporna Numpal for his son-in-law, and young men told of the affection of Flint for his father-in-law.

But at Linidis there was a freshly made grave. This was across the river from the deserted house of Semporna Numpal. In the enforced presence of unwilling witnesses the expedition opened this grave, and there discovered the decapitated and dismembered body of Walter Flint.

Not until then did the witnesses find themselves able to recall the violent scene which had taken place when Semporna Numpal and his relations had met Flint's angry pursuit with the mortal blows of swords and spear thrusts. And not until then did they recall the dancing and feasting and celebrating which had honored the event of the taking of his head.

Hastily then, with horror at having their worst fears realized, and with an indignation which outran every other emotion, the expedition closed the accusing grave, and prepared to follow the fleeing Numpal and his guilty relations. Before leaving the scene of the murder they warned the Linidis natives that the expedition would return later and burn their houses and destroy their crops, in retribution for their deceit and implication in the murder. Taking the *perahus* of the Linidis people from them, the expedition started down the Kalabakang River in these.

It was raining, the river was in flood, and the dark overtook them before they had come upon any sign of Numpal. They stopped for the night in a deserted Murut house, but sent Dyak scouts on ahead in an effort to locate the fugitives. Very shortly the scouts returned. They had found a very fine longhouse down the river with hundreds of people gathered in it, and there was a great celebration. Semporna Numpal was there with his wife and daughter, and his family, and his family's family. The men were dancing and singing and the gongs were beating, and the rice beer was rising in the throats of the drinkers, and sinking in the great *tapai* jars.

As the Dyak policemen scouts told the expedition of what they had found, the Dyaks' eyes sparkled fiercely and they rubbed their swords hungrily and patted the butts of their guns. The expedition decided to go down the river and surprise the exulting Muruts before daybreak of the next day. But meanwhile the river rose and crept into the old longhouse where the two chilled white men waited for the dawn. Fires washed out, and blankets and mats were soaked, and finally they and the Dyak policemen were driven from the house into their boats, which in the height of the river's flood had to be moored to the roof of the house. There in the open boats they crouched, and the only light was the lightning and the only sound was thunder.

They dared not ride that flood in the dark, but with the first hint of daylight they started again down the river, shivering and half drowned. Following the lead of their scouts they turned out of the Kalabakang River and up a tributary river known as the Pegan. In the almost darkness they could just sight the longhouse in the distance. They landed stealthily downstream, left their boats hidden in the heavy creepers of the riverbank, and struggled through the mud, back into the jungle for some distance, in order to come upon the Muruts by surprise from the rear of the house. Finally they waded into the clearing at the back of the longhouse, and were within a hundred yards of the house when the Muruts first saw them. Then just as the house burst into life, with shouts and whoops and cries of *"Amok!"* the expedition fired. From that time on each person had either to kill or to be killed. The Muruts had men. The white men had guns.

It was only twenty minutes. The guns of the expedition swept through the longhouse from both ends. Blood poured through the floor, and raced down the tall stilts and oozed in the mud below. The men of the expedition fought for their lives, which they succeeded in saving, but between one hundred and thirty and one hundred and forty Muruts, including women and children, were killed. Those who ran from the house to the river were shot down and cut to pieces. With the exception of four women and three children who crept into the jungle wounded, all who were in the house when it was surrounded died. It was only twenty minutes.

The longhouse blazed and then it was embers.

The Dyak policemen wiped their swords, and slung

the Murut heads which they had cut from the bodies over their shoulders.

Then the expedition of inquiry proceeded down the river.

An eye for an eye, and a tooth for a tooth, the native understands. But as the story lives up and down these rivers, as the story passes from mouth to mouth, it seems to prove to the musing natives that the white men took not an eye for an eye, and a tooth for a tooth, but a hundred eyes and a hundred teeth, in the Murut longhouse one rainy dawn on the Pegan River in 1890.

Thus died Semporna Numpal's branch of the Tengara Muruts?

A Hundred Teeth and a Hundred Eyes

Two respectable-looking, betel-leaf-chewing elderly Muruts talked to us at Kampong Kalabakang later that day. Four women and three children, they reminded us, had crept into the jungle wounded. Two of these were the grandchildren of Numpal, the offspring of Flint and Lingud. Their names were Alipin and Ohdohn. The two respectable-looking elderly Muruts shifted their squatting from foot to foot, tightened their sarongs, and said, "We are Alipin and Ohdohn."

"How do you know?" we asked.

They pointed at the old woman who squatted near, with fallen breasts and straggling hair and blackened lips. "She," they said, "is Lingud."

"The story is very terrible," I said.

"Yes, it is," my husband answered. "But that story is one reason that you and I can travel on this river to-day without danger to our heads."

13. *A Blue Umbrella*

It took us an hour and a half that morning when we left
Kampong Kalabakang to stow ourselves and the *barang*
into the small boats for the first time. Harry and I used
four Murut *perahus*, and our party consisted of twelve
Tengara Muruts acting as boatmen, Puasa, Unggib, and
Kadir from the Forest Department, and Harry, Arusap,
and myself.

Winki wanted only one Murut *perahu*, as he was using
three boats of his own. In his party there were six Muruts,
his own Dyak foreman, his boy, and himself. Throughout
the trip our numbers varied with the changing of boatmen
at villages, the picking up of sick people who asked for
treatment, the meeting of native friends, and the recruiting,
on Winki's part, of new *kulis* to take back to the oil survey
work on Sebatik and at Tambisan.

Our *perahus* were native-made boats with rounded bottoms, about twenty feet in length and just wide enough
for one person, of unstable equilibrium, and obviously
pervious to water. When overloaded with luggage, as

they were now, they looked perilous. The *barang* had to be stowed in order to balance the boats, and quite without regard for comfort. Later in our travels I managed to arrange some of it so that I could occasionally stretch out flat on the top of it, and look up to the trees and the heavens, and give thanks that I could for a few minutes take the weight off my haunches, and the corkscrew out of my back, even if I tipped the boat over. But most of the time we squatted in the bottom of the boat with our loins aching and our buttocks wet from the water that was always awash there.

Now we were ready, blue umbrella, basket of eggs, wife, boy, and Conservator of Forests.

Now Winki was ready. Cross-legged in his *perahu* he sat, his survey instruments before him on a portable table top, two chickens cackling on his bedding roll, the Swiss flag floating over all. Big moment this, packed with emotion and sentiment. Farewell . . . farewell . . .

"Tickets, please!" shouts Harry.

> "Punch, brother, punch,
> Punch with care,
> Punch in the presence of
> The pass-en-ger."

And so we left Waterloo Station.

Each man ploughed his paddle. The water pushed against the *perahus* as the river in spate opposed us. But the Orang Tua had spoken truly when he said, "My men are strong."

My men are strong!

The white man builds the roads and follows the coastways, speaks the laws and rules the land. But the native knows the strength of his own arms, the endurance of his legs, the fortitude of his naked body, and the wit of his leaking *perahu* — an old patched *perahu*, a tipping and swaying and waterlogged *perahu*, but a *perahu* which travels to the heart of the country to make river and jungle his alone.

I looked back at the kampong women standing in the sunlight on the black mudbank. Three things faded slowly in that memory: the black pupils of their eyes shining in their faces; their lips, red with *sireh* juice, like cerise flowers blooming; and the fluttering notes of their treble voices blowing like leaves on the wind.

2

We had been traveling since six o'clock in the morning. Then the rain had come before we made camp in the afternoon. No one had been dry all day. Now we were crawling into our camp beds for the night.

"The tent *is* leaking, Harry; the rain is pouring in over my *bongon!*"

"It will stop when it gets thoroughly wet."

"Well, I'm not going to let it get thoroughly wet." I started to lift my *bongon* towards the bed.

"The *tent*, I say. When the *tent* gets thoroughly wet it will stop leaking."

"It will be too late then. Everything will be soaked. Just feel my bedding. Aren't you going to do something about the tent?"

"There's nothing to do. That African safari cloth isn't waterproof until it's wet. It's only leaking badly over your *bongon* because you allowed the *bongon* to touch the tent, and that always makes a tent leak." Harry lay philosophically back on his cot.

"Well, it's leaking over your *bongon* now," I said with satisfaction.

"Cripes! So it is." His *bongon* was pulled towards the centre of the tent with rapidity.

"It may be an African safari tent to you, Harry, but it's only an irritation to me," I said, putting up my blue umbrella.

"Look out with that umbrella, if you must put it up. Don't poke it into the tent or you'll start another leak."

"It will keep me and the pillow dry, anyway," I said, squatting hopefully under it on the cot. "What became of that big tent we used to take with us?"

"That old piece of brown sailcloth? That never was a tent. It was just the sail off the *lipa-lipa*."

"Well, it kept the rain out anyway. I wish this tent had never left Africa. The water is pouring in under the beds now. It must be coming down from that slope behind the tent. What's that under your bed, Harry? It looks like the Leica!"

"Cripes! I thought I put that back in the *bongon!*" Harry rescued the Leica, and tenderly wiped it dry with his sarong. "Put it in your bed, Old Thing — that seems to be the driest place."

I took it to bed with me. The rain was blowing in from both ends of the tent. I had rolled back the ends of my mattress, and I sat like Noah in his Ark in the waters of the flood, except that Noah may not have had a blue umbrella. I tied a sarong about my head to keep my hair dry, and placed bath towels over the bedding to absorb the top moisture. The rain came through the tent cloth in a mist and dripped off the edges of the umbrella. I could think of nothing to look forward to until coffee in the morning.

I dozed that way in a cramped position all night. When Harry called me at five o'clock the next morning the rain was still pouring. He had been up at regular intervals in the night to point his flashlight at the rising river. I had had chills and fever all night, and had lost my voice from the dampness, and I was, when we awoke in the morning, in the stage in which I wished that I had never come.

Tactfully, Harry didn't ask me how I felt, or try to be cheerful, but just poured three large cups of boiling coffee for me, and got my dry clothes out of the *bongon.* Kind words, coffee, and dry socks did wonders, and by the time we were in the boats and going up the river, with the detestable safari tent packed out of sight, I felt better. The first sunlight fell on the river by eight-thirty, and it was such a lovely warmth when it came through my jersey that I felt like the coming to life of a cold clay statue.

We soon found that the Kalabakang River was flooding so badly that we had to turn up the mouth of the Tiaggau, although we had hoped not to do so. The rapids were not bad yet, but the going upriver was slow and uneventful. We made an early camp before three o'clock in order to be sure of getting the shelters up before the rain started. Rain came daily before three o'clock, and usually by two. The tent was still soaking wet from the night before, and I hoped that it had achieved the proper amount of wetness which African safari tents require in order to keep out the rain. The men collected large *keladi* leaves, which have the quality of waterproofed velvet, and are about a foot and a half in diameter, and made eaves out of them to extend from the back and front of our tent, in order to break the force of the rain. By four o'clock our wing of camp was in working order, the *kulis* had their own shelters up, the *bongons* were stowed under *kajang* mats, the fire was burning in the kitchen *sulap*, and Harry and I were drinking hot chocolate, the first refreshment we had had since morning coffee at five-thirty.

Winki pitched his tent at some distance so that we should all have privacy. He had his own hours for getting up and going to bed and eating his meals, and he had his own especial food. He followed his own theory of travel, and we followed ours, and the theories were quite different. We found that we all got on very well indeed together, as long as each one did what he wished to do.

Arusap went hunting just before dusk, and returned in ten minutes' time with two barking deer, about thirty pounds each. He is a skillful hunter, but we all admitted that two was good luck. The Muruts greeted the return of the successful hunter with admiration and enthusiasm, and brought up their suggestively empty stewpots. Medical reports of North Borneo state that the diet of the natives is deficient in meat and animal fats, but it certainly wasn't that night.

Harry held a medicine-box dispensary every night for the men. Many had ulcers, several had yaws, a number of them had fever, and all, to judge by the answers to our questions, were constipated. This surprised me, as they lived in a state of nature and exercised constantly, and I had always heard that constipation was a complaint of civilization. Probably if we questioned them further we should find that they had acidosis, arthritis, and hemorrhoids.

3

"Fried bananas for breakfast! Fancy that!" said Harry early the next morning as we paddled down the river past Winki's camp. Sure enough, there was Winki sitting at his table in front of his tent, and eating what was, we were sure from our rude and caddish personal observations of the past, a meal of fried bananas.

We waved at him as we paddled by, and he waved at us, and probably he was telling himself, "Nothing but coffee for breakfast! And don't they look it!"

About an hour after this Winki's flotilla came tearing down the river, and passed ours. This always happens within the hour, and demonstrates to us that it does not retard the speed of travel to wait for one's breakfast. Shortly afterwards again we passed Winki prowling barefoot up and down on a stony beach. Occasionally he would pick up stones and smack them to bits with his little geologist's hammer. His legs were brown and his shorts were ragged and he only looked scientific from the neck up.

Harry halted our boats beneath a tree that was in flower, to collect specimens. Unggib was the official tree-climber. The obvious thing to compare Unggib-climbing-a-tree to was a monkey, but no monkey could know the conscious triumph of his performance the way Unggib did. Like a prima donna holding a high note, Unggib would hold his perilous poses just long enough for applause, but achieve the whole ascent quickly enough to show his skill.

246

A Blue Umbrella

I reminded myself those days of the Fukien-ware Kuan Yin that the Chinese peddler brought to our house one day. At every house where the peddler had stopped he must have patiently unboxed and unwrapped her, and set her up on her little pedestal. If she had been mine I should have wanted to throw her down and break her nose, or give her away to be rid of her. But not so the peddler, and carefully, painstakingly, at each house he must have unpacked her and set her on her pedestal.

I am like that porcelain Kuan Yin when I sit in our *perahu* and wait every afternoon for the men to build our camp. And when the camp is up I am carefully unwrapped and mounted on my pedestal.

However, during the hours of travel there was nothing idolic about me. Travel up the river was beginning to be one long fight up a succession of swift rapids. Part of the time the men hauled the boat up the side of the river while we crawled and climbed over slippery rocks. It was slow going.

When going through rapids Unggib would swim by the boat with a lighted pipe in his mouth. His rôle in the party was changing. From the village half-wit he was developing into the soothsayer. Harry said that the men believed he had supernatural contact with the spirit world.

Harry shot two wild pigs. The Muruts loaded them hilariously into the last boat. They love pig, especially after it is a little bad. Puasa, who is a Mohammedan, was disgusted, and made them stop and let him get into another boat. Kadir, who is a pagan by birth, but is studying under Puasa to become a Mohammedan, also put his nose in the air. A pig always makes trouble in camp. I remember the last time on a jungle trip we had trouble because Puasa left some flower presses to dry over the fire, and the *kulis* cooked a pig over the fire, and the flower presses dried in the smoke of the pig, and Puasa refused to handle the flower presses after that.

In the stretches between the white rapids I lay on my back in the bottom of the boat and looked up at the pale sky through a fresco of feathery *mengaris* trees. The river was walled by the forest. I did not see trunks and limbs and branches of trees, but one solid mass of green. The vines hung down from the trees like skeins of matted silk in a woman's sewing basket. Our biggest rapids that day were Karandulang and Mansalong, and we passed the mouths of Large Makandut and Small Makandut rivers.

We made camp by three, and it rained, and the tent still leaked, so we left the bedding in the canvas bag till we were ready to get in bed. It is not so bad to have a bed get wet after you are in it, but it is very discouraging to climb into an already wet one. Before we went to bed I washed handkerchiefs and underclothes, and dried them over the fire inside the tent.

Most of the sick stomachs which we treated with salts the night before were cured, but the patients returned with other ailments. One *kuli* had diarrhoea so badly that his boat made little progress. Harry suggested that for this reason all those with digestive ailments who had taken salts should go in the same boat the next day. Harry was afraid some of them had dysentery; and if so we could do nothing for them, as we had no treatment and could only give a sedative for temporary relief. All the fever patients that we treated with quinine had improved. I made a note that Harry and I must not forget to be tested for malaria when we returned to Sandakan, as most of our *kulis* had it and there were a lot of anopheles mosquitoes about — at least they stood on their heads when they bit.

The men were becoming individuals to me, and I started a sketch of Apul, a good-looking young Murut who wore only a loincloth. He stood quietly when I worked and paid little attention to me. The other Muruts were much amused, standing in the background and whispering and scratching themselves and spitting *sireh* juice, and laughing in childish falsetto tones which were very disarming.

4

We left camp in the morning under a clear bright sky which we had learned meant rain in the early afternoon. We made rapid progress up the river as the water had risen enough to give clearance to some of the rapids. We hoped to reach the *pengkalan*, or landing place for the jungle carry-over, that night. There we would leave our boats and start on foot over the watershed. Early in the morning we had asked the Orang Tua if he thought that we could reach the *pengkalan* by five o'clock in the evening, and he had said yes. By noon, with a dark sky ahead of us, Harry consulted him again.

"You say that we can reach the carrying place to-night, Old Man?"

"Of a certainty, Tuan, we can reach it. It is but two hours away."

Two hours later, with the sky more threatening, Harry resumed the conversation. "How long now before we will reach the carrying place?"

"It is but two hours away, Tuan."

"So you told us two hours ago."

"Then probably it is only an hour away, Tuan."

An hour later we return to the conversation. "How long now before we reach the carrying place, Old Man?"

Old Man studies the scenery more carefully and says, "It is perhaps three hours away now, Tuan."

It becomes obvious that we are getting no place by measuring in hours. "Do you think that we can reach there by dark to-night, Old Man?"

Old Man looks at the sky, which is black, at the river, which is rising, at Harry, who is scowling, at the moderately possible camp site which we are passing, and says diplomatically, "Perhaps we could reach there, Tuan, but then again probably we could not reach there, Tuan."

"Have you ever been to this carrying place, Old Man?"

"Certainly, Tuan!"

"How long did it take you to get there after you left the mouth of the Tiaggau River?"

"Let me remember carefully, Tuan. We stopped for one day to visit our friends who had the longhouse near Karandulang Rapids, and there was a good harvest of *padi* there and much fine rice beer and we had many matters to discuss, and that took us two days. And then we went to collect gum pontianak in the jungle with another friend and that was four days, and then we met a friend who had shot two pigs and we stopped to eat them with him and that was five days, and then . . ."

"Never mind, Old Man. We camp here."

The men got the tent up and the *kajangs* over the *barang* before the storm came. Then almost instantaneously a strong wind came up the river valley and quickly swept the storm to the east, and we felt only the tail of it. Before the dark came the rain stopped, and Arusap went hunting. He returned to camp carrying a spectacular bird with long luminous blue wattles and a pure-white, long-feathered tail. To see such beauty brought to death frightened me, and when Harry saw the bird he was furious, for Arusap had shot a Bulwer pheasant. The pheasant is very rare, it is a difficult bird to hunt, it is difficult to get a license to shoot one, it is protected by all of the game laws, and Harry is the Game Warden.

Poor Arusap!

When Harry quieted down enough to ask him why he had shot it Arusap answered, "I like it. My people think it is very fine. My people wear its feathers in the hair. Its flesh is sweet. I shot it for the Tuan's dinner."

Item, one Bulwer pheasant, stew for the Game Warden's dinner.

The Muruts, who had all gathered around to admire the pheasant, listened then to what was probably their first exposition of the game laws of the country. They all said, "Good, Tuan," and "Yes, Tuan," but they continued to stroke and gloat over the white tail, and to look admiringly at Arusap.

Shortly after that Winki dropped into camp, and Harry was diverted from the pheasant by a discussion between himself and Winki as to the best jungle footwear. Winki and Harry represented two different schools of thought, and each believed implicitly in the superiority of his own school.

Winki always wore heavy leather hobnailed boots in the jungle with heavy wool socks which were a cuff length higher than the boot. But when traveling in his boat, or when in camp, or any place except in heavy jungle, Winki went barefoot. This, he said, was the ONLY WAY. Winki had bites, sores, and ulcers on his legs.

Harry wore nothing heavier than rubber-soled canvas sneakers, and he usually went barelegged. He said that wet leather boots made his toes crack. He never went barefoot, however, because of the danger of hookworm. His way, Harry said, was the ONLY WAY. He also had bites, sores, and ulcers.

I didn't belong to any school of thought because I was never convinced of the correctness of the shoes I wore; whatever shoe I was wearing always seemed to be the wrong shoe at the time. Leather boots gave support and protection to my feet, but were burdensome. When they filled with mud and water I found it unbearable to drag them along on the end of my tired legs. So I wore rubber-soled canvas tennis shoes like Harry's, not because they were good but because anything else was worse. At least they were lightweight, they didn't hold the water, and they could be removed and the mud emptied from them quickly. They gave no protection to the feet and were slippery on wet rocks, and in an emergency I would take mine off and walk barefoot on the rocks, but as my feet were tender I could not do this for long. About the camp and when traveling in boats I went barefoot like Winki. I also had bites, sores, and ulcers on my legs.

The need of a high leather boot for the protection from snakebite was unappreciable. The natives were always barefoot, and such casualties among them were rare.

Whenever Harry and I met a new type of jungle boot

we had it copied, wore it once, and discarded it. In this manner we had tried lace boots, gillies, short riding boots, high canvas shoes laced down the back, and ordinary oxfords. We always returned to Chinese canvas tennis shoes as sold in Sandakan for fifty cents Straits. I took half a dozen pairs with me on a trip, sometimes discarding them daily as the tread wore off or the rocks cut through. This lightened my luggage but added weight to Arusap's, as he would always pick them up and carry them back to Sandakan to use himself.

I had not had my culottes, which were designed to protect me from *kurap,* out of the *bongon* once. I knew that the less clothes I wore the better for actual jungle tramping, but I had not realized that this would also be true of boat travel. But I soon found that shorts were the only possible garment when squatting in the bottom of a leaking *perahu,* or wading in rapids. I envied the Muruts their loincloths, which dried quickly, and the invulnerable quality of their skins which a lifetime without clothing had developed.

One disadvantage of wearing shorts was the long expanse of leg which was left bare and resulted in scratches in the jungle, bruises on the rocks, bites from sand flies, wasps, mosquitoes, leeches, and finally a number of patches of *rengas* poisoning from rubbing against the leaves of the *rengas* tree.

5

Harry and I were having a bath, and not before we needed it. I had smoothed a flat place in the gravel bottom of the river pool so that no sharp stones stuck into me, and I was sitting there with the water up to my chin. The current flowed by the pool and was just strong enough against me so that if I eased myself up in the water I started to float away, but if I sat tight to the river bed I could rest against the current. It was a moment to be well content. Harry was working energetically on himself with the red antiseptic soap. Then I worked on myself, and then we threw the soap back onto the riverbank. We could see Winki's head upstream on the other side of the river where he was pottering about his own little beach in front of his tent. Then I saw that Winki's head had turned towards us, and then he started to run down the bank and was shouting at us. At first I thought that he was just being sociable, and had chosen an inopportune time. Then I heard what he was shouting.

"There's a crocodile in that pool!"

It was tactless of Winki. I could not have the same feeling about sharing a bath with a crocodile as I did about sharing one with my husband. But I did need a bath, and if nobody had said crocodile to me I could have gone on happily, and probably without interference from the crocodile, sitting in the bath. But now that I had been said crocodile to, the bath became a dangerous river.

Winki, it seemed, had seen the crocodile lying on our beach and disappearing into our pool several times the day before we arrived.

We had arrived there at the *pengkalan* that morning, eight days after we had left the launch below Kampong Kalabakang. We pitched our camp on the near side of the river, as we saw that Winki was on the far side. Later in the day Winki warned us that he had seen elephants on our bank of the river the night before, just where we now had our camp, and that was the reason he himself had crossed to the other side. We had wondered why he hadn't camped there, as it was obviously the best place.

So then Harry pointed out to Winki that Winki's camp was in the line of a number of very large dead trees which would probably fall if there was a storm. And then I pointed out that none of these impending dangers was half as menacing as the sand flies, which, now that dusk had come, were terrible. So then we all had a couple of gins, and none of our troubles seemed so imminent.

6

When we had decided to make our camp where we did the next afternoon, Puasa had looked pessimistically at the river. We were on a high beach extending below the bluff of the river's bank. It was covered with grass and shrubs, and small trees, and appeared to be above the high-water level of the river. To build camp on the bluff above meant clearing a number of large trees. Harry said, "Make camp."

But Puasa looked sagacious and foreboding and said, "I am afraid of a flood."

Harry called the Orang Tua. "Will a river flood cover this beach?"

Old Man, also looking sagacious and prophetic, studied Harry to see what answer he wanted, while he pretended to study the beach, the river, and the sky.

"Probably there will be no flood, Tuan."

"But is this beach covered by flood?"

Then Old Man remembered that he was tired and that large trees were difficult to fell, and after studying the river and the sky and Harry for a moment longer he declared that he remembered distinctly that that beach was never covered in time of flood.

But Puasa continued to be noncoöperative. "I fear a flood, Tuan. Do you not remember the great trip when we went to look for gold, Tuan, and three times the floods came on us?"

"Don't be an old woman, Puasa. It's only one night, and we'll take a chance," decided Harry.

Winki and his men arrived half an hour later. Their minds followed the same series of doubts and deductions as ours had, and they arrived at the same conclusions. As we had our tent pitched on the best level stretch they had to camp on the peak of the small beach, which placed them on a level four feet higher than ourselves.

It had been a bad day for me. Any day in the jungle from 6 A.M. to 3 P.M. is a bad day for me, but that day even the men were tired. We were now crossing on foot the watershed between the east-flowing and the west-flowing rivers. We had thought to find some trace or blaze to mark a path of habitual native travel. But apparently the only habitual travelers were elephants, and when we followed anything we followed elephant tracks. Although I saw fresh elephant dung I had difficulty in believing that elephants had tramped through that seemingly unbroken jungle just before us.

Everything in the jungle that day united in a malevolent effort to defeat me. I was always hurrying because the pace was always a little too fast for me, and when I hurried I slid and stumbled and then I got behind, and then I hurried more and slid more and was more behind, until the man in front of me would be lost to sight. He might only be ten yards distant, but he would be lost to sight, so dense was the jungle. And then I wouldn't know which way to go, and the green crepe of the jungle would drop over me like a mildewed mourner's veil, and I would stand still, defeated. And then I would sit down gloomily and wait for the *kulis* to overtake me, and pretend that I was waiting on purpose and not lost from the men in front, and they would pretend that too, but they knew.

A hundred times I had told myself, "Never again, never again, never again," pulling myself out of the mud, spitting bugs out of my mouth, pulling off the leeches, "never again will I go on a jungle trip!"

By three o'clock, if I had been asked, I could have proved to them by the look of the river, by the color of the sky, by the foliage of the trees, by omens, portents, and signs, that any camping site was a good one. So when we made camp on our grassy beach we were all in accord except Puasa, who still persisted in looking unhappily at the river and muttering about "when the Tuan and I had three floods on the gold hunt, and he was almost drowned, and I was almost drowned."

There was a beautiful place in the river to bathe, but it was just in front of Winki's camp, so we put up the "Look the other way" signal. That's my pink bath towel, and all the men look away from and stay away from my pink bath towel. There was a fallen tree wedged into the bank and reaching over the river and touching the water.

The river was so swift that we couldn't keep our feet but had to hang onto the fallen tree with both hands, while our bodies drifted out behind us just below the surface of the water. To float in this swift-running water was like moving fast without making any effort, and our bodies when we looked back at them were like figures on a Lalique vase. And then we got out of the water and stood on the bank to rub the soap on, and got back in the water again, and this time when our bodies swept out behind us soapsuds floated down the river, and the very last of the jungle mud washed off, and I forgot that I was never going to take a jungle trip again.

By six-thirty we heard thunder down the river, and called for our food early, hoping to get through eating before the rain. We didn't. We ate corned beef, rice, and tinned carrots, sitting in the drizzle which always came through our tent. The beds were open, but we left the bedding in the bags to keep it dry until we were ready to crawl in.

The storm rolled up the canyon and broke on the hills surrounding us. Between cannon balls of thunder came the crash of dead trees falling in the jungle. With each flash of lightning the Muruts whooped an answer, and the whoops were exuberant and welcoming. I had just opened my bedding roll and was sitting on it in my nightgown with the blue cotton umbrella over me thinking how cozy I was, and what a lot of merit there is in corned beef, when Winki suddenly appeared in the tent. The rain dripped from his tow hair and slid off his sunburned bald spot, and his sarong was hauled high between his legs for action.

"I move my *barang*," he said excitedly. "I measure the

river. It rises three feet. I send everything to the upper riverbank."

I could see his Dyaks, then, filing by in a flashlight procession, carrying his things. The lightning played on them like floodlights. They hurried, not quite running because of their loads. I watched them to the river's edge. Each one went in with a shout, nearly disappeared, struggled, and finally shoved head and shoulders up above the rushing water. They formed a chain, half swimming, half pulling each other, singing and chanting, and got the *barang* across.

Winki stayed in our tent for a minute looking worried. Harry called for Arusap and started immediately to send our *barang* up to the river bluff. Then he placed a pole in the mud by the edge of the river to mark its rise in order to gauge whether or not we must leave camp ourselves. I sat under my umbrella and didn't believe any of it.

Harry went to the water to look at his marking stick, and the stick was out of sight under water. "We must go," he said.

Still I sat under the umbrella. It wasn't until I heard Puasa's voice shouting in the distance, and the Muruts singing the words with him in Malay so that it almost made a chant, that I knew I was in a flood. They sang: —

"The Mem go first, the Mem go first, the river
    runs strong,
The Mem go first, quickly bring the Mem,
The river comes fast, the river comes strong,
If you wait the Mem cannot cross.
Quickly bring the Mem, the flood comes;
The flood, the flood, flood, flood, flood, flood,
    flood, flood!"

The dazzling illumination of the lightning photographed the picture of Puasa and the Muruts racing down towards us from the upper bluff of the river where he and the *kulis* had wisely made their own camp for the night. With the increasing violence of the storm they had known that we were in danger, and had now decided that the time had come to rescue us.

But I didn't want to be rescued. I didn't really believe that the flood would reach us, and I thought that the Puasa-led demonstration was like a lifesaving drill with a women-and-children-first theme, fine in theory but a great nuisance in practice. So I sat quietly in my nightgown on my bed under my umbrella amidst the confusion.

Then suddenly the men were all in the tent and pulling the canvas off the ridgepole, and everybody was shouting at me, and Harry was getting annoyed, and he grabbed the blue umbrella away from me and shouted, "Don't be a damn fool, or we'll all get drowned!"

And I shouted back, "Well, I'd rather drown than die of a cold from being rescued in my nightgown!" But I was half out of my nightgown by then. I rushed so quickly into my jersey, shorts, and shoes that there was hardly a naked moment. There were so many people around me participating in things that I had the feeling that I was lost to sight. I got into my leather coat then and even remembered to find the belt, and crammed any loose possessions I saw into my *bongon*. Before I went to sleep every night I always put everything I could inside the *bongon* for a quick morning start, so there wasn't much out except my nose atomizer, which the Muruts had always thought was very amusing. I pushed the plugs in the ends of that so the medicine wouldn't run out, and packed it into the box, shoved it into the *bongon*, and put the lid on tight so it wouldn't leak. Then I took my flashlight, and we were ready. Meanwhile the tent had disappeared from over me, and the river was filling the front tent holes.

What had been a beach to be walked upon half an hour before was now a river separating us from the upper bluff.

Harry held on to me and I waded in, still mentally poohpoohing things. But waist-deep the water poured against me, and I almost lost my feet, and entirely lost my cynical attitude towards the flood. I tried with all my strength to stand against the river and could not do so, and Harry braced himself and held me, and together we could stand, but we could not move. Puasa was reaching towards me from the end of a chain of men extending from the upper bluff of the river. When they saw that I could not move against the flood, slowly Puasa and the chain forced towards us through the waters. Then Puasa reached out for me, and made me another human link in the chain, and then the chain, with Puasa shouting constant directions of "Quick, quick," and "Careful, careful," pulled slowly back towards the bluff again, and I was rescued.

I stood on the top of the bluff and looked back at the line of men behind me, half swimming, half wading. Our *barang* was passing over their heads from man to man. There came my open bed, the *bongons*, the tent and the tent poles, and the blue umbrella. Unggib's head was just above water, and he still had his pipe in his mouth. They all looked happily excited, and at intervals they whooped and shouted.

Before the tent could be put up the men had to cut down trees and clear a place on the upper bluff. Now by flashlight in a storm they had to do what had been too difficult to do in the afternoon. I stood on the bluff under my blue umbrella and tried to think of some way that I could help, but every idea I had was thought of first by somebody else. Arusap was trying to light a fire and I held the umbrella over it, and then I kneeled down and blew on it. But if I kneeled down to blow, Arusap had to hold the umbrella over it. And as Arusap is a stronger blower than I, I finally resigned myself to being nothing but the blue-umbrella holder, while the rest of them rebuilt the camp.

I turned the flashlight back towards our old camp site and saw that it was under water. Four feet higher, on the peak of the sloping beach where Winki's tent stood, a campfire still glowed. Every so often I could see Winki's bare feet in the light of his own down-turned flashlight walk down to the edge of the water; then the flashlight would sweep the rising river; then it would illumine his feet again and the feet would go back to the tent.

When our tent was up we started locating our possessions. This had become a familiar moment to me, this picking up and dusting off the household gods after the outdoor gods had destroyed the house. Everything turned up this time except Harry's cigarette holder.

Arusap had our small fire going under the umbrella, and he boiled a kettle of hot water and made tea. Harry told Arusap and Puasa and Unggib to bring their cups and we gave them tea before we took ours. They tried to refuse it, and perhaps they didn't enjoy it, but we meant it as a gesture of gratitude and as the mark of a bond between us, so they humored us and drank it. Harry gave cigarettes to everybody, and the Muruts melted away to lie down under their *kajang* mats. Having no clothes on, they did not seem to be as wet as we did, and appeared quite comfortable. Long after I had crawled into my damp bed I could still hear the Muruts chanting and giving an occasional faint whoop at the fading streaks of lightning.

Heroic phrases ran through my mind about these men, phrases that may have been remembered verses of poetry. But the men were real, and the phrases were artificial.

There's greatness in them, I thought. And I went to sleep to dream that Winki was swimming in the river with his clinometer in his mouth and I was swimming behind him in my nightgown and holding the blue umbrella high over my head.

The camp had the same feeling of relaxation the next day which exists in a family after a successful wedding party — everybody still eating chicken salad and wedding cake, tolerant and good-humored, but not accomplishing much.

The river had fallen again and Winki's camp had come through the flood with a foot to spare, although he had sat up all night watching the river. He was moving camp one day's journey ahead of us now, as we were short of carrying *kulis* and had to move our camps in relays. The plan was for him to send the men back to us the next day.

I spent all day drying, smoking, and singeing things over a large campfire. Everything was wet — camp beds, mattresses, and clothing. By the time I finished the smell of smoke and fire in the bedding was enough to arouse a fire horse.

I was alone all that day in the camp with Apul, Nulang, Melasi, Uman, Isat, and the other Muruts. They put wood on the fire for me, and brought water up from the river, and laid my washing out on the sunny rocks, being careful to stroke the wrinkles out of the pieces so that they would dry smoothly. They turned Puasa's drying flower presses carefully, and they put Arusap's kettle on the fire for him so there would be hot water when he came in from hunting. Between chores they sat under their *atap* shelters, and ate half-cooked pig, and picked it out of their teeth, and smoked and talked, and sometimes they sang. They seemed to be singing in parts, and it made me think of the university Glee Club singing under the stars in the Berkeley stadium in my university days. Perhaps that wasn't beautiful, and perhaps the Muruts' singing was not beautiful, but they both seemed beautiful at the time. There is a strain in young strong male voices that is very touching; a strain that is not in women's voices. Young

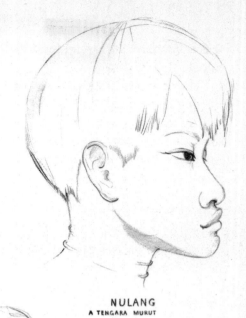

NULANG
A TENGARA MURUT

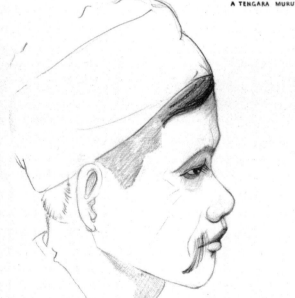

ISAT
A MELANO DYAK FROM
LUNUD VILLAGE — AND A
MOHAMMEDAN

men sing for their own great joy, women sing to be heard; young men sing with the flow of the blood in their bodies, with a great hunger for living, and then with a hunger satisfied.

Arusap came into camp that night disgusted. It was the second day that he had hunted without bringing home. It was not his fault, because with Winki's camp moving in front of us the game was all scared up. But Arusap wanted meat to feed to his Muruts, and not to get it made him bloody-minded. He has these spells when something upsets him, when he retires into being a noncoöperative dunce. It isn't premeditated on his part, but it is like a second nature which overtakes him in spite of himself. Ordinarily he is so responsive and so quick to interpret my ideas that I know immediately when Mr. Hyde has come upon him. One physical symptom of this condition is that he never steps over anything, but walks right through it. In this manner he walked through the campfire that night, then through the tent supports and guy ropes, through the opened medicine box and my clean washing, and arrived before me and asked me what we wanted for dinner. He spoke, and although the words were polite, the glum tone of his voice said, "There was to have been deer steak for you and the Tuan, and now there isn't, so nothing that you eat will be any good, and you might just as well not eat."

"Open a tin of stew and make curry," I said.

"There is no stew, Mem."

I knew that there was stew. "Then make fried corned beef and sweet potatoes."

"The corned beef is gone, and there are no sweet potatoes." That again, I knew, was the voice of Mr. Hyde.

"Make fried rice, then," I said.

"What shall I put in the fried rice, Mem?"

If there is one thing that Arusap thoroughly understands making it is fried rice, and he, like every native, knows that its ingredients are anything and everything that the cook can find in camp. Nevertheless I said, "I'll look in the *bongon* and see what there is."

I took out a tin of sardines, of sausages, a box of raisins, and some white onions, and gave them to him. The rice was to be boiled first until it was fluffy and dry, and then placed in a large skillet and fried, and while the rice was frying the shredded sardines and sausages and the raisins and onions were to be mixed into it.

Sometime later, after much more time than Arusap usually devotes to a meal, two large stewpots arrived before us. Fried rice is never in a stewpot. I lifted one lid and saw beautiful white rice, but it was not fried. I lifted the other lid and saw a ghastly combination in which the sardines had stewed into a state of apparent decay, the sausages had melted into grease and gristle, and the raisins looked up at us like shriveled black eyeballs.

I looked at the stew in surprise for a minute, while Arusap stood by and looked over my shoulder with what seemed to be a mutual surprise. We both felt that he had no more willed it to be like that than I had. So I hid my surprise from Harry and pretended that this was a new kind of stew. Harry ate it, and said it was good.

When we were in bed and the petrol light was out, I

watched Arusap washing dishes in the light of his kitchen fire. The glum look spread over his face like a clay film. After a minute he stepped over to the Murut *sulap* and spoke, and then I saw Apul get up, and the two of them returned together to the dying kitchen fire. Arusap took the shotgun and silently left camp, but Apul squatted over the fire and fanned it with the lid of a *bongon*. As Apul squatted there I had seen his picture in many picture galleries. He was Primitive Man Makes Fire. The red and gold of the fire flickered over him in waves of sudden color, and then again he would be dark and shining, and the shadows that hid around his strong features would be very black. He was intent, with the complete absorption of a child, and he was lovable as a child is, whose whole heart and mind are in the occupation of the moment.

When the fire flamed high he would stop his fanning to examine the pictures on the tins of food which were about him, pictures of carrots, tomatoes, peaches, cherries, sausages. He picked each tin up and scrutinized it attentively, then replaced the tin and returned to his fire-fanning.

I heard Arusap calling to the barking deer, then. The call is made by blowing softly through a folded leaf. Apul heard the call also, and looked quickly up from his fire. Then came a shot. Soon, from beneath my tent flap, I saw Arusap's bare legs joining Apul in the firelight. They talked in Murut, and Arusap's voice was dull. Arusap had evidently put up a deer but had not hit it. Apul went to his *sulap* and returned with his knife, and Arusap took the gun again, and they disappeared together into the darkness. The fire burned dimly then and the pictures on the tins faded out, and far away and very faintly I heard again the sound of savage lips blowing through a leaf to call a wild deer in the jungle.

THE WILD MEN FROM BORNEO
OR
THE WILD GENTLEMEN FROM BORNEO

I wrote in my journal about that time.

Now that I was seeing Arusap every day with his own people, I realized what a long way he had come from them. In twelve years spent away from his village he had covered centuries. He had learned to think with his mind as well as to feel with his body. At home I was often annoyed with Arusap for his failure to achieve the standard of efficiency of Chinese servants. But now that I saw him with his own people I saw that he had in his individual lifetime encompassed a diuturnity of learning.

He has accepted electric refrigerators, flying machines, warships, and submarines. He has accepted both the white man's laws and his idiosyncrasies. He has accepted a belief in the importance of the unessential possessions with which we surround ourselves. And although he has accepted the white man's own high estimate of the white man, I do not think that he has accepted the white man's underestimate of the brown man.

At times Arusap can think through the mind of a white man. Yet he can still return to his own people, and be one of them. He has taken on none of the superficial veneer which among white men separates the small-town man who makes good in the big city from the small-town man who stays at home. He has a simplicity of mind which makes both white and brown ways seem right to him. I frequently recognize that he is being tolerant with Harry and me, that he knows better himself, but humors us in our whims.

7

I told Harry that I thought our Muruts were as amiable and pleasant persons as I had met in a long time and that I couldn't imagine being afraid of them. Harry then said that as recently as 1925 these pleasant persons were conducting regular and systematic head-hunting and warfare as a part of their daily life.

Then I remembered the day when Harry had shot a wild pig on the riverbank as we went by in our boat. The pig went limp and his head flopped forward and his eyes rolled upwards, but he wasn't dead. With a joyful yell Apul jumped out of the boat and carved off the pig's legs, and sliced pieces off him while he was still squealing. Harry called to him to kill the pig quickly, and then Apul did so because Harry told him to, but not because he saw any reason in stopping the pig's suffering.

Our Muruts all showed an uncomplaining acceptance of pain in their own physical ailments. They had an unimaginative indifference to suffering in others, and a stoic acceptance of suffering for themselves.

When they thought in terms of themselves they gave death violently and accepted violent death, for that was their way. But when they thought of white men they did not think in terms of themselves. They thought of us as strange persons whose strange lives were ruled by strange standards. If these were the standards we liked they were willing for us to have them, and they accepted any incidental benefits which came to them by way of these standards. This was the mood in which they went to Harry to ask for medicine for their ailments. We had the medicine and they were willing to be benefited by it, but if the medicine had not been there, and we had not been there, they would not have complained — they would just have accepted.

They did not judge me by their own standards, and say, "Here is a woman who does nothing. She doesn't harvest the rice, or work in the fields for her husband, or nurse his children, or build his fire. Why should we do her bidding? Let her get out and work for herself."

Instead they thought, "Here is a strange person from a strange world, and we will make no attempt to understand her. Perhaps her husband may find some use for her in that strange world from which they come. Meanwhile, we Muruts are good-hearted men, after our fashion, and they seem good-hearted persons after their fashion, so let us all be amiable together." And so they build my fires.

As long as we remain people of our own world they do not force their world on us. But if we try to invade their world we must accept life on their terms, for they will be thinking of us then in terms of themselves.

14. *Jungle Mud*

WE were still crossing the watershed and walking through heavy jungle. At nine o'clock, after three hours of walking, we stopped on a bank of a stream and waited for the *kulis* to catch up with us. I was having chills and fever again, and I tried to find a spot where the sun would come through the trees. But the sunlight had no warmth, it was like a pale lemon liquid spilled over the ferns. I couldn't stand the chill, so I took Arusap and walked on ahead. I like walking behind Arusap. He tries to make it easy for me, and pretends to lag when I lag. He knows that I walk blindly along behind the man in front, and he picks his steps accordingly. When we are in Sandakan I am responsible for him, but when we are in the jungle he is the responsible one. I am afraid that I am not as tactful with him, when I am in the lead, as he is with me.

It had been raining all night and the leeches were bad.

271

Like the waving tendrils of the vines they reached out at us from every leaf. They inched cunningly up my legs trying to get under my shorts. When I pulled them off they fastened onto my hands, and then I rolled and squeezed and pinched them till they burst. Harry has a book called *Hints to Travelers* which says that leeches do not go above the knee, but the leeches have not read the book.

Then for the first time I met *lintahs*, or game leeches, in the Biyudun River. Harry and Puasa and the *kulis* had overtaken Arusap and me, and we were all wading a tributary stream just where it entered the Biyudun River when Melasi, one of the Muruts, screamed. That was the first sound of pain or fright I had heard on the trip. Melasi was standing on one foot with his pack almost falling in the water while he struggled to pull a large buffalo leech off his other foot. These leeches are almost impossible to remove unless you hold a lighted match to them, and when you are standing in the middle of a fast-running river with a falling pack it is not easy to light a match. Melasi finally got his leech off with a knife. It was about four inches long. I got out of that stream as quickly as I could.

We arrived that night at the carrying place which marked the end of the trip across the watershed. We found Winki's camp there. He said that he had had a bad trip the day before with rain all day and many leeches. I knew that if Winki said "many leeches," it was so. We got our camp up just before the rain came. The river was flooding, which made our nightly bath exciting. Harry sent the Orang Tua on ahead of us to Kuala Biyudun to arrange for more native boats to take us down the river.

Meanwhile Winki came over to visit us and we started

rather nervously to count our provisions. We found that
we were both going short on rice for the *kulis*, and on
personal supplies, as the trip was taking longer than we had
expected. In an endeavor to travel light I had not taken
anything extra as I sometimes did, and I found that our
tinned supplies were ample for only ten days more. We
had thought we might get rice as we traveled along,
but the country proved to be so sparsely inhabited that
we had not been able to do so. We told the Orang Tua
to try to bring us rice from the village at Kuala Biyudun,
but we were not sure that he could do so as the natives
there ferment much of their rice into rice beer.

By five o'clock, when the Orang Tua had not returned,
we decided that he must be drunk on rice beer in the house
of a friend, and would not return that night. Harry, Winki,
and I were condoling with each other, and drinking a
peg of gin, when we heard welcoming shouts from Apul
and Nulang. Thus announced, the Orang Tua wove his
way into the firelight, and proudly reported that he had
obtained the loan of three small boats for us to go down the
river in. The Old Man had the polished mahogany glow,
both physical and spiritual, which comes from the recent
meeting of a Murut with a quantity of rice beer.

The realization that we would be traveling down the
river the next day reminded us of the fact that our Tengara
Muruts from the Kalabakang River would leave us to return
to their own village as soon as we acquired the new boatmen
on Biyudun River. So when the Orang Tua sobered up
later that night Harry made the bill out to him for the
wages of each of his "children." The account covered the
work of each man and the use of each boat, and extra

wages to cover the time of the return journey back to the village after the men had left us. The Old Man and his children stood around us and looked wise, while Harry struggled with accounts and worked it out down to the last penny, which was not easy, as every few minutes somebody remembered a new item which changed the account. Harry made the chit out to the Old Man to be paid by the District Officer at Tawau upon the first visit of the Old Man to that district. The Orang Tua could not read what the chit said, but everybody seemed perfectly satisfied.

Upon inspection by flashlight the last thing before going to bed we found that the three *perahus* were very small and very leaky. We decided that in order to lighten the load we would send the luggage by boat, and go on foot ourselves through the jungle again. My heart sank, for I had hoped that my jungle walking was finished for the time.

2

And then I find, in looking back over my journal of that trip, some brief entries as follows, each one marking a day: —

Make camp three o'clock. Pouring rain since noon. Too tired to write.

Make camp one o'clock. Pouring rain all day. Dead tired.

Make camp two o'clock. Pouring rain and electrical storm. Too tired to write.

Well, if our matrimony can stand this trip it can stand anything!

Make camp two o'clock. NO RAIN!

What a day! Too tired to write and too wet to care!

HOW I HATE JUNGLE TRAVEL!

Jungle Mud

That was a day which started badly but ended well. We were still traveling through the jungle, but sending our luggage on by boat. I was becoming very tired and each day seemed worse than the one before. I felt an almost physical nausea when I fell in the jungle mud. This day I could not even keep Harry in sight. It seemed equally impossible either for him to slow down or for me to speed up. Again and again I lost sight of the person ahead of me, and fought the trees, and missed the blazes. When we followed down a river bed I always missed the blazes which marked the place where the trace left the water and ascended the riverbank again. Once I rolled down the mud-bank and ended with my face in the mud. The *kulis* fell back in a discerning way, and pretended that it was a clever acrobatic stunt. But I was past pretense, and the tears rolled down my cheeks from anger with myself.

By noontime we had reached the carrying place on the Nepagan River and I was cheered by the thought that the rapids of the Kwamut River would soon be before us. We said good-bye then to most of our Tengara Muruts, as they were to return through the jungle to their own village. I felt sentimental about it, but no one else did. Apul and Melisang stayed with us as they were going down to Kuala Kwamut.

We were met at the river by three very small boats sent up by the headman from Lunud Village. These *perahus* were inadequate to our luggage or personnel, not to mention that of Winki, who had not yet arrived at the carrying place. We saw that we should again have to relay ourselves downstream. As we were the first to arrive we took the two best boats and left the poorest one for Winki. We put what we could of ourselves in the two *perahus*, leaving part of our luggage to be returned for the next day. When loaded the boats sank almost to water level, so that they not only leaked, but shipped water consistently. Although Harry and I bailed all the time we could not keep up with the water. After each rapid we had to draw to the riverbank and empty the boat, but in contrast to the grind of jungle travel this inconvenience was nothing. Actually shooting the rapids was lovely, a wonderful feeling of painless precariousness, whereas travel in the jungle was a painful certainty. We had four new boatmen who were Iban Dyaks from Lunud, and were covered with *kurap*.

At three o'clock we arrived at the place where the Nepagan River empties into the Kwamut River. It seemed to me that the Kwamut was faster in its upper waters than any Borneo river I had seen before, and distinctly more forbidding. On the other rivers we had been people of some importance, but on the Kwamut we had neither weight nor substance. As we sped down the river Harry was watching for a place to camp, and we saw a pleasant high bank with a Murut house standing on it. With difficulty the men paddled our small boats out of the current of the river and over to the bank. As we waded through the mud and climbed up the riverbank, we saw that the house, which stood high on stilts above the mud, was deserted. "Here," said Harry, "is Ye Old Family Tavern for the Keiths." And we climbed the notched log which served as a ladder and entered the house.

That was one of the nicest houses in my life. From the moment we entered it, it was friendly, and everyone who entered the house adopted its congenial manners. Arusap, who was excited at being in a house of his own people again, said that it must have belonged to the chief of the village.

"But why did he leave it?" I asked.

"The roof has fallen in, Mem," Arusap answered.

"But that is easy to fix," I suggested. "We can even patch it up ourselves before to-night."

"It is taboo to these Muruts," Arusap answered, "to repair their houses. When a house falls apart it is fate that the owner should move."

"Those little packages that are hanging from the roof, Arusap, what are they?"

"I do not know, Mem, and it is taboo to touch possessions left hanging thus, because the owner may intend to return for them."

"Is it taboo for us to stay in the house?"

"No, if a man has no house of his own then it is good that he should use the house of his friend."

The floor of the house was eight feet above the ground, and made of narrow strips of split bamboo laid over cross-beams. As the bamboo was rotten with age we took care to step where the planks supported it. We balanced the legs of our camp beds on these plank supports, and getting in and out of the beds without tipping them off the plank was a feat of equipoise. The middle of the bark roof had fallen in and a large-leafed vine grew over the outside of the house and down through the roof inside. Sitting inside the house we could pick the leaves from the vine, and these Arusap sometimes cooked for a vegetable.

There had been bark partitions in the house to divide it

into cubicles, but these were only remnants now. I asked Arusap to describe the uses of the various rooms to me, and following his description I drew a floor plan to illustrate the text of his story, showing little Murut figures at their daily occupations. Each time I thought that I was finished he would introduce a new member into the family. Finally after I had reproduced two young Murut men having a cockfight in the bachelors' hall, the house was so full that I had to stop. Arusap looked over my drawing of the household then, and he was disappointed, because he said that the cocks looked like hens and not like cocks.

The house stood in what had once been a pleasant garden. There were bananas, green pineapples, sweet potatoes, tapioca root, *sayor manis* (a form of sweet greens), and six-foot *keladi*. Arusap knew how best to cook these things. He washed them carefully, soaked them, and arranged the leaves according to shape and size, and our vegetables before they were cooked were as ornamental as the flowers in a bowl. He introduced us to the delicate flavor of green pineapple fried with rice, as a vegetable. The first two days we had an abundance of green stuff and everybody came in with his hands full. And then we had to go further and further from the house, until finally we had eaten our way through the cycle of the garden, from ripe to green, and were back to tins of Army Rations again.

The area of the whole house was about as large as that of our living room and dining room in Sandakan. Staying in this house for four days were Arusap, Puasa, Unggib, Kadir, three Dyak boatmen, Harry, and myself, but never once did anybody seem to be in anybody else's way. There

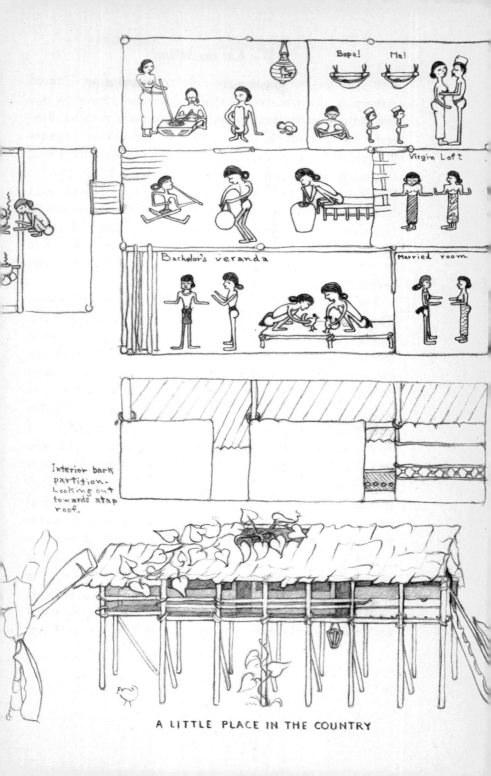

Bapa! Ma!

Virgin Loft

Bachelor's veranda

Married room

Interior bark
partition.
Looking out
towards atap
roof.

A LITTLE PLACE IN THE COUNTRY

was a long box filled with earth in one end of the room that was the kitchen, and in this box the men made the fires for cooking. As we all ate at different hours there was always a pot simmering in the kitchen.

That corner of the house which Arusap had described as the married quarters we allocated to be our bathroom. We hung a palm-leaf mat and a bath towel over a rope to make a wall. We used an empty gasoline tin for a bath-tub and an empty fruit tin for a dipper. As the floor of the house was pervious to water we just stood on the floor and poured the bath water over ourselves. Although the other seven occupants of the house were on the other side of the precarious bath towel I never felt any lack of privacy. Their desire not to intrude upon me was the greatest protection I could have.

One problem that was more difficult than that of baths was the sanitary engineering arrangements of our usually one-night camps. I could write a treatise on the toilet difficulties to be faced by one woman who travels with thirty men, with a dense jungle behind and a swift river in front. When the men wished to respond to nature they had only to locate and avoid me, but I, between Winki's followers and our own, had thirty individuals whose ways I must avoid. If I went into dense jungle, by the time I was out of sight of camp I was also lost. Every day Harry would have the men blaze a path away from the camp for me. That was my path then, and supposed to be avoided by others. But walking down that path in the dark, in the pouring rain, with leeches, and insects, and possible snakes, was enough to make one constipated for life.

While staying in our Murut house Harry told Unggib

to clear a path away from the house for me. Unggib cleared the path in the direction of Winki's camp, so I was between the two camps with people coming from both directions. After that I realized that no one except myself understood the finer points of jungle sanitary plumbing. I knew the theory of it, but was no good at the construction. The men could construct, but they had no theory. If we had ever gotten together with the ideas and the labor we could have produced a super comfort station.

3

We spent four days in the Murut house while we waited for the flooding Kwamut River to go down, and for the promised boats from Kasuyun Landing to come up to us, as the boats could not come up while the river was flooding. Meanwhile the Orang Tua was trying to negotiate for sufficient boats from Lunud Village to take us down the river in case the other boats should be delayed indefinitely by flood. If we procured boats from Lunud we might be able to go down the river to meet the other boats several days before the flood would allow them to come up the river. At the moment, we could travel neither up nor down the river for any distance because of flood.

We had only one small *perahu* left in the camp, as Harry had sent the other two up to Lunud to bring back provisions and more boats. Harry and Winki took turns hating each other, according to who had the use of the one small boat — the one who didn't have it hating the other, and the one who had it being smugly happy. After observing the way Harry, Winki, and I all reacted on each other under

stress, I began to understand why shipwrecked and marooned persons turned to cannibalism.

We went to visit Winki's camp one evening. It was only
about five hundred yards away, but ordinarily we did very
little dropping in on each other. This evening, the third
one at the Murut house, we wanted to find out what Winki's
plans would be if the boats didn't turn up the next day.
His tent stood on a near-by spot of high ground, the site
of another deserted Murut house, but a house that was too
dilapidated to use. The day we had arrived we had taken
the best house for ourselves.

The walk to Winki's camp was through mud along the
riverbank, and then across a wide gully with a dead tree
across it. Winki heard us coming and he came out of his
tent and shouted to us to cross by the fallen tree. My only
jungle accomplishment is walking across gullies on fallen
trees without falling in. Winki greeted us with six days'
beard. He had taken a vow that he would not shave until
the boats arrived to take us down the river. His pointed
face was emphasized by the shadow of his beard, his eyes
had blue shadows under them, and he looked rather fragile
in his thin shirt and his tightly wound sarong. He didn't
indulge in many luxuries, and the fittings of his tent looked
frugal to me, and pathetic. It wasn't pathetic, because he
didn't care about having many things, and the luxuries
which he really wanted, such as a fine camera, good guns,
a folding camp chair and table, he had. And he himself
wasn't pathetic, because he liked his life. But it was hard
for me to realize just how he could do so, because if I had
not been with Harry I should have hated that life of rough
living. I was not by nature a pioneer woman.

We Eat the Wind

Harry and Winki talked it over and decided that they would have to give up the trip to the bird's-nest caves at Timbang Batu, as we were already six days behind our schedule. If we fell too far behind our schedule Government might send out a rescue party, which would be annoying both to Government and to us, if there was nothing to rescue us from.

After we returned to our Murut house we had another bad thunderstorm, and after the storm the sand flies were terrible. I said nothing about them at first because I was used to being told that it was my imagination. But Harry was lying in a sarong and reading when suddenly he jumped up and shouted, "I can't stand these bloody things any longer! Puasa, build fires under the house!" I looked up mildly, not understanding at first, and then I realized that Harry's imagination was biting him also.

Puasa built three smudges under the house, one under the place where I was sitting, and although the sand flies persisted I did at least get my bottom warm. It was a great treat to have my bottom dry and warm because it never was in river travel. When I was squatting in the bottom of a leaking boat it was wet all the time, and I could not get it dry because it always had to be sat upon.

We ate our dinners sitting over the smoking fires and each of us holding a smoldering torch in one hand, which we waved as we ate. The sand flies were uncontrollable. They were so small one could hardly see them individually, but they came in clouds and attacked every exposed portion of the body. The sensation was that of being stuck all over with pins. Within a couple of hours the bites swelled and itched more violently than mosquito bites did.

Jungle Mud

For days after we were bitten the bites would itch every night at dusk. The sand flies were so small that they went through mosquito nets, and although we were using special double nets which were supposed to be proof against them, no net really was. When we got into bed that night the net was full of them, and I sat for twenty minutes holding smoldering sticks of wood over the bed until I got rid of some of them.

I had a wonderful night's sleep, and dreamed that I was in a very smart shop at home buying beautiful clothes, and then I went to a beauty shop and had myself completely redecorated, manicured, shampooed, and massaged, and emerged looking very nice indeed, so nice in fact that nobody recognized me.

4

Unggib had a face of great solidity. It had two expressions; one was glowing good humor, and the other one was worried concentration. It took him some time to shift from one expression into the other and I seldom saw the muscles of his face actually move to negotiate the change. One said something to him while he was wearing the expression of good humor, and a long time afterward one discovered that he had shifted into worried concentration, then later again, about the time his face had shifted back to good humor, he would produce the remark that went with the look of concentration. His pipe never left the corner of his mouth even when he swam by the boat in the rapids. The first time I saw him in Sandakan I had thought that he was ugly, but when I saw him in a native boat I saw that he was ornamental in the manner of a figurehead. He had *kurap,* and the scaly effect of the disease on his skin made him look like a merman.

In our Murut house Unggib developed unsounded depths. He told us stories about other Murut longhouses, and yarned amusingly about native customs and fables. He found an old nose flute in the corner of the house which had been left there by its former owner. He would lie on his back every night with his knees crossed and blow through his nose on the flute while a small, timid tune came and went. It was a tune like a tame mouse playing in the corners of the old house, and quickly disappearing down its hole if you looked at it too closely.

Usually Unggib was shy, but the night he returned from Lunud Village he was not. He brought triumphantly back with him three chickens, five *gantangs* of rice, a promise from the Orang Tua that he would send boats to us the following day, and a bellyful of rice beer. That bellyful of beer transformed Unggib from the simple jester into the inspired priest of his people. His mouth overflowed with proverbs and prophecies. His two expressions raced back and forth across his face without settling, his words never stopped, and when we went to sleep that night we could still hear him orating to his sleeping companions. It was then that I learned there had been one disappointment in the triumphant pilgrimage of Unggib to Lunud Village. Lunud Village had had no virgins.

Along with the welcome news that Lunud Village would send us two *perahus* the next day Unggib brought the less pleasant news that the seven boats Harry had instructed the D.A.D.O.[1] to send to us at Kasuyun Landing

[1] Deputy Assistant District Officer.

had by mistake gone up the Kasuyun River. There they were waiting for us at the carrying place for the bird's-nest caves at Timbang Batu. This meant that they were from three to seven days away from us, the time depending upon the condition of the river.

When Winki visited us that evening and we talked over this news we all managed to be thoroughly upset about it. It meant that we should have to relay our two parties in the two or three small boats that Lunud Village could furnish us, until word had reached the other boats that they should come to meet us. Harry and Winki decided that the Lunud Village chief should take one boat the next day, go after the seven waiting boats at Timbang Batu, and send them back to meet us. Meanwhile we should our-selves be traveling down the Kwamut River, if the Kwamut River was navigable. The river was falling now, and we went to sleep praying for a dry night.

The chickens cackled all night at the foot of our beds as a cheerful reminder of fresh food, and we awoke the next morning to find that the sun was shining, and Unggib had again become silent. By ten o'clock two small *perahus* and one fair-sized one arrived with the chief from Lunud Village. The chief was dressed in a dirty white tropical suit of European cut, and was wearing spectacle rims without glasses. He brought his flashlight with him, which had neither battery nor glass bulb, and these he suggested we might supply for him.

By eight o'clock that night the men and boats had not returned to us. Winki came to see us looking very wor-ried, and we drank the last of the gin, and we all gave up hope of the return of the boats that night, and consequently of our departure the next day. It was a depressing moment, to see the last of the gin disappearing, and to face another day of waiting with the possibility of another flood and indefinite waiting again. In the depth of this despondency we heard a shout from the river, and Unggib and Arusap rushed from the house to welcome the returning boatmen, whom we received like heroes. They had taken our *barang* to below the large *wasoi*, or waterfall, and hidden it. They promised us that if the good weather held through the night we should all join the luggage at the waterfall the next day.

We had loved the Murut house — for four days; but always in our minds had been the nervous realization that although the rest was pleasant, it was not accomplishing our trip. Now at the thought of action we all revived. We had a party meal — stewed chicken, rice, baked tapioca root, and a tin of peaches. We couldn't eat much because we were so excited, but it was a festive gesture to have both chicken and fruit, and we knew that the others would enjoy what we left of the food. Eleven of us slept in the house that night, counting the Dyak boatmen. I listened for a long time to the sound of their whispers and their bare feet patting on the bamboo floor.

The next day we were moving again. There were eight of us in the *perahu* and a lot of luggage, and the gunwales barely cleared the water. We bailed constantly and once again my bottom was wet.

We came through six long rapids, and the men had to get out and climb over the rocks in order to lighten the boat. The Dyak boatmen showed wonderful skill in managing the boats. Each time before we swung into the strength of the rapids the Melano Dyak at the prow of our boat would turn back to me with sparkling eyes, and whoop and wave his paddle in the air. But after that one splendid gesture his body and mind became part of the *perahu* and he lived and breathed with his boat. Half the time he was in the water, swimming with his canoe, pulling it, dragging it, jumping onto water-buried rocks to swing it aside, and then leaping back into it and paddling, poling, and guiding it. The boat was constantly shipping water, and after every rapid it had to be brought to the bank and bailed out.

We arrived at the large waterfall before noon and found that our *barang* was safely stowed in the crevices of a rock cliff high above the water. The waterfall was lovely. According to Winki's measurements, which are always disappointingly correct, the longest straight drop in a series of minor steps which form the rapids was only twenty-two feet. The insignificant measurement gives no conception of the beauty or spectacular effect of the long valley of white water which we saw before us.

Our boats could not go through the waterfalls, and our luggage had to be carried down the clifflike banks of the river over a series of perilously slippery rocks until we arrived at a bank of rocks at the foot of the falls. Here, almost in the spray of the waterfalls, we planned to wait until our seven lost boats should come up the river to meet us. Meanwhile we sent our Dyak *perahu* back up the river to get Winki and his *barang*. We knew we were taking a long chance in isolating ourselves without boats on exposed rocks in a flooding river, hoping that seven hitherto lost boats might arrive before either nightfall or the river did. However, like many long chances which one deliberately takes, after having looked ahead and speculated upon the foolishness of such, this one turned out well.

Arusap was the first to sight five strange *perahus* coming up the river, and the psychological effect upon us was that the sun shone immediately. With the arrival of those *perahus* we would at last have adequate and legitimate transportation, instead of boats which were begged and borrowed from their unwilling owners.

With our usual ungenerous gesture we took three boats ourselves and left two for Winki, one to wait at the foot of the waterfall and the other to follow in the wake of the Lunud boat which we had just sent upriver for him. That boat had to be literally drawn up the rock sides of the waterfall over the same route that our luggage had come down by. If I had not come to know Dyak boatmen I should have said this was impossible to do, but with a Dyak nothing in his boat is impossible to do. I watched in admiration while the men carried the boat up the slippery sides of the waterfall across the same rocks over which I had been lowered with the aid of a rope. As soon as Winki's boat arrived at the eddy of still water, above and to one side of the waterfall, we took to our own boats in the river below. The good weather and favorable water were too transient for us to wish to dawdle.

Now it was gentlemen's travel indeed. With three *perahus* for ourselves I could have an eight-inch-square plank to sit on, instead of squatting on my heels. We found that it was very restful not to have to bail the boat constantly, and there was a pleasant sense of security in not having the water flush over the sides. No impressive ocean liner ever gave a traveler a greater feeling of luxury than my little seat in the *perahu* gave me.

I was very conscious that day in going down the river so swiftly, of the feeling of traveling with the will of nature, rather than against it. In jungle travel I was always fighting an antagonistic element, and everything tried to retard me, but on the river the speed of the current embraced us.

We made camp by three o'clock, still without rain. With the change of boats we had some new *kulis* and with these new natives came a new set of pains and aches and sores for Harry's medicine box to deal with.

Meanwhile Winki had not yet come down the river.

The next day was the Sunday that we had been due back in Sandakan. Instead of having our Sunday-afternoon nap in our big bed in Sandakan we came through the longest succession of rapids on the Kwamut River. Sometimes the boatmen made me get out and walk on the rocks for fear that the boat might capsize. I fell on the rocks, and finally skinned my thigh and was angry with myself and everybody else about it. Puasa would keep handing walking sticks to me to help myself with, and I always had my hands full of walking sticks when I wanted to hang onto the rocks. When Winki overtook us at noontime with four *perahus* I was well prepared to be annoyed with him for turning up with one more *perahu* than we had. He said he had bought the new one at Lunud Village.

There was one good incident. Kadir, Arusap, and Puasa were in one boat together. Kadir is a forest guard, a wild-eyed native lad who has been taming down since Puasa decided to make a Mohammedan out of him, but not all the wild is out of him yet. He had the prow of the boat, which is the key position in the rapids, and instead of following in the procession of our boats down the side channel in the rapids Kadir swung his boat into the centre of the rapids to pass the rest of us. Instantly the boat was taken from his hands by the river. It shot forward, into and under waves, while Kadir's black hair swept back in the wind and he paddled desperately to steer. Arusap, who was paddling in the back of the boat, wore a look of indignant surprise on his face, but Puasa in the middle bailed madly with his head down, as if he did not dare to look about him. They went by us in an instant, and disappeared around the bend of the river, like a runaway that tears through the town and leaves people standing on the street corners shaking their heads and predicting destruction. We rounded the turn in the river with pessimistic fears. There on a stony beach were the three mad horsemen. Full of water and almost sinking, their boat had been thrown onto the beach at the river's bend. Puasa was scowling, and scolding Kadir, and opening his own *bongon*, and getting out his wet bedding to dry, and looking thoroughly disgusted. Arusap looked politely annoyed. Kadir looked as if he didn't know whether he had been a fool or a hero, but he didn't take any more middle channels after that.

By two o'clock, when I was tired and cross and hungry, we struck the longest and worst rapids of the day. The boat pretended to be a flying fish, staying out of the water completely part of the time, and then skimming under water and emerging into the air and shaking the drops from its tail. But when the men had to draw the boat along by the bank, they insisted that I get out and climb over the rocks. While we were crawling on all fours on the moss-covered rocks a violent downpour of rain struck us. The prone position of crawling was not a good one in which to seek protection from the elements. When we returned to the boats I found that my leather coat and the

bedding roll were also soaked by rain, as the men had forgotten to cover them with *kajang* mats. We made camp by four o'clock in a continuing downpour, and everybody was in a bad temper. That was worthy of comment, because although I was frequently in a bad temper the rest of the camp usually stayed cheerful. Harry hated me, I was cold and miserable, the campfires wouldn't burn because the wood was wet and Arusap had lost the rosin, and we couldn't get anything to eat until nine o'clock that night.

Perhaps I could be heroic against great trials, but I am not stoic about daily discomforts. I was finding it difficult to hold to my original vital mood of high adventure. I didn't want that mood to be dissipating itself into the petty moods which are so easily invoked by leaking tents, wet blankets, sore legs, and fever.

5

We had been traveling in jungle for two days while Harry inspected possible forest areas. All that day had been a nightmare, but we were in camp at last. I had peeled off my wet clothes, but Harry's still stuck to him like skin. I was sitting on the edge of the damp camp bed and rubbing alcohol on my bare legs. "I wish this leech bite would stop bleeding," I said, "I can't put on my nightgown because if I do I'll get blood on it and then I'll have to wash it, and I can't wash it because I can't get it dry in this rain even over a campfire, and anyway I've already burned up two nightgowns over campfires."

"Wear it with the blood on it then," said Harry.

"No, I can't." No, I thought, the men can wear anything with anything on it, but a nightgown with blood on it marks you for a woman, and I can't be a woman on this trip. And yet, damn it, I am.

"Your leech bite will never clot unless you stop pulling those ropes of dried blood away from it."

"I know, but I hate seeing the dried blood on my leg." I gently picked at the long red creeper, trying to detach the rope without reopening the bite.

"Did you get the leech that did it?"

"No. I was sitting here on the bed with my leech-control precautions temporarily relaxed, and the bastard came up the leg of the bed and went up my shorts. He sucked full and fell off before I noticed him. I expect to have leeches in the jungle, but it's pretty thick to have them come and get into bed with me."

Harry's stockings were matted with blood as he peeled them off, and the leech holes were clustered about his ankles. "Here's one at work now. Ho, George, here's where you get yours!" He lit a match and held it to the leech, which let go in the flame, popped at the end, and belched blood.

"The sand flies are awful to-night. I hate them more than the leeches," I mourned.

"I sometimes wonder why you come on these trips," Harry said. "I go because it's my job, but what's the sense of your coming when you're not comfortable?"

"But I don't want to be just comfortable all my life!"

"Oh? What do you want?"

I stopped picking at the leech bite, and thought. In my mind I saw a shelf of women's faces that all wore the same expression. The bodies that went with the faces wore soft rubber corsets, and the minds that went with the bodies had sagging muscles.

"I guess I'm afraid of too easy living. That's part of it."

"Oh?"

The "oh" didn't urge confidences.

I wanted to say: "Can't you see that I admire you, and want to see the things that you see, and do the things that you tell me about? And can't you see that this country is

293

only good for people who give to it, as well as take from it?"

I wanted to say: "I don't want to be a parasite on the country, I want to be a living part of the country. I want to talk the language, and know the natives, and laugh with their jokes, and smile with their joys, and sigh for their troubles as you do. I want to come down its rivers and go through its jungles. I want the mud, and the rain, and the leeches, and the discomforts, and everything that this trip is . . . except sometimes my body doesn't do it very well."

And I wanted to say: "But even if my body doesn't do it well, I will beat it in the end with my spirit. Only please, please, please don't hate me when my body stumbles, and whines, and complains, because it's doing the best that it can."

That was what I wanted to say. But people don't say things like that. Devoted husbands don't hate their wives. Decently reticent people don't talk about their spirits. And proper-minded persons are uncomfortable when confronted with such confessions.

"Oh? What do you want?" came Harry's question.

"I don't know, but I guess that spirits aren't as reliable as guts, Harry, and you've got guts."

"Tra — lalala — lala — lala — " he hummed, but the hum was an amiable one.

I returned to rubbing my sore legs while I held the Devotional. Every night while disinfecting my bites I held a catechism of Body and Spirit. This night there were no beating of wings and triumphant cries. Spirit's wings were drooping and wet.

"Just let me crawl quickly into bed with Body," she begged.

"This morning you were brave enough!" I said. "Your wings were dry and they fluttered. And Body had nice dry shoes and a dry jersey to put on. This morning you said you would not ask to stop and rest all day. Not if it killed you!"

"Yes," whined Spirit, "but Body said, 'Why kill yourself!'"

"Rubber corsets for you both," I pronounced.

"What are you babbling about corsets for?" said Harry. "You don't wear them."

"I babble for the same reason that you hum."

I basked in the warmth of his returning informality. Perhaps he was going to be fond of me again. I knew that I had been very aggravating on this trip, and I didn't blame him for being annoyed with me. But I wished that he wouldn't be, because it didn't stiffen my backbone any.

When it rained at night and the tent leaked it was no worse for me than for him. But I put up my umbrella, and shifted my cot, and huddled, and looked dejected, while he lay serenely quiet and read a book. When it rained all day and the *perahu* leaked, I was obviously wet, and chilled, and miserable, but he always smiled.

Everything in the jungle bit me until my skin was raw, and I couldn't sleep at night for the scratching, and I said so. He was covered with leech bites and inflamed scratches, but he always slept as soundly as a crocodile on a sunny bank.

I stumbled and fell often while walking in the jungle, and when I dragged myself up coated with mud, I thought he looked at me with silent disgust. At such times I hated his resilient step and his untiredness.

These days I walked just in front of the carrying *kulis*. As long as I kept ahead of the *kulis* I knew I was moving as fast as the camp could move. But this wasn't thrilling and proud the way racing along far ahead of the *kuli* line with Harry was. But I had ceased being thrilling and proud when he began to be mortified by me.

We didn't talk together so much now when we came into camp. He hummed to himself in a controlled manner while in the tent, and then went back with the men and laughed and joked with them in Malay and Murut. I could hear their soft tones and their laughs, and I felt closed out. I must not go back with the men because they would be bathing and eating and making themselves comfortable in the ways they could not do when a woman was about.

Then I would comfort myself with hanging my little mirror, and getting a cup of warm water, and trying persuasively to push the wave back into my hair. All day long my head was bound in a tight red bandana. My face, my arms, my long thin hands, my long thin legs, were burned a monotone of coffee brown. Out of this monotone of background my eyes scarcely showed in the daytime, they were so grotesquely squinted to close out the rays of the sun. It was only in camp at night, when the lamplight and the firelight shuddered softly, that my eyes had a place in my face. And then they didn't matter because Harry didn't look at them any more.

The only thing that I did on the trip that was any good was my drawing. He thought that was fine. It looked like 'em, he said. I got out my drawing pad then to finish my sketch of Apul, and sent Arusap to fetch him to come to the tent.

Before I sat down I brought burning logs from the campfire and made a small smudge in the tent at my feet. I put on dry shorts and wrapped Harry's sarong around my bare legs, and tucked a scarf inside my jersey to cover the space between hair and collar, and the tender triangle between ear, jaw, and neck. It's not just my imagination, I told myself, when I can see the big bumps they make on me.

Apul arrived in his loincloth. Compared to him I looked like an advertisement for winter sports. Apul stood unconcernedly in the hard white light of the gasoline lamp, and smoked and scratched while I worked.

The Happy Savage and his White Goddess! I said to myself, and I enjoyed the irony of my phrase. I talked soundlessly to myself as I worked. That long, looped hair makes him seem not feminine, but more masculine, I thought. Those Mongoloid cheekbones and strong eye sockets would be good to model. I never saw such a determined jawbone. Probably a very weak character, really, and like putty in the hands of his wife!

He is naked, but he doesn't look undressed. Neck rooted in bull shoulders. Neat, compact, hard little hips. He is beautiful, and he doesn't know it. Body probably functions perfectly. What would it be like to have a body like that? What would it be like to be Apul's wife? No, the idea is as perverted as to imagine myself lying down with a six-year-old, or Apul as taking to bed with a Freudian complex. No, I wouldn't like to be Apul's wife. But it must be very relaxing to lie with somebody purely because your body wanted to, without any of the other things mixing up in it. It must be very simple never to have any introspective probings, I thought.

Apul opened his mouth and spat betel juice on the ground.

And very appropriate! I thought. That's what he really thinks of us. Probably he's wondering what white men can find in white women.

Apul shifted his position in the hissing white light, and the hard shadow swam across his nose and poured over on the other side of his face. The black pools that were shadows under his nostrils, the black triangles that were shadows in the curling corners of his unbelievable cupid's-bow mouth, the unimaginable shining black of his large eyes, the black of the long hair wound into the oiled bun, all these blacks were deeper and more astounding blacks than I could possibly reproduce with my soft lead pencil.

Apul shifted again full face to me, and the shadow swam off his face and poured down his neck.

"Will you give me some coconut oil?" he asked.

"We haven't any coconut oil. I'll give you some olive oil, or tinned butter, if you want it for cooking."

"My people like coconut oil for the hair." Apul touched his looped bun proudly.

Hair oil! Pomade! That's what we should have brought for presents! I thought. So Apul, my simple savage who had no vanities, asked only one thing of our civilization — coconut oil with which to dress his hair!

"Olive oil is good for hair also," I answered. "I will ask Arusap for an empty tin and give you some."

"Very well, I will try it."

APUL
KAMPONG KALABAKANG
After dressing hair with my olive oil

MENUKUK
ORANG TUA OF KAMPONG KALABAKANG
A respectable old man

I continued to draw, while we awaited the arrival of the olive oil. Soon Arusap brought a cigarette tin full. Apul sniffed it.

"The smell is different. This has a bad smell."

"That is because it comes from a different tree than the coconut tree. But it is very good to use on hair. My people use it," I said.

"It does not smell good."

"Very well, do not use it then. But give it back to me because my people value it highly, even to cook with."

"I will try a little." Apul retained the tin.

"I am finished with the picture now, Apul. Take a cigarette." I held the sketch for him to see.

Apul nodded his head noncommittally at it. He discharged the cigarette smoke through spreading nostrils, scratched the leech bites on his buttocks, flickered his long, artificial-looking eyelashes, and then said, "My friend Melisang would like you to make his picture also."

"Melisang is the one with the hair cut short, and the coat and trousers of the white man?"

"Yes, and my friend Melisang has also a cigarette lighter."

"Tell Melisang that I will draw his picture if he will take off the coat and trousers of the white man, and put on again the loincloth of his own people, the Muruts."

I wrapped up my sketching pad in the waterproof cloth, this being dismissal for Apul. He stood a moment longer fondling the cigarette tin and sniffing the oil, and then left. He walked beautifully. From the point of view of anatomical drawing his muscular back was perfect.

Harry came into the tent then, and I showed him the

picture of Apul. "You do get a likeness all right," he said. I felt that my picture was being hung in the Louvre.

A *kuli* came up with a sore foot and asked for medicine; he had driven a stake through his foot between two toes. The boy was uncomplaining and laughed about the accident, and he trusted Harry to make it quite right. Harry cleaned the hole and soaked it in disinfectant.

The boy sat on the ground fomenting his foot in his rice bowl. With great amusement he called to our attention the absence of one toe from the foot, a toe which had been lost years before in the overthrust of his chopping knife. I thought that such an accident to myself would have been no laughing matter. But with the natives, catastrophe held amusement, and it was only polite for us to share his amusement.

I looked at Harry and thought, I wish you would look at me like that — with approval and admiration. But then, I couldn't do that — run a stake through my toes and laugh about it, and then sit at your feet and look at you with worship because you put lysol solution on it.

Harry repacked the medicine box and found that my eye-wash bottle had leaked again. It was always doing this. At first I had felt humble about it, but now I got mad about it. It seemed always to be in Harry's way. I almost threw it away now in a temper. Then I corked up the leaky bottle again. Damn it! To hell with his fussy old bandages that he says are getting wet!

Arusap brought us an extravagant meal. There was the brown native rice with a nutty flavor, and a sauce pot full of stew made from Harry's barking deer, with just enough curry in the gravy to make it exciting. There were long, roasted tapioca roots, crisp and brown outside from the fire. These I liked to eat with butter, breaking them up with my fingers and pretending they were hot French rolls.

"There is no meat as sweet as barking deer," Harry pronounced happily to Arusap.

"Yes, Tuan," said Arusap approvingly. "My people prize it also."

I ate with excitement. I was ravenously hungry every night. We thought it was wasted time to have a meal in the middle of the day, so we ate nothing from the time of the pot of boiling coffee at 5 A.M. until late afternoon after camp was up. So I ate deer stew now until I almost hurt, and when I finished I was already looking forward to the next night's meal.

It's the high spot, I thought. I used to think it was the drink of gin that was the high spot. But it isn't. It's the food when you're hungry. No, maybe it's the hot bath when you're cold. . . . No, I think it's just being able to lie down inside the mosquito net and quit pretending to be lion-hearted. Well, I can do that now. I crawled into my small camp bed.

Harry crawled into his small camp bed, the older camp bed, with the tippy legs, and the thinner mattress, and less-warm blankets, and the singed pillow, and the second-bests of everything, because he had given me all the bests. The mosquito net hung about both beds. One side of the net was still wet from last night, but that was the side he took.

"Are you warm now? You can have one of my blankets," he said.

301

"No, I'm fine."

"Did your leech bites stop bleeding?"

"Not yet. Perhaps I'm a haemophile."

"Did you hurt yourself when you fell in that stream to-day?"

"Considering it was me falling, I did it quite painlessly."

"How's the old body? Ready to push on to-morrow?"

"*Yah-lah!*"

"To-morrow will not be very hard. We did our last day in the jungle to-day."

"I don't really mind jungle travel, Harry."

"Good old thing!"

So he had stayed fond of me! Even when I was mortifying, and aggravating, and puny, and dejected!

Decently reticent people don't say things, but I was sure now that they felt them!

I lay under the blankets and listened, while the rain and the trees talked to themselves, and the river paid no attention to any of us.

I looked towards my sleeping husband. I reached out and touched the hardness of his bones, and the touch pleased me. That strength was mine also. And then I saw that it was part of being husband and wife that, in the same way his strength was mine, my weakness was his, and hurt him. If I had been somebody's else wife he might have thought I was pretty good in the jungle.

To-morrow I'll not even look dejected, I whispered. And when I get home I will be just a woman again for a while. I'll go up on the shelf of women's faces, and adjust my expression, and wear soft rubber corsets, and be just a wife. And I'll use rouge and lipstick again, and that softens the shape of my face, and makes my eyes look nice. I'll wear my prettiest dresses. At home he shall think well of me, because as a woman I'm all right. But as a man, or an adventurer, or a pioneer, or a wilderness breaker, I'm just a washout. . . .

I'm just a washout! . . .

But anyway, I did it. Nothing can take from me what there is in me of this trip. Better, maybe, than rubber corsets. . . .

Then I saw, as clearly as though those weeks of travel had been thrown on a screen with a camera, I saw, and went to sleep still seeing . . .

I saw again a long river breaking often into white rapids, and the morning's first sun lay kindly on its violence. It was a seldom-traveled river, but I saw twelve people on it. The people were so small compared to the river that you scarcely noticed the difference between the people, which were the white and which the brown. You scarcely noticed the difference between the two white people, the one that was Harry and strong, and the one that was Agnes and weak, because the difference was between the river and the people.

I saw that the boats were nearing white rapids, and the noise of the fighting water was great. Everything hurried towards it. The *perahus* were like joyful fanatics rushing to be sacrificed in it. Naked figures arose like priests, for the boatmen stood to greet it. The figures shouted, and it was only a little noise lost into the roaring sound of it.

Then the sides of the *perahus* buried in froth, like thin wafers churned into milk. The water was over the boats, and the *perahus*, which had seemed so willing for sacrifice, struggled now to resist it. The naked priests who stood in the bows fought with paddles against it; now that the sacrifice had come the martyrs were not willing.

The minutes lasted a long time. Then, like disillusioned disciples, the frightened *perahus* were racing swiftly away again, the priests were kneeling humbly in them, and the rapids were safely behind.

The *perahus* drifted swiftly then, fanatic desire was gone from them, and the shouting priests were quiet. Everything rested. The sun was hot and straight overhead, but the shade of the trees of the riverbank lay over the boats. The smell of Dusun tobacco came from rolled newspaper cigarettes, the sweet tune of warmth and contentment cried in the air like a small wild animal.

The *perahus* drifted slowly, then. The golden fur of a frightened stoat flashed against the leaves of the jungle wall. The white tail and the blue wattles of a pheasant showed. A Tengara woman stood in the sunlight on the river's bank with naked breasts and shining shoulders.

And there I stopped, because it seemed to me that all my life I had been waiting to know just these things — rivers, and rapids, and sunlight, and tunes like small wild animals, and the color of breasts of women who stand in a golden sun.

And there I stopped, and went happily to sleep, and left the two little people still coming down the big river.

15. *A Pioneer Returns*

By six o'clock that night we began to plan what we would have to eat. We would have toast. If there was a shop at Pintasan, and if the shop had bread and a tin of butter, we would have toast, hot thin buttered toast, lots and lots of it. And we would have sardines, not one tin but at least three, and the sardines would be fried until the grease was out of them and they were very crisp and their tails curled up. And we would have three tins because we were only four days away from Sandakan now, and we no longer needed to hoard our tins, and we did actually have the sardines, so at least we were sure of them. And we would also have tea — not thick body-building cocoa, but dainty, ladylike, little-finger-extending tea. We would, if the shop at Pintasan had tea. And we would not use the celluloid cups which had absorbed the flavors of toothwash and antiseptic and coffee and cocoa into their very fibre. We would take turns drinking from the one porcelain cup, which would make the tea so much hotter and cleaner and more luxurious, for this was to be a meal for gourmets and epicures. If Pintasan had a shop.

"Do you think we will get there by eight, Harry?"

"By nine at least, the way the men are paddling. They're digging right in." Harry stuck his head damply out from under the *kajang*-roof shelter of our boat. "When will we reach Pintasan, Nulang?"

"Eight *tanjongs* further, Tuan."

A *tanjong* is the answer to both "How far?" and "How long?" As a native measures distance on a Borneo river, a *tanjong* is a hairpin bend, and one *tanjong* is from the end of the hairpin around the bend to the other end. The answer "Eight *tanjongs*," to Harry's question, might mean any length of time according to the size of the hairpin.

The rain poured off the unprotected backs of the men in front of me. They had unwound their headcloths and draped them over their heads to shed the water, and the rain ran down the long folds of cloth like water off the roof of a shed.

"Are you very cold?" Harry asked me.

"No, just some. My central zone is radiating nicely, but the ends get cold. But never mind, we'll have a hot bath when we arrive at the launch at Pintasan, and a dry bunk to sleep in. I'm going to sleep in the cabin just for the feeling of four walls again."

"If this rain continues," Harry said, "I think I'll sleep in the cabin too. A dry bed for a change won't hurt my feelings."

I scrooged back under the *kajang* roof of the *perahu*, and felt grateful that the Penglima who had lent us his boat had had a wife who liked to travel in the protected luxury of a floating harem.

We had arrived at Kuala Kwamut early the afternoon

before. It was the first sophisticated port we had touched since leaving Tawau four weeks previously, as Kuala Kwamut was frequently visited by District Officers and Government medical dressers.

The Penglima, or native chief, who had heard we were coming, met our *perahus* with much ceremony. He proved to be a very punctilious person, who was, compared to us, exquisitely dressed. I had looked especially disreputable as I was sunburned to a crisp and plastered with dried mud from river wading. The Penglima, who represented Government at Kwamut, was known as the D.A.D.O. He offered us the Government office to sleep in and we gladly put our camp beds there. This office was used as a court of justice for the district, and beside my cot stood a witness box with a chair in it, and the rail of the witness box was convenient to place my mirror on when I combed my hair. Before I left the office to appear in public I changed to gray flannel trousers and a clean jersey, in order to bear the white woman's burden more creditably before the crowds (fifty natives and Chinese) of Kuala Kwamut.

Winki and his men did not arrive until about six o'clock. It seemed that his boat had struck a rock and overturned in the last strip of bad water on the Kwamut. His men had managed to bring the boat and most of the *barang* safely to the shore, but had had to stop for some hours to dry their things on the rocks. Winki had ruined his Leica and lost a number of his pictures. I was sorry it happened to Winki, but relieved that it hadn't happened to us. A trip like this develops the instinct of self-preservation more than any other instinct.

Winki's outboard motor had arrived at Kuala Kwamut

to meet him, and he told us that he would be going down-river to Pintasan in two days' time by motorboat, to meet the launch at Pintasan. As Winki had five *perahus* and twelve *kulis* to tow, and expected to hire twelve more *kulis* at Kuala Kwamut, he would not be able to tow us, as he had expected to do. We decided to leave in our *perahus* the next morning, in order to arrive at the launch at Pintasan when Winki did.

When the Penglima heard that Harry and I were continuing our travel by *perahu* he insisted that we should borrow his covered boat. After a good night's sleep in the courthouse we were ready to leave Kuala Kwamut at six in the morning, with the sun just showing on the river. When I saw the sun instead of the usual rain I wasn't so pleased with the borrowed *perahu*, for it was like Noah's Ark compared to the naked little boats we had been using. Judging from the small size of the peepholes in the wooden sides of its haremlike walls, I decided that the Penglima's wife had not cared for scenery. But it would have been ungracious not to accept the well-meant offer of a vessel obviously more impressive than our own, and Harry said that if anything happened and we failed to meet the launch, this larger *perahu* would be one in which we could sleep.

By the time we had our *bongons* in the boat it hardly looked possible for us and our four men and the five boatmen to get in the boat too, much less to sleep in it. But packing people and luggage into boats is like packing suitcases; the longer the container is packed the more space there is.

All of Kuala Kwamut had come to the landing to inspect our luggage and ourselves, and see us off. This was my moment. I had saved, through flood and mud, one entire change of clean clothes. I had clean white shorts with ironed creases in them, a white jersey, white socks that were not mud-tinged, and one last pair of new canvas shoes. I was favorably impressed with the three-inch mirror's-eye view which I had had of myself that morning, and with my cleverness at being able to present such a good appearance at Kuala Kwamut.

The Penglima's boat was moored at the landing. When the river was low, as it was at present, the landing was at the water's edge, and there was an expanse of mud for a hundred yards between the landing and the bank of the river. A trestle of single logs which were laid end to end across this mud connected the landing with the top of the riverbank. Conscious of the temptation to fate which my clean clothes offered, and of all of Kuala Kwamut watching me, I followed Harry very carefully along this single-log track. When I reached the end of it Harry looked back at me with approval. I knew he had been thinking, "It's just the sort of place where she would fall in."

I arrived at the last log, and there was one loose plank which balanced between it and the landing. With intense concentration and the caution of an infant taking its first step, I stepped on the wrong end of that plank. The plank tipped like a seesaw. I dropped into the mud and sank to above my knees. All activity in Kuala Kwamut stopped. It was like a motion picture which suddenly halts, leaving the people on the screen in grotesque atttitudes of suspended animation. Everybody was overwhelmed by the happening, including myself. Harry gave one horrified look back at me, and then left the woman and the crying baby and went to the front of the trolley car and pretended that they did not belong to him.

I was quite helpless until the Penglima and his number one recovered from the shock and came back to me. Then each took hold of one of my legs above the knee, and by levering on them alternately they got me out.

They say that violent emotions release poisons in the system, and I was so angry with myself that I felt physically ill. I was too emotionally exhausted even to swear. My legs were coated with black silt, my clean clothes were spattered with it, my shoes had stayed in the mud, and my shins and knees were bruised. I sat on the edge of the landing and washed myself as well as I could, with the assistance and advice of the Penglima and several old women of the village. Nobody laughed, and I don't think they even wanted to laugh. They were completely overawed by the downfall of the white race.

After that I had no advice to give upon the bestowal of luggage in the boats, or the placing of bedding rolls, or any of the little things that I had formerly thought I had such good ideas about.

2

Perhaps if I had approached the Kinabatangan River from the Sandakan end, without having first come down the Kwamut, I should have felt more admiration for it. But after the majesty of the Kwamut, the lower Kinabatangan seemed hot, slow, and muddy. Although the headwaters of the Kinabatangan are as beautiful as those of the Kwamut, from Kuala Kwamut down to Sandakan the river showed the unattractive results of native shifting cultivation which has done away with the tall trees and forests.

The native farms which we occasionally passed on the riverbank were pleasant-looking, and had vivid flower gardens, but there was no evidence of industry in the agricultural line. As we passed one of these farms Harry said, "I wouldn't be surprised to see most of this land farmed by the Chinese in time, and it might be a good thing for the country if it were. The Chinese have energy and the natives are lazy."

"I should hate to see this land occupied by the Chinese. I don't see why the natives shouldn't be lazy if they have enough to live on without working," I replied.

The pro and con of the native-versus-Chinese problem is something we discuss regularly. Whichever premise one of us begins with, the other one takes the opposite side. We are equally good with both sides of the argument, but our sympathies, with which reason has really little to do, continue to remain with the native.

Our boat swayed precariously as we traveled. She was top-heavy to begin with, she was overloaded with luggage and with people, and Arusap and Puasa, who were too reticent to lie in the bottom of the boat with us, were perched on top of the luggage, where they acted like ballast which, instead of being in the hold of a boat, is hung from the masthead. I am not nervous in an open boat, but I felt that I should not like to be capsized inside this walled seraglio. Harry agreed that the boat was acting unreliably, and finally made Arusap and Puasa lie down inside with us. Puasa, who is a very strict Mohammedan, was shy about being near me because I was the Tuan's woman. He was always very deferential in his attitude towards Harry and did not approve of informalities. Arusap took these matters more simply. He would not offer to sit in the same part of the boat as we did, but when Harry told him to do so he said to himself, "If the Tuan asks me to, he wants me to. That's that." And then promptly laid in the bottom of the boat and went to sleep and snored.

By one o'clock the rains came. The four of us crouched closer and closer in the bottom of the boat. Each one had his occupation. Harry read a collection of modern short stories and said that he didn't like them, they were all about nothing. Arusap smoked his pipe, Puasa sharpened his knife, which is an inexhaustible occupation for him, and I rubbed my bruised legs, which is an equally inexhaustible occupation for me. By six o'clock we had arrived at the sardines-and-toast-for-dinner stage, by eight o'clock we had arrived at the anything-for-dinner stage, and by nine o'clock we had arrived at Pintasan. By 9.01 o'clock we had arrived at Pintasan and discovered that the launch was not there. There was only one launch on the river and that was the Chinese freight launch belonging to Yong Soon. After inquiry they told us that our launch had come up the river to meet us three days before, on the flood waters, but when the river had started to fall, the launch had been afraid to wait for us and had gone down again. I saw in my mind, then, the instant disappearance of dry bed and hot bath, and I felt sure when the launch was not there that there would be no shop at Pintasan, and if there was it would not have bread or butter or tea.

A Pioneer Returns

It was now dark and still pouring rain, and under such conditions it would be almost impossible for us to pitch our tent and make camp. If Harry and I slept in our own boat our men, who had been paddling since 6 A.M., would have no place to sleep and no protection from the rain, nor would the men who were following us in the other open boat. Harry said he would go ashore and ask the Chinese shopkeeper to open an empty shop for us to sleep in, as he remembered there were several old shacks at Pintasan. He left me in the boat, to wait for the result of his inquiries. I was in the dark, with the exception of a tiny kerosene lamp such as the Chinese use, over which I was trying to warm my hands.

Ten minutes after Harry left I saw a flashlight coming from the land across the trestle of logs which led down to the landing. Then the figure of a tall Chinese appeared on the landing where our boats and the Chinese launch were moored. I began uncurling my long legs and pulling myself together, as I thought I was about to be invited to come ashore to a shelter. The Chinese, however, directed his flashlight on the Chinese launch beside us and called out to the men there, "Here's a letter for Sandakan."

The man in the boat leaned down to take the letter, and then said in Malay, "Did you meet the Tuan from Sandakan?"

"Oh, yes," said the Chinese. "He came to the shop and said, 'I am Tuan Keith from Sandakan, and we are on the river in a small boat. We would like to sleep in an empty shop. Will you open one for me?' And the shopkeeper said, 'The shops are full.' And the Tuan said, 'Then may we sleep here in this shop?' And the shopkeeper said,

'This shop is also full.' And the Tuan was angry and said again, 'I am Tuan Keith from Sandakan!' And the shopkeeper said, 'Very good, Tuan Keith from Sandakan, but this shop and all the shops are full.' And the Tuan said, 'Where is the native clerk? I will go to the native clerk.' And the shopkeeper said, 'Very good, Tuan Keith from Sandakan, go to the native clerk,' and the Tuan went off very angry."

Then the young Chinese, and the other Chinese who were listening, laughed heartily at the discomfiture of Tuan Keith from Sandakan, until one of the men on the launch remembered me, and said, "Be careful; the Tuan's wife is down there in the boat." At this the flashlight was directed on our boat, where I was discovered, an ignoble sight in muddy shorts, fondling a flickering Chinese lamp for warmth, and looking like nothing they would ever recognize as a white woman. I knew then that if empires were to be built I was not the kind to build them, for I should always be discovered in ignominious positions. The flashlight stayed on me for a long minute, while the laughter stopped, and perhaps the Chinese were as uncomfortable as I. Then they left me to my dark boat again.

After some minutes flashlights approached again over the trestle of logs from the landing. This time it was Harry and Arusap who came, and as soon as Harry spoke I knew from the triumphant tone of his voice that we should all sleep under a roof that night, but I asked no questions.

"Come very carefully," Harry said, "because it's slippery in this rain. You will have to walk over the trestle, and then the men will take the boat down to the landing and bring the *barang* up from there."

A Pioneer Returns

Walking over that slippery trestle by the light of a flash, in heavy rain, after having sat for fourteen hours in a small boat, took all my attention. Harry kept looking back at me anxiously, remembering my morning mud bath, but I made the trip safely.

"The Chinese wouldn't give us a place to sleep," Harry said grimly, "but I found the native clerk, and he turned out to be Moumim, the son of old Majid in Sandakan, and he is going to put us up overnight in his house."

"Son of old Majid? You mean that Sumatra Malay who was a gardener and whom you were always angry with? The one you said was no good? The one you said you were going to fire, only he retired of old age first? His son?" I asked.

Harry laughed. "Yes, his son. Coals of fire, eh?"

We walked for ten minutes across a swamp before we came to a lighted house. Then Moumim himself came down the steps to greet us, and a little boy with a shining face said, "Greetings, Mem," and a barking dog was held back by friendly hands, while we climbed up the steps out of the rain. Instead of being a native *sulap* this was a Government-built one-room wooden house, as Moumim was the representative of Government at Pintasan. I saw that the verandah was used as an office for Government business, which business appeared to consist of receiving Government circulars and posting them on the office walls where the cockroaches made tracks on them.

I stopped on the verandah and asked for water to wash the mud off my bare feet before we should enter, and Harry also took off his muddy shoes, while everybody said, "Never mind, never mind," and gave us to feel that the dirt off our feet was really rather desirable. While I was washing my feet Moumim stood back and smiled diffidently. I saw that he was young and strong, with fine white teeth and brilliantly shining eyes. He was taller than the average Malay and had extremely well-shaped, long legs. Although I learned afterwards that he was often in trouble with Government about money matters, his face was of such integrity that I have always believed his financial difficulties were a matter of difference in attitude of a Malay and a European in regard to the importance of details, and not a matter of dishonesty.

Inside the house a small partition had been built to make a sleeping room for Moumim, his wife and child, the Javanese housekeeper, and the friend who lived with them. The space behind this partition was offered to Harry and me as our room. We could see that this was where the family slept and we tried to refuse, but Moumim insisted that we must take it. Moumim bustled his family out, leaving the room with the two beds in it for our use. One was a huge iron bedstead with a native mat on it and a mosquito net which followed the splendid curves of a Turkish dome as it draped in scallops from the overhead framework, while the other bed was a simple sleeping arrangement which consisted of a couple of planks laid across two sawhorses. When our own camp mattresses were brought up from the boats we told Moumim that we would place them on these planks, and would not use the iron bedstead. At this auspicious news the bedstead, looking like a Sultan's palace on wheels, was speedily trundled from the room to the other side of the partition, where all five of Moumim's household appeared to be going to occupy it.

A Pioneer Returns

We did not wish to sleep in the bed for fear of bugs, but I reverenced Moumim in that he had tried to give us not only the half, but the whole of his kingdom.

Moumim said that all our men could be accommodated on the verandah and in a small backhouse. Meanwhile the men had brought up about a third of our *barang* from the boats, and although it was the wrong third, we were not in a mood to complain. It was then nine o'clock, and when I heard Harry asking Arusap to bring him a cupful of hot shaving water I thought it a tribute to a strong morale. I was even inspired to clean my teeth, and to try to push a wave into my hair with the last of the shaving water. While we were performing these delicacies of toilet, and putting on dry sleeping things, the members of Moumim's household went quietly in and out removing their own belongings. We all pretended not to see each other in unseemly poses, and thus avoided embarrassment.

We knew that our boatmen were short of food and I told Arusap to give them tins of Army Rations, and then to bring us what food he found first in the *bongons*. While we waited I wrote in my mind many flourishing Malay letters to Moumim, in which I thanked him for his hospitality, and sent him, in my imagination, gifts of great value, which he was delighted to receive.

I looked around the room then and made a list of the sort of things which Moumim and his family appeared to value. And the list was as follows: Sweetened condensed milk in tins, flesh-colored face powder, *tokalon* hair oil, brilliantine hair dressing, eau de cologne, perfumed pomade, face cream, flashlight batteries, bottled Indian curry powder, cigarettes, playing cards, and strips of bright silk and cotton.

317

And then Arusap brought in the food. There was hot chocolate, and rice, and sardines.

"Bloody good, eh?" said Harry.

And it was — probably even better than tea and hot thin buttered toast.

We got into bed then, and the bed was dry, and that was the highest compliment that I could conceive of to apply to any bed at that moment.

And after we returned to Sandakan we did write the Malay letter of gratitude to Moumim, and sent back the things which I had written on my list.

3

He lay in the sun on the mudbank at Lamag. He was brilliant and handsome, with a skin of a clear yellow ochre color with shining black markings, almost the colors of a sunflower. But he looked more like a griffin than a crocodile. If a flame had come out of his mouth I should have known he was a griffin.

We were in the smallest *perahu* and could approach the mudbank silently. While we were doing so Harry got out the .22, and I got out the extra cartridges, and the Leica. As we neared the bank I snapped pictures, expecting at any moment that the creature would move for the water. But he paid no attention to us, and I thought for an instant that he was dead. Then his eyes blinked. I realized with the blinking of those eyes that a crocodile, even in his most innocent moment of lying on a bank, still looks malevolent and leering. Perhaps his looks influence his personality.

As Harry had only the .22 with him in the boat, we waited until we were about fifty yards from the crocodile and then Harry emptied the magazine at him. The crocodile threw up his head and beat in the mud with his tail, and tried terribly to struggle towards the water, but he could not move his centre of gravity. He was terrifying and hideous and pathetic in his dying malignant ferocity. Harry refilled and reëmptied the rifle twice down his open gasping mouth, and the crocodile must have died then,

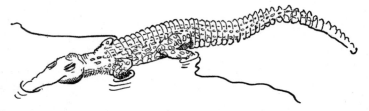

but he still didn't stop beating with his tail. Then Puasa jumped out of the boat and stabbed him in the chest, and Melisang grabbed the flaying tail and cut the tip off it for a good-luck charm. They roped the crocodile then by the jaws, and tied him to the boat so that we could tow him behind us.

All during that trip we had seen large crocodile runs down the riverbanks, and the men had described the size and strength and ferocity of the crocodiles who had made the runs, and the men had seen the crocodiles, and Winki had seen them, and Harry had even seen one bathing in our pool, but I had not seen them. I looked at this creature now trailing in the water behind our boat. He had been killed by the hand of man, and a flame had not come out of his mouth, so I knew that he was not a griffin, but only a crocodile.

Our Muruts said that this surprisingly vivid coloring was common to the crocodiles who lived far up the rivers. The river-mouth crocodiles which I had seen before were only a drab mud color. When Harry skinned the beast we found he had a very fine hide. I tried to help at the skinning but I did not like the muscular reaction which made him continue to jerk even with half of his skin off. As it was taboo to Arusap's tribe of Muruts to touch a crocodile under any circumstances, Arusap stood by with nothing more helpful than advice, while the sweat poured off Harry. It was a small crocodile, only about six feet, but that seemed large when it came to the skinning.

As crocodiles are a menace on the Kinabatangan River and are known as "bad" there, it is not taboo to the natives to kill them. But on the Kalabakang River the crocodiles are known as "good" ones, and it is taboo for anyone to molest them. Because of this mutual agreement of nonaggression between the crocodiles and the people, if the crocodiles are molested they will retaliate by becoming "bad." We would not have shot a crocodile on the Kalabakang River as that would have been an overt act, and might have ended the good relations between man and beast there. However we are never allowed to say "crocodile" on any of the rivers, as the natives believe that the mention of the name will attract a crocodile and may incite him to violence. For this reason a crocodile is always referred to as "Grandfather."

Harry's men were pleased with the crocodile incident. It

vindicated the .22 rifle, which was known as "the Tuan's *phit-phit-phit* gun," because it did not make as impressive a noise as Winki's big gun, or the old shotgun which Arusap used.

Just as we had sighted the crocodile on the beach we had also sighted the launch lying in midstream off Lamag Landing. In the excitement of the crocodile I had forgotten that this was the moment I had been longing for. I even forgot to be conscious of any happy last minutes of being in our small *perahu*. Suddenly I found myself standing on the deck of the launch and knowing that the exciting part of the trip was over. And it was already like having eaten something strange and full-flavored; while it is in your mouth you do not know whether you like it or not, but the minute it is down you know it was delicious.

I went below to bathe. There we were on the launch, and the sleeping in *perahus* and under *sulaps* and under tents and under *keladi* leaves was ended. A roof, four walls, and a wooden bunk were ours. The rub of paddles against the sides of boats would soon change for the thump of Diesel engines. The tip and lift and sway of *perahus*, the untamed coltishness of *perahus*, would be disciplined behind the steady and heavy pound of machinery. The roar of the rapids was a long way off, the sun on the river was hard to feel, the breeze in the face that smelled of wild cattle, and the sickish, sweetish smell of dead pig, and the strong, delicious smell of the smoke from the fire — these were only words written on paper. My nostrils would be clean of them now. I went back on deck. I was clean, I was bathed, I was dry, I was comfortable. But I wanted to cry.

Perhaps I was tired. That was nine o'clock in the morning, and I lay on the deck and slept until five in the afternoon. When I woke up then I heard the put-put of Winki's motorboat. I looked up the river and saw the whole Swiss Navy sweeping towards us. The Swiss flag with the white cross on the now-faded red background floated above the outboard motorboat, and Winki sat cross-legged

under it. His head was wrapped in his white bandana, and his face was very thin, and he looked hard-used and heroic. Trailing behind the motorboat swung a long buffalo tail of nine *perahus*, towed one behind the other. Eight *perahus* hung in a straight line, but the ninth swished restlessly like the very end of a buffalo's tail. There were twenty-four men in the boats, as I counted them then. The men were using their paddles to guide the swishing tail, but when they saw us on the launch they flung up their paddles in greeting and shouted jubilantly. Drops flew from their paddles over their tattered clothing, back over their thrown-back heads, down on their smiling faces, and over their friendly bodies. It was a fine moment, and I wished that I could have held it.

Then Winki climbed onto the launch carrying his Swiss flag. He was grinning widely and looked like the youth who bore mid snow and ice the banner with the strange device, and I wanted to sing "U-pi-dee . . . U-pi-da . . . U-pi-dee-i-da!" Then Diesel engines began to throb and we were moving. Then came sunset, the heaviness of the night descending, and the soft kind tones of the men who were lying on the decks, and for me sleep, sleep, sleep.

When I awoke the next morning, my first thought was, "Push on," and then, "No more need to do so; the launch does the pushing now."

Before we left Sandakan we had sent a package of clean clothes up the river to Lamag to be delivered to us on the launch. I opened the package that morning. There was a pair of clean, starched, and creased culottes. In Sandakan culottes are considered very sportsmanlike attire. I put on the culottes. After four weeks in shorts I felt as feminine in them as if I had been wearing a garden-party gown. I hadn't used make-up for four weeks. I put on a little rouge then, and a little lipstick, and a little more, and I was really startled by the effect. Dashing! Almost pretty! . . . Just, of course, if you looked quickly, and then looked away again. I swished my starched culottes. It was rather fun being a woman.

All that day everybody on the launch took it easy. We had about fifty men on board, counting Winki's twenty-four, our party of eight, and the crew of the launch. Most of them had little to do but lie on the deck and talk. Winki's men vied with our men to tell the tallest tales, while the men of the launch encouraged both sides. I listened shamelessly to their accounts of our adventures.

Winki's man said, "Your Tuan's gun says *phit-phit-phit*, my Tuan's gun says *pommm-pommm-pommm!*"

Arusap said, "Never mind! My Tuan's gun shot the crocodile!"

Puasa proudly described his fear while going through the rapids. He has made a virtue out of it. "My heart beat my sides. I was very frightened. For twenty-eight days I was frightened. When we came to bad water I would get out and walk on the banks, over the rocks, through the jungle. I am a man of the jungle, not a man of the river."

"Was the Mem afraid in the rapids?" This question came to Arusap.

"She was not afraid, but she was often angry," answered Arusap. "At first when they came to bad water the boatmen made her get out and walk on the rocks. They were afraid that if the boat would turn over the Mem would drown, because probably she could not swim, and even if she could swim probably she could not swim in such bad water, and if the Mem drowned the Tuan would be angry, and that would be bad for the boatmen. So when we came to strong rapids the boatmen said that she must walk. But when the Mem walked on the wet rocks she fell many times. That made her very angry."

Puasa interrupted here. "I cut sticks for her to help her, and she threw them away, and again she fell, and again she was angry."

Arusap continued, "So one day the boatmen took the

boat to the shore for her to get out and walk while they went through the rapids. But she sat in the boat and said, 'Go on! I would rather drown than break my legs crawling on wet rocks. Go on! From now on I sit in the boat. Go on!' So they called to the Tuan to come to ask her to get out of the boat. But still she said, 'Go on!' And the Tuan said to the boatmen, 'Never mind. You'd better go on.' And we did go on, and after that the Mem always sat in the boat through the rapids."

And sometimes they made a Malay nursery rhyme of it all: —

"What does the Tuan who seeks oil do?"

"That Tuan strikes the rocks."

"What does the Government Tuan do?"

"That Tuan looks for trees."

"What does the Mem do?"

"The Mem follows the Tuan who looks for the trees."

"Why does she not stay in her house in Sandakan?"

"She does not like to stay in her house in Sandakan."

"What does she do when she follows the Tuan who looks for trees?"

"She does not do anything. Her heart desires to eat the wind. That is the way that it is."

"*Baik-lah* — very good, that is the way that it is."

"*Yah-lah*, very good, that is the way that it is."

We came out of the mouth of the Kinabatangan River and went slowly into the sea. I had forgotten the peace and rest of the sea. I had forgotten the size and color of the descending sun seen in a great open space. I had forgotten the depth and weight of the black cloud balls that the sun would leave when it fell. I had forgotten the sound of the open sea which is so different from the hurrying of rivers and rapids, and the soft sound of thunder which is heard in the distance, and has no urgency to come nearer and is only the pleasant beat of a distant gong. I had forgotten the brilliance of lightning which is seen without alarm. And I had forgotten the smell of the sea, which is the cleanest and finest of all smells.

I had been seeing everything from under *kajang* shelters, from between tent flaps, down narrow rivers, through tree trunks, and stippled with treetops. Everything had been cut and framed and pictured. Coming into the harbor now was like leaving a picture gallery and stepping into the open air.

So we went slowly out to sea to follow the deep channel in to Sandakan.

Part IV

WINDS OF HOME

16. *With a Shining Star*

I LIKE to climb the hills in Sandakan in the early morning, and the hill that is nearest to us is a burial ground. It is leased by a Chinese burial company and covered with crumbling graves, and the bones of some of the dead disintegrate in open jars by the headstones. Paper money is on the headstones, and small bowls stand close with rice in them, and seats are built near by upon which the departed spirits may rest when they return to visit the dead.

On my climb I have two stopping places. High up the hill is the grave of Kwang Loong Lee, unknown to me in life, but in death occupying the best view of the hillside. He looks and listens by the Sulu Sea, and I do likewise with him because his spirit seat is a comfortable one. I am indebted to him for much hospitality, and for the smooth surface of his tomb upon which I have written many words.

Further on, on a separate hill in unclaimed ground, is the pagan grave of Arusap's babe who lived for so short a time in our household. He lies very close to the sky with only a thin red layer of Borneo clay between him and the tropical sun. He has already been made one, I think, with all beautiful things.

There on the top of the hill I stop. The wind of the northeast monsoon is in my face as I look across the jungle to the Sulu Sea. The sea both isolates and connects our island of Borneo. If I travel far enough, for days and weeks, my home shore will come in sight. Then the mass in the distance will become places and people, and the people will be persons with dear faces, met once again. When I left home those faces smiled bravely, but when we meet again it may be permissible for us to cry.

The meeting comes soon now, for my first tour in the East is almost finished.

We exist in the East at present with the knowledge of changing conditions, and the awareness that life may not be the same again. Now in these last months before our leave I wish to become deeply conscious of everything in my life out here.

When I was very young I was sometimes very happy. It was the proper state of affairs and not the occasion for surprise, and if I wasn't happy it was a matter to be resented. I have learned differently now. For that reason I wish to stop and rejoice at and mark with a shining star these present years of happiness in Borneo.

17. *The House of Friends*

WITH youthful swiftness Fi-fille came towards us across the lawn, using the private path that leads between the Chinese Consulate and our garden. She carried in her hand the blue paper of the Consulate war telegrams which came to her father, the Chinese Consul, and which she often brought to us.

At the same moment in which I saw Fi-fille I saw the tall Japanese Consul appearing from the public path at the other corner of our lawn. The painted-on-silk figure which tiptoed beside him, the high spikes of her French heels tapping elegantly into the turf, must be the animated Tokyo wife of whom I had heard. They came towards us smiling.

The smug hostess expression faded from my face. The Japanese Consul and his wife were our invited guests for tea at what would be our first meeting. This afternoon I could not welcome Fi-fille. The Sino-Japanese war situation was just entering a crucial phase, and to entertain together the families from both consulates would be a social stupidity which was almost a rudeness.

Rapidly the International Situation advanced across the turf towards us, unaware as yet that it was a Situation. Fi-fille's casual glance did not recognize the Consul, and she herself, in saffron-colored jersey and skirt, was, at first glance, any smart young woman.

As simultaneously as if they had measured their steps beforehand, the three arrived at our doorway. Hoping that this moment in my life would never repeat itself, I stepped forward to greet them.

"It is indeed a great pleasure that we meet."

I turned to the bowing Consul. "Good afternoon, Consul, we have been anticipating knowing you. And do you know Miss Genevieve Ou, the daughter of our Chinese Consul?"

Austere wonder appeared in his eyes at my introduction, and the air became full of unspoken exclamations. Fi-fille's face grew bright with confusion, now she was understanding the situation. It seemed to me then that the tinge of rouge and lipstick on her oval face added no more sophistication to her countenance than does a turquoise ribbon to a kitten.

The Consul recovered first, and gripped Fi-fille's coral-tipped hand. It lay in his slender fingers like the wax hand of a window manikin. Fi-fille had apparently lost connection with it, and I wondered vaguely if the Consul might toss it away when he had finished.

"Fi-fille, this is the Consul's wife."

With easy grace Madame veiled the questioning in her face, and extended her hand. The Consul transferred Fi-fille's hand to Madame, who touched it daintily and then returned it to Fi-fille, at whose side it swung abandoned.

The next difficulty was to negotiate our doorway. I stepped back and gestured for Madame to enter, and she gestured for me to enter, and I gestured again for her to enter, and she deprecatingly held back for me to enter, but I stood firm. Protesting, she then stepped over the sill first. I then gestured for Fi-fille to enter, as I was the hostess. She gestured for me to enter, as she was an unmarried girl. This dilemma we usually solved by entering doorways together, but to-day she was determined on etiquette. I gave up and preceded her. Meanwhile my husband had solved his doorway problem by stepping around the corner to the French window, and forcibly injecting the Consul through this before him.

Fi-fille sat on the divan by my husband. Her face had become an exquisitely molded bisque mask. The expressionless young woman I saw there was a stranger to me. I could not tell whether she was deliberately handling the situation thus, or whether she was in a trance of embarrassment.

The face of my husband beside her was another mask. The yellow, livery look of many years in the East now for the moment possessed it painfully. Distress at the awkward situation had strained away into tightness the amiable laugh lines which usually show at the corners of his eyes. I read his thoughts behind his mask, but hoped that nobody else could. He was a conversational loss, and husband and friend together formed an unrising dough in the social sponge.

I searched for a conversational loophole. "You have lived in San Francisco, I understand, Madame?"

"Since one year. But only a little do I speak English. You will pardon?" Her voice tinkled out the words with a diminutive sweetness which suited her small stature.

"My wife desires to learn immediately to speak better English." The Consul's voice was clear and decisive. I noticed that although he was very tall, he was not un-Japanese-looking. His bones were Oriental and shapely, and without fleshy padding. His face was like a fine-boned and beautiful skull with parchment molded over it. The death mask of a samurai, I thought.

"You find our isolated Borneo very quiet after San Francisco, Madame?" The question was inane, but the pauses were worse.

"Ah, quiet, yes. But there is movie here in Sandakan. I like movie. And you, Madame Keith, you have been to Japan?"

"Yes, but we were only there for one week."

"You like Japan, yes?"

"Yes, indeed, Japan is very beautiful," I said helpfully.

"You were there in cherry-blossom time?"

"No, we were there in October."

"Ah, chrysanthemum time."

Tea arrived. With the passing of cream and sugar, sandwiches, biscuits, and tarts, with the comforting occupation for our hands, the scene became almost social. I saw my husband's mask becoming pliant with the warmth of tea.

And then Fi-fille refused tea. She hurled a belligerent "I do not care for any tea!" like a bomb into a nursery. It burst among us, and its fragments shot up and exploded the comic-strip balloons which still floated inoffensively above our heads with our amiable pleasantries on them. Our social phrases came tumbling down, and the descending fragments scratched our bright surfaces.

Conversational *rigor mortis* ensued. I passed the flower-decorated cakes to Madame, who removed one tiny pink one from the tremendous plateful.

"And does not the other lady enjoy tea?" she questioned.

"She says she has had her tea. Fi-fille, why don't you speak French with Madame? Madame speaks French fluently, I believe."

This bait dropped by Fi-fille without a nibble. I passed the cakes to the Consul. He would not have any. I passed them to Fi-fille. She would not have any. I relinquished the overwhelming plate with the one tiny pink cake missing. I never again wanted to see sandwiches, cakes, or tea.

Just as I gathered myself together to reopen Japan, the Consul's eye fell on the milky jade of the large Sung celadon plate which hung on the wall, the one with the highly embossed acanthus blossom, of which we were so proud. The eye of the Consul sparkled from out his samurai mask.

"You collect?"

Even without words the answer was in the glow which came in my husband's eye. Expression wrinkled his mask.

"A little, Consul. And you?"

"I also have the spiritual joy, the financial misfortune,

335

to collect." The Consul was over by the plate, gently removing it from its holder, smoothing the ancient surface, feeling its oyster gloss, touching reverently the embossed acanthus. My husband was beside him, unable to conceal his pride of his treasure.

"It is genuine, Consul. You see here . . ." They turned it over, and then back. "Nine hundred years ago some old boy turned, and worked, and molded . . . this leaf, this petal, this stem," tracing them lovingly, "perfected this oval, and to-day we have them still. That's what gets into the bone about this early stuff. It's that feeling that throughout centuries men have handled and valued this, and that for centuries to come other men may do so. It is our link with the past. Don't you feel that way, Consul?"

"Indeed, yes. It makes us one with the ages."

I thought that I had heard these phrases before some place, but my husband and the Consul seemed quite satisfied with their originality.

"And you are happy also that your husband collects?" questioned the Consul's wife of me. We exchanged sudden laughs. We saw that both of us understood that the wives of collectors live on the verge of bankruptcy.

The Consul and my husband disappeared into the library, and I knew what this meant. The best pieces of Sung were there.

"Diplomatic relations with Japan saved by Sung celadon!" My mind carried a front-page newspaper article with this joyful streamer. "Ceramics save the day! Sung, and Ming, and blue-and-white, play their part in keeping world peace. Siamese ware and early tradeware, blanc de chine and famille rose, snuffboxes and medicine bowls, pots,

336

jugs, and pitchers, all gather at International Conference to make the world safe for collectors. Wives excluded, and the wolf not allowed at the door!"

Now that the samurai mask and the angry-husband mask had disappeared amicably together, I felt that I could deal with the female situation. Almost with gusto, I eased us out of our seats and towards the hall. Madame was an obliging creature and quite content to be disposed of in any way I suggested, but Fi-fille was still enveloped in her aura of obstinate tragedy. Slowly we negotiated the hall doorway, again an almost insuperable obstacle for our gentilities.

"This is a native blowpipe used for poison darts. It is a favorite Borneo weapon," I described.

Madame acknowledged this gracefully, and then stepped over to a hanging native skull, the trophy of a head hunt.

"And do these Borneo men still hunt heads?"

"Sometimes."

"But that is not civilized, I think!" She shuddered away.

I caught Fi-fille's glance, and felt what she was thinking of Madame's comment. Fortunately, she did not say it.

I chose the double doorway through which we three might step at once, and we went out to the garden. We all said that the view was wonderful, wasn't it! And what tree was that? That was the African tulip tree, the *Spathodia campanulata*. And what rose was that? That rose was an hibiscus. And did that white lily have a fragrance? No, that white lily was a scentless orchid. And wasn't that wonderful to have orchids growing all about! Yes, that was wonderful, but we still liked geraniums. And would we all like to walk down and see the *wah wahs? Wah wah* was the native name for *kelawat*, and *kelawat* was the Malay name for gibbon ape, and if Madame loved the animals she would surely like to see the *wah wahs?*

Slowly, slowly, slowly we walked.

"Oh, Hermie! Oh, Anjibi! Ooooooooh! Whooooooo? Whooooooo?" I made *wah wah* noises. "They go to bed very early, and now that dark is coming I am afraid I cannot get them to come down."

"Oh, but the baby one! Can I love him in my arms?" begged Madame.

I entered the cage, but Herman was nervous with strangers about, and hung out of my reach, and jibbered at me like an old man with unmanageable false teeth. Madame and I made supposedly enticing noises. Herman, Anjibi, and Fi-fille looked at us with common scorn.

"If you will come over some morning I can get them down for you. They are more playful in the morning," I apologized.

We returned to the house, and we all looked at the clock. "You pardon, please, if I call to my husband in Japanese?" queried Madame. I pardoned gladly, and she called.

"My husband! It grows dark. Surely we have been here a long time. Surely we have said everything twice. Surely it is time to go home. Come away from your plates and your bowls." Her voice tinkled it out in music-box Japanese, but I knew every word that she said.

"Yes, yes! Indeed I do forget the time when we collectors are together. But now I come." The samurai mask appeared from the library, accompanied by Harry.

"Good-bye!"

338

"Good-bye!"

"Good-bye."

"Good-bye."

The sloping path lost them to sight. Then Fi-fille turned quickly to me, and I saw that the delicate mask of her expression was breaking.

"Oh, you must be angry with me for coming! Oh, please do not be! I am so sorry, but after I was here I did not know what to do." The clear skin flushed with unmanageable emotion, and a lock of shining, irresponsible hair fell forward out of the well-arranged permanent wave.

I remembered then an old Chinese proverb I had read, "When riding a tiger it is difficult to dismount."

But Fi-fille had dismounted from her tiger now, and in the place of a militant Amazon there was just a small girl who had been too distressed all afternoon for tea and her favorite cakes. My heart recalled the childlike defenselessness, the youthful eagerness, I had seen in her face in the afternoon sun.

I took Fi-fille's hand and I held it tightly, while I urged her ahead of me into the lighted room. I called for the afternoon cakes again, and we searched attentively for her favorites. I called for a watered vermouth for her, and lighted a cigarette, and then while we sat and smoked we looked about us searchingly. The parlor of horrors had vanished. And I saw, and Fi-fille saw, that this was the house of her friends.

2

From the evening when I first met the Chinese Consul, and Madame Ou his French wife, and Fi-fille and Georges, the young daughter and son, I connected them in my own mind with my family group at home. And the better that I came to know them the more they came to be for me the symbol of family life in Sandakan. I went often to the Chinese Consulate, for Fi-fille and I discovered a mutual attachment, Georges and I practised the tango, Madame Ou loaned her French-style periodicals to me, and the Consul discussed with us Chinese nationalism and gardening. I went often, and always when I entered the doorway there I felt as I had felt in my own home in the United States, that family affection is a fire which warms all those who come near it.

The Consul himself spoke the Mandarin dialect of Chinese, the dialect of the diplomats, but he also spoke French perfectly, and French was the family tongue employed by all of them in their home. I used to try intensely, when the flames of their French licked around my head, to bring back to my memory the small amount of French which I had one time known, but always instead Malay words sprang to my lips. But Fi-fille and Georges, who spoke English very well, would dart with their agile tongues in among the French phrases, and pluck out those of significance, and translate them into English for me. By reason of this erratic method the conversations at the Consulate were always very alive, very fluent, very well illustrated by gestures, but principally made comprehensible by virtue of our mutual desire to understand one another.

There in that home I found many beautiful possessions which I admired, of both Chinese and French origin. And I not only found cosmopolitan treasures from Peking and

from Paris, but I found in the Consul and Madame themselves qualities of being which came from equally distant
sources. But never was there anything in those differing
qualities which failed to be predominated by the bond of
affection between them. Madame ruled her end of the
dinner table with a generous elegant gesture. The Consul
ruled his end with an unobtrusive low-spoken word in
Mandarin, but the rule of both was to the benefit of both.

And great among the qualities which I found in that
home to admire was the quality of sincerity to their friends.
And among those friends, whom to me it was unaccustomed
pleasure to meet, I found ever more fuel for the fire of my
interracial warmth.

Not all Asiatic homes are open to Europeans, and not
all European homes are open to Asiatics, and to Eurasians
sometimes the homes of neither are open. But when a home
welcomes all, as the Consulate did, it welcomes people
whose stories are writing the future of their races, but
whose lives are tangled.

I watched many stories begin at the Chinese Consulate,
and many of them are still without ending. There was the
Chinese doctor with an Edinburgh degree, who brought to
Sandakan his wife, a smartly dressed young Spanish woman
born in Gibraltar. He practises in Sandakan still, but she
has returned to Gibraltar with their baby.

There was a young Eurasian nurse who came to Sandakan from Singapore. Her mother was Siamese and her
father was English. When she first saw our semi-Siamese
cat, Mary, she picked her up and laughed and said, "You're
like me, kitty, half and half!" I had read that the Siamese

Eurasian women were often very beautiful, and when I met this girl I saw that it was so. She was also intelligent, industrious, and ambitious. Her story is only beginning.

These and many others came to the Chinese Consulate, while through companionable buoyant evenings we gorged on Madame Ou's lavish French dinners, or at cheerful Sunday tiffins reveled in the salty tang of her Marseilles bouillabaisse. And those days were happy days, it seems to us now, as are all days before impersonal disaster becomes personal, when looked back upon.

Then coincident with the growing imperativeness of the war in China the dinners and tiffins began to abate, and I thought that it must be the war situation, which it could reasonably be. Some time passed without my visiting the Consulate, and then suddenly as a shock the answer came to me. Unexpectedly one afternoon I happened upon the Consul in his garden when I had not seen him for some weeks. He smiled, he was most courteous as always, we said good-day, and I passed on, but I had seen that he was very ill. A few days later Fi-fille came up and told us that her father must leave immediately for Hong Kong, where he would probably have an operation.

The afternoon came when the Consul was to sail. We asked permission to go with his family on the launch which was to take Madame Ou and the Consul to the Hong Kong boat that lay in midstream. At sunset the boat weighed her anchor and moved slowly towards the harbor's mouth. When we on the launch below looked up and watched the ship out of sight I could see to the last the Consul's smile, which seemed to me celestial upon his beautiful and aristocratic face.

I had always drawn a comparison in my own mind between the Consul and his family and my own closely knit family, but I had little known the coincidence which was

to work out in our relations to draw that comparison more deeply and more sadly.

Within a few days after the Consul left we had news of him which had been radioed to a passing Borneo-bound ship. The message said that the ocean passage was very bad and the Consul was growing weak. Then came news by wireless from Hong Kong — the captain of the steamer had forced his engines to their utmost speed, had brought his ship in to Hong Kong a day ahead of time, and the Consul was safely in the hospital. Then came the news, just eight days after he had left Sandakan, that the Consul was dead.

Five days after that I received a cable to say that my own father had died in the United States.

And I do believe that these two fine men live on, in the hearts which they leave behind them. And I do believe that to create love in the hearts we leave is the richest legacy.

18. *Two People Whom We Like*

I SHALL always remember that night because it marked for me the closing of the carefree epoch in Borneo. The war in China, terrible though it was, still seemed like somebody else's trouble, and we ourselves had not yet become aware of the acuteness of the situation in Europe. From that night on every event contributed towards a disintegration in me of the sense of security in life.

My husband had been reading the Singapore *Straits Budget* that night as I dressed for dinner, and he read aloud to me this paragraph, "It is with horror and distress that the civilized world views the unequaled atrocities and inexcusable brutalities of Japan in China."

"I wish you wouldn't read those things to me just before we go there," I protested. "Why must the Consul and Madame be Militant Japan, and not just two people whom we like?"

Two people whom we like — the phrase was to recur to me many times thereafter, and sometimes sadly.

The distance to the Japanese Consulate was short, but all the way down the road, as we walked in the path of the warm, fervent moonlight, I was seeing the fragile face of the Japanese Consul with his kindly, half-anxious smile, and the delicate porcelain face of his wife. As the musky laburnum blossoms fell on the path before us I saw those friendly faces stamped out with the staring words, like the label on a poison bottle, "Don't trust them!" The air was warm and scented, and as we turned into the Consulate I was resenting all contentious thoughts.

The Consul came hospitably down his driveway to greet us, and when his eyes looked into mine I started with relief and almost spoke my thoughts aloud: "But the atrocities and brutalities! They are not here."

Before the lighted doorway stood his wife. She smiled at me, and again I knew that this was a woman whom I liked. She wore a deep blue kimono which matched the great sapphire stone on her finger, and even her *zori* were blue, with sapphire soles and bright blue straps which came between the toes of her little white-cottoned feet. I guessed that it was in courtesy to me that she had worn the kimono and left her Parisian dresses hanging in her wardrobe, for I had said with admiration to her once, "No Western dress has such dignity and beauty as the kimono."

The Consulate itself was built in Western style, and inside the house the furniture was also modern. Straight-angled, flat-planed, glass-topped, metal-cornered, it was like fine machinery. So much for Western influence. But all one wall of the room was a vast jade-colored painted-on-silk sea. Two fat gray fish swam lazily across it, while down on the jade water dropped the evanescent, paler-than-pink petals of cherry blossoms. Only a Japanese would have painted so much jade sea, such small plump fish, and such a perfection of pink petal blossoms.

Another wall of the room was a painted-on-silk forest. Not the limbs and trunks of trees, but a shimmering mass of cornelian leaves, dripping and moist with the rain. As Madame bowed in her long kimono, with the painted forest wall for a background, it was as if I saw her in her own country, with the paper walls of her Japanese house thrown open to the autumn, while outside in the rain on the hills glowed all the maple trees of Nara.

Seeing her thus, I wished that I might always see her so, against her own harmonious background. And I wondered then why it was that when man has become in harmony with his own surroundings he is still willing to put himself at a disadvantage by trying to adapt the surroundings of others.

After dinner she and I were expected to devote ourselves to women's topics of clothes, food, painting, and needle-work, or to listen and nod assent to the words of our husbands. This disposition of the evening's entertainment was deftly settled by the Consul. "We will listen to the Tokyo broadcast while our wives are looking at their women's magazines," said he.

So we two wives sat together on the divan, and docilely picked up the Japanese pictorials. Madame translated the Japanese title of the one we held as the *Women's Club*, and we turned through the advertisements slowly. We came to Petal Blossom Complexion Powder, and I asked Madame

if she sent home to Tokyo for her cosmetics. When Madame said yes, she did, and I agreed with her that I did too, our husbands pricked up their ears.

"Why," ruminated my husband sagely to the Consul, "do women believe all these advertisements about how to become beautiful?"

"Why, indeed?" agreed the Consul.

Two People Whom We Like

But she and I laughed together deprecatingly, pleased at our own foolishness, and then smiled cunningly at each other, secure in our own wisdom. Was not the object of our sex to please, those laughs said silently. And if so, was it not a good object? And would not the world be more pacific and happy if the object of our husbands' sex were also to please?

Just then the radio interrupted with a Tokyo announcement which swept us out of our women's world to which we had been relegated. The announcer had switched from Japanese into English and he was describing Japanese victories in China — sweeping victories, glorious victories, victories which dropped from his tongue with such ease that they scarcely seemed to have been fought for. Following this came further enthusiastic description of vigorous onslaughts, triumphant attacks, fearless reprisals, and successful affronts, coming in such effortless syllables from his mouth that there seemed to be no broken bones behind them.

And then came the casualties, followed by the statement from the radio, "The ashes of the hero dead will be brought home for interment on native soil. A war monument will be erected in Tokyo to them, to these the dauntless dead, the immortal hero dead, who will live forever in the memory of their country. . . ." Zealously, imperturbably, the pronouncement went on. The voice was maddening. I turned to Madame to cry out against it. But she was looking down, and her face was very sad, and she sighed and said, "My husband's brother . . ." and stopped.

"War! . . ." I cried.

"War . . ." she answered.

349

But we could go no further.

Again the radio became compelling, and Madame and I dropped our magazines. Although the announcer was having difficulty with his English pronunciation, his accents were vehement and sonorous. "And still the army pushes invincibly on. Like an onrushing wave our heroic men sweep after the retreating Chinese. Despite the Russian incident which our brave soldiery are dealing with so dauntlessly . . ."

The Consul broke in on the radio excitedly then. "Those Russians! But they can do nothing against our men. They are helpless before us! We are winning tremendous victories!"

Meanwhile the Tokyo announcer was working himself up into a paean of admiring victory: "The dauntless, the fearless, the fierce, the bold soldiery, like the samurai of old, sweep on to victory! Victory our war cry! BANZAI! BANZAI! *Banzai!* Banzai!"

As the radio voice faded Madame and I sat motionless. She wore the kimono, and I the Western dinner dress, but drops of blood from our hearts would be of the same color.

There must be something that we can say, I tell myself. I will say to her, "Do you want this?" And she will say to me, and there will be tears in her voice, "Please, no!" And thus joined in our desire we shall find the words in our woman's world, in our sisterhood, to stop all this. But we do not find the words.

Slowly we become conscious again of our husbands, who are still sitting by the radio. The Consul is still talking about beating the Russians, and my husband is saying that it cannot be done as easily as all that. And if they had tin soldiers

350

and a map with flags it is obvious that our husbands would be fighting the battle on the carpet.

The room relaxes. I smile then at Madame, and my face has a stiff feeling as if it had set in a mask of sadness from which it is difficult to break. She smiles back at me from behind the same sad mask.

Very soon then my husband and I leave, to walk home under a clouding moon, in the fragrance of a night which has become melancholic.

2

On the map the island of Borneo appears to be isolated from a European war. But draw an imaginary path across that map from Germany to Japan, and from Japan to Borneo, and that path destroys our peace.

Our coast line is unfortified, the country is without defense. In Sandakan there are seventy-five Europeans. There are fifty "volunteers." The defense problem was dealt with in the words of a senior administrative officer here when asked what he would do if a Japanese cruiser landed an armed party. He said he would ask them up to tea.

In time of war women face the possibility of evacuation, and everybody faces isolation from communications and supplies, food shortage, and indefinite separation of wives from husbands, either for civil or for military purposes.

It was the day after the failure of Mr. Chamberlain's second flight to Berlin. People had waited all night for the radio relays from London, and then electrical storms had made the broadcasts unintelligible. I sat at my desk in the afternoon and looked down at the Japanese timber ship in the harbor below me. If she weighs her anchor, I thought, word will have come to her by radio, and that will be the beginning of war. At three-thirty I heard the anchor chain

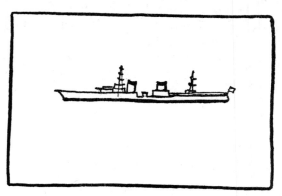

grind. I watched her moving towards the sea. I marked her slow progress by the anchored British Hong Kong steamer. She moved quietly, stealthily, as an enemy ship would move. I watched her sadly, thinking, This is the end of peaceful Borneo, life will not be like this again.

Then I saw that although she seemed to move, she had not left the frame of my window. Slowly I realized that it was not the Japanese boat which was moving out of harbor, but the British steamer I had used as a marker, moving up the bay to a better anchorage. Thankfully I looked again at the battered black timber steamer, now lying so innocently there, not now an enemy, not now an alien rushing from hostile waters.

19. *Fever*

I FOUND a note in my typewriter, when I went back to it many weeks later, which marked a period of long lassitude that preceded the coming of fever: —

I am so tired and listless now that I wish I could go in a painless daze from coffee in the morning to the first drink before dinner at night, and then to bed, only to become conscious again in time for coffee in the morning. Even the typewriter has become an enemy. My mind is unable to encompass the interval between now and the coming of leave. I only know that I am so tired.

And then I began having fever every day. It came by nine o'clock in the morning and lasted until dark, obsessing every thought and action as if I were drunk with it. Every evening by six o'clock it loosened its hold, and by eight I felt all right, but as if I had worked hard all day and earned the right to rest. By midnight it would come again, and by four o'clock I would sweat, and then fall asleep. I would arise in the morning feeling weak but not ill, and by nine o'clock fever would possess me again.

I was trying very hard to finish my book before the date of our leave should arrive, and I knew even before the coming of fever that I had barely time enough to do so. But after I was ill I would lie on my bed with the sweat standing on me like the cold damp on ice-box fruit, while I tried to hold a tablet of paper and tried to think, and I could not think, except of the heat inside me and the pouring of water out of my body.

Then one morning my chills increased and I felt a violent nausea. Arusap and I watched with annoyance while the mercury in my thermometer climbed steadily up. There seemed nothing to do about it but break the thermometer. This I did, but Arusap meanwhile had taken matters into his own hands and had telephoned to Harry to come home from the office, and Harry had called the doctor again, and in a very short time I was driving down Hospital Road in a red silk kimono and a nightgown. And when at last I crawled into the high white bed on the open hospital verandah I was grateful indeed to be there.

I was a suspect for typhoid fever, but whenever anyone thought of a new fever I was a suspect for it also. As there is no bacteriological laboratory in Sandakan local diseases are usually unnamed, and our tropical fevers, of which there are many, can seldom be classified. To all practical purposes I seemed to be having typhoid, but my daily diversion for some time was touching my chin to my chest to prove it was not spinal meningitis, furnishing drops of blood to show it was not malaria, and supplying spots of spit to eliminate diphtheria. For a while then I was not interested in making notes on my condition.

2

At six o'clock one morning I opened my eyes to see Ah Yin standing by my hospital bed with tears rolling down her cheeks. "How you feel to-day, Missee?"

I couldn't describe how I felt. After trying to vomit at half-hour intervals for two nights and two days, I was feeling the necessity to do so again.

"I think you very sick, Missee," she said sadly.

I thought so too, and found nothing comforting to say about it.

Slowly she circled my bed, pushing in my hot protruding hands and feet, pinning them firmly under the blankets and tacking them down with a twist, the tears trickling down from her face onto the bed while she did so. Then she stroked my pillow flat, felt my forehead, held my hand, and said, "You can eat, Missee?"

"No."

For five minutes she stood there by me and she was crying still. Then she left, and I was sick.

At nine o'clock I again felt the power of eyes upon me and unwillingly opened my own. Arusap and Ah King stood by the bed. Arusap wore his new head cloth and the magenta and yellow plaid sarong which I liked so well, and Ah King wore clean white Chinese trousers and a starched tunic. As soon as I opened my eyes Arusap spoke, with the sombre eloquence of one who delivers a funeral oration.

"We know that this day the Mem is very ill. When Ah Yin returned from the hospital she said it would be well that we should hurry to see her. I wished to do so immediately, but the Tuan had not yet had his bath water or his breakfast, and I remembered that the Mem had always told me to take care of the Tuan when she was not with us, so I waited to give the Tuan bath water and food before I came.

"The Mem is now very sick, and because of this we are sad at home, and we do not eat and sleep. It is indeed a very strong fever that you have, and perhaps you must remain in the hospital for a long time. But never mind that if you grow well again.

"To-day I have come to tell the Mem that she and the Tuan are as a mother and a father to me, and that we in their house are like their children." Arusap stopped.

I had known before that Harry was spoken of by Arusap as being father and mother to him, but I had never anticipated being raised to this category myself. It was the final tribute, and I reckoned that I must indeed be very ill. I gathered myself together for the response which I knew must be made to this honor, only hoping that I could suppress the necessity to be ill again until after they had left. "That is indeed very good, Arusap," I said. "The Tuan and I likewise look upon you as a father and mother look upon their children."

Arusap answered, "Mem," and stood silent, while Ah King made inarticulate mutterings which we understood to mean that she wished to be included in the family too. After a moment Arusap said, "Peace remain with you,

Mem," and they left. But peace did not remain, and I raised myself and was ill.

At noontime Ah Yin was at the bed again. She opened her large shopping basket and produced a tin of cigarettes, then saw that the cigarettes by my bed were untouched, and mournfully repacked the new tin and said accusingly, "You very sick, Missee, if you not smoke. You eat to-day, Missee?"

"No."

"Maybe hospital food not good, Missee. To-morrow I bring you food from home."

"No, Ah Yin, I cannot eat."

A long silence while tears fell upon the bed, and then Ah Yin said comfortlessly, "You not eat, you die, Missee."

But the next morning I was better. When Ah Yin arrived at six o'clock I was drinking a cup of tea. She saw this through the doorway before she entered the room, and a look of delight beamed on her Chinese face. In that look was a superhuman quality of selfless joy which made me feel that she was smiling at me from the ranks of the angels and the archangels and all the company of Heaven.

3

It is such a struggle to come to life again when one is ill! Can the original creation have been any more difficult than this?

Through the blue tropical shutters of the hospital came the first streaks of morning light. The late mosquitoes were still buzzing outside my net and the night light still glowed in the hall. Inside my head ash cans were being banged about, the back of my neck was being sawed on by two men with a large-toothed saw, my stomach had been trod upon by an elephant, and my backbone had been run down and rolled over by a steam roller.

I was just taking all of this sadly into account when Nurse Topsy came to the bed and thrust a brown Filipina hand through the opening of the mosquito net and grasped mine and shook it vigorously. "Happy New Year, Mrs. Keith! Happy New Year!"

Happy New Year! I thought. Am I expected to live through another year feeling as I do?

"Are you feeling better to-day, Mrs. Keith?"

Am I! Well, nobody ever felt worse than I, and lived to tell about it.

"Well, well, that's fine," says Nurse Topsy as she looks at the thermometer, "just fine. The doctor is coming early this morning, and you must be ready."

Here comes the doctor. "How is the patient this morning?"

"Much better, Doctor," says Nurse Topsy blithely. "Her temperature is going down, and she slept last night."

So they call that sleep, that horrible struggle I had all night with demons and devils! Well, let them have their jokes.

"That's fine, Nurse. We'll soon have her up now. Feeling better, eh, Mrs. Keith?"

"No, I feel horrible."

"Yes, yes, of course. A long fever always leaves you that way. Weak, of course, but we'll fix that with a good tonic."

"Doctor, I don't think you can ever wind me up and make the works go again."

"Yes, yes, of course we can. A good tonic, and your leave is coming in only a month's time. You need a change. You've done too long without leave, that's all. This is your fifth year now."

"Then you really think I am over the worst?" I am cheered in spite of myself.

"Yes, certainly you are. A month from to-day we'll put you on the Hong Kong boat, and by the time you get back to the United States you'll forget all about this."

"Do you think I'll be able to travel in a month?"

"Of course, of course. Did you think we were going to let you die out here?"

I am ashamed to admit it now, but exactly that idea had been in my head.

"I must be off," says the doctor. "There are other patients more ill than you now. Well, cheerio, and Happy New Year!"

Maybe it's going to be a happy new year, after all!

I came home from the hospital then. I looked about our house. How could I possibly prepare for the eleven months we should be away in the short time then remaining before we sailed? The question was answered for me within the week, when I returned to the hospital with another high fever. I decided then that it was not in my horoscope to prepare for things.

This time it was malaria, which had settled in my glands and liver, and had not shown up in blood tests. During the weeks of my first stay in the hospital I had worried about not being able to finish my book before leaving Borneo. But when I returned to the hospital I ceased to care about anything except to get well again, and to be able to catch the Hong Kong boat on February fifth,

headed for home leave in a country where the milk came out of a cow instead of a tin. I came out of hospital five days before the boat sailed feeling scarcely able to travel. But there was just one word of advice that everybody gave me — "Don't miss the boat."

The day of departure we went on board at dusk. From the bay I looked back to where our hill rolled up to the sky, behind the lights of the town. There was a light in our house where my husband's relief was then living. Up there on that hill other ears than ours would be hearing the bullfrogs glunk in the tall damp hedge and the night birds call in the jungle, other bare feet than ours would be under the drinking table, and other voices would call for drinks and food in the hot, sweet, tropical night. And in the mornings the *wah wahs* would sing and no one would stop to listen.

We looked up at the light on our hill. We wanted our leave, and we knew that we needed it. But we felt that night when we sailed from Borneo that we were not going home on leave, but we were leaving our home.

20. *Home*

WE were on the *Empress of Canada* in Hong Kong Harbor.

"There's too much luggage!" Harry said, and the words were somehow familiar.

There was my wardrobe trunk, Harry's favorite abomination, standing boastfully against the wall with its chest swelling out like a fat woman in a pullman aisle. There was Harry's steamer trunk, hiding modestly beneath a bunk as a well-trained trunk should do, and there was his small sheet-metal trunk with the manuscript of his Murut vocabulary and his favorite books, lying docilely beside his other trunk. There were two legitimate suitcases with clothing, there were two zipper bags with dutiable goods, and one large suitcase with dutiable gifts. There were our two brief cases, each one fighting to be on top, and my portable typewriter, and the golf clubs, and the duffle bag with

Home

Harry's Ming porcelain wrapped up in my rabbit coat.
And there was the large, very large, Chinese-made extension suitcase which held my manuscript.

"Can't that manuscript suitcase go in the hold?" Harry
asked.

"No," I answered. And Harry said nothing.

When I had had fever and had worried constantly about
not being able to finish my book before our leave came,
Harry had promised me that I should take it all home with
me to the United States, down to the last scrap of paper.

"All those drawers- and drawersful of half-written
notes?" I asked. "You mean I can take all of that home?
And all those stacks of what looks like scrap paper to anyone else? And all those papers in clips? And my sketches?
And my Malay dictionary? And the Handbook? And the
Malay pantuns and songs and the Jawi reader? And the
sheets and sheets of stuff that I might never use at all, but
maybe I might? All of that?"

"All of that," Harry had promised. So now the Chinese
extension suitcase stood in the cabin. It had extended to
such proportions that it would not go under the berth, it
would not stand between the beds, it would not fit in a
corner, and it would not go in the closet. The suitcase
stood, and Harry said nothing.

My plan was to work on the manuscript all the way
across the Pacific, and to have it emerging in a coördinated
state by the time we reached British Columbia. During the
first few days of the voyage I upset everything in the cabin
daily by opening the Chinese suitcase and sitting and nibbling tastelessly at the edges of the sheets which lay on top.
At each nibble it became less appetizing.

Meanwhile Harry vacationed in the smoking room, occasionally returning to the cabin full of the beer of human kindness, only to find me dyspeptic on undigested manuscript. Then after three days, like a vaccination, the virus of vacation took. I strapped up the Chinese suitcase and sent it down to the hold, and gave myself up to watching the exile's return.

Oh, that trip across the Pacific! Oh, the cold again! Hong Kong was cold, Shanghai was cold, Kobe was cold,

Yokohama was cold, the *Empress of Canada* was cold! Or maybe it was I that was cold. The only time I was warm was sitting in a hot bath or drinking whiskey, and once I took the whiskey in the bath with me. My body hurt with the cold, but it made me live again.

And oh, the food! Red-blooded Canadian beef; liver that had no cirrhosis; kidneys without Bright's disease; apples, oranges, pears, and grapes which could be distinguished one from the other by flavor as well as by shape; vegetables which did not have to be labeled and indexed in order to reveal to the consumer their identity; and one head of lettuce per day per Keith, and NO tins.

Home

Oh, the women in furs again! And a real dance orchestra, and hot water running out of the taps, and an enamel bathtub with a drain therein, and all the luxury of a luxury liner, and we two people in the lap of it! Ships have carried passengers before, but never two more contented ones.

2

"And the natives," we explained to our English friends, "will paddle out to greet the ship in kayaks and birchbark canoes. They are a white-skinned race of more than average stature, with Aryan features and simple ways. Clad in the skins of the wild beasts which they have shot in the Canadian Rockies, and adorned with the beads and bracelets which the traders from England have brought them, they will look alarming, but they are not dangerous. Be surprised at nothing, however, for we are about to touch at our first port on the North American Continent."

The next morning we came into harbor at Victoria, British Columbia, and if the natives of Canada were a disappointment to our English friends, at least early spring in Victoria was all that we had promised.

I walk down the quiet streets of Victoria wanting to shout and sing, filled with a joyful vigor again. It is the old wonderful feeling remembered from all the happiest moments of my life, the joyful feeling that went with me on the hilltops of Borneo and came down the Borneo rivers. At last I no longer carry the listless carcass which has burdened me through weeks of fever, and the blood awakens in my quiescent flesh. This is no whiskey stimulation, this is coming alive in a spring world — a spring world after four years and a half in a land without seasons. The crocuses bloom. How happy they make me! The sun shines. How beautiful it is! The rain falls. How cozy our fireside! And the milk comes out of a cow, not a tin.

Everything in the world about me shares in a great vigor. I recognize now as never before the tremendous aliveness of the people of this continent, a germinating aliveness which makes it impossible to catalogue them. People and positions flutter out of their pigeonholes and refuse to be documented. Wives wash their husband's underwoolens in order to ride in handsome motorcars; plumbers talk philosophy and philosophers do the plumbing; the man who paints the pantry borrows the anthology of English poetry and the man who compiles the anthology paints his own pantry.

Conversation here is not English dinner-table conversation. It leaps nimbly from the subject of unemployment in the Canadian provinces to the submarine habits of the goldfish who swim outside in our garden pond; from the topic of delayed menstruation in the tropics to the making of blackberry jelly in the fall; from the threat of war in Europe to when will the neighbor's bitch have pups. It is not English dinner-table conversation, but it is very alive and very invigorating.

From Victoria, British Columbia, to Los Angeles by train is two nights and two days. Two nights of boring in and out of sleeping berths like a maggot in a cheese hole; two days of crawling in and out of Ladies' Rooms like a constipated caterpillar; of watching female hair, teeth, eyebrows, lips, and cheeks vanish from their owners to lie disabled, impotent, in shelves above the washbasins; two days of squeezing by the bosoms and bottoms of fat people who stand in the aisle, and of stepping on the feet and suspenders of men who undress by their berths; two days of asking the pullman-car porter persistently, When do we reach Portland, please? and Eugene, please? and Klamath, please? and Shasta, please? and Oakland, please? and of trying to get off at each flying station to telephone home, feeling that I cannot wait longer, now that I am so near, to hear the sound of those dear voices again. And finally asking, And When Do We Reach Los Angeles, Please? And then we do reach there. And a traveler has returned.

A traveler has returned — to the greetings of people she loves, to the warmth of affections withdrawn from, to the circle of arms that was hers at her birth. These be three enduring things, and for them a traveler gives thanks.

And so I am home in America. A traveler returns, but he is never the same; he returns, and what he returns to is new. And if he comes from an outpost of the British Empire, and from jungles and swamps, and from Eastern languors and tropical calm, then a traveler returned is momentarily confused by life in the U.S.A.

I read the headlines: "Ape Man Bites Woman"; "Phantom Burglar Robs House"; "Girl Sobs Story of Killing Father for Affection"; "Arsenic Widow Marries Victim's Son"; "Actor Divorces Fifth Wife Because He Loves Her."

Life here seems to be lived in headlines; love is in electric lights; vice is illuminated with neon signs; crimes are the biggest and best; men test their strength by the number of live goldfish they can swallow within the hour, by the number of girls they can kiss within the day, by the number of women they can marry within the year. Quiet affection and unblazoned love lie moth-eaten in the bottom drawer. The digit "one" is at a discount, nothing under five counts in marriages, and when the man bites the dog it is appetite, not news.

These are my people and I am proud of them, but not when I read the headlines. But I know that behind those headlines, like a clear flame which is distorted when seen through the glass of a cheap lamp, burns a fine and great energy. Burns the same great energy which our forefathers set sail for this once stern and rockbound coast, which made our grandfathers move in covered wagons across this once uncharted soil, which made our fathers build New York, Washington, Boston, Chicago, San Francisco, and Los Angeles on these once unbroken and un-ballyhooed acres. Burns the same great energy which makes the United States to-day the potentially greatest, the most exciting and dangerous, place in the world, far more so than the Borneo jungles.

This is my country and I am proud of it. For I know that here is a fertile clay which teems with the very bacteria of life. Everything flourishes in this clay, grows to the tallest degree, flowers to the hugest size, and reproduces in the greatest number. On such a fertile clay guard well what seeds may fall.

A traveler has returned, and he wishes to tell what he sees. But there is the same risk in writing about this country as there is to the around-the-world journalist who writes about Borneo — the risk of seeing only the elephants and the rhinoceroses, because they are SO big. And that is the way with the United States, and with Borneo — unless you look closely you may classify them by their elephants and their rhinoceroses.

Home

People ask me if I wish to return to Borneo. People ask me if I like our life out there. The answer is that I like our life as we live it better than I like anybody else's life of which I know.

I like the black nights of Borneo when the air smells of tree buds and wet leaves, when the only sound is the bark of the frogs and the tock of the nightjars in the jungle, and the only company is our own, and the only words are ours. I like the quiet days at home alone, days in which I am not ambitious, energetic, or noteworthy, but just am. It takes time and solitude to exist, and we have those in Borneo. I like the jungle trips, when I come to know the things I have wanted to know — the Stygian gloom of the *nipah* swamps, the murky green of the rivers, the beautiful excitement of the rapids, and the mellow color of sunlight on the backs of naked men.

I like our coming home on leave. We hurry through space, over oceans, across continents, and pass through all conditions of climates, people, mental attitudes, manners, and morals. One day my feet are too big for my shoes and the next day the shoes drop off in the cold; one time my dress is too daring and the next time it's dowdy; in one place I am being careful not to shock the people and in the next place they are shocking me.

I am glad that we come home on leave to a new continent, to these United States of America, where we may see life written with headlines again. And while I am here I like being the woman who came from a long ways off — Was it Bermuda or Buenos Aires? Siam or Central America? China, India, or Africa?

When I left the United States to sail for Borneo in 1934
I said to my husband, "This is a moment of great joy. I
will remember it all my life." That was almost five years

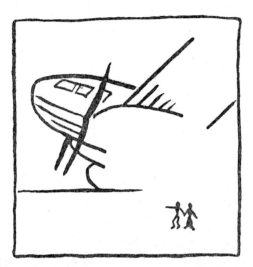

ago, and there are things now which I understand, and accept, which I did not know then.

I know now that in that land to which we are returning
there will be two people there together, and they will be
everything to each other, or they will be nothing. I have
learned now that it is not easy to leave children, and the
people you love, to grow up, or to die, in a distant land.
And I know now that when in that last moment I stand on
the deck and look back at the dear faces which say good-bye
to me I shall be embracing in my mind the fact that such
farewells may be eternal. Then everything in me will say,
"How can you go!" But I shall go.

I shall go, because I know that when we sail again for

Home

Borneo this fall I shall feel the same deep emotion of happiness from which I spoke five years ago. But my lips will not need to utter the words this time when I turn to my husband, for we both know now without speaking that to journey together is happiness.

THE UNITED STATES OF AMERICA — 1939

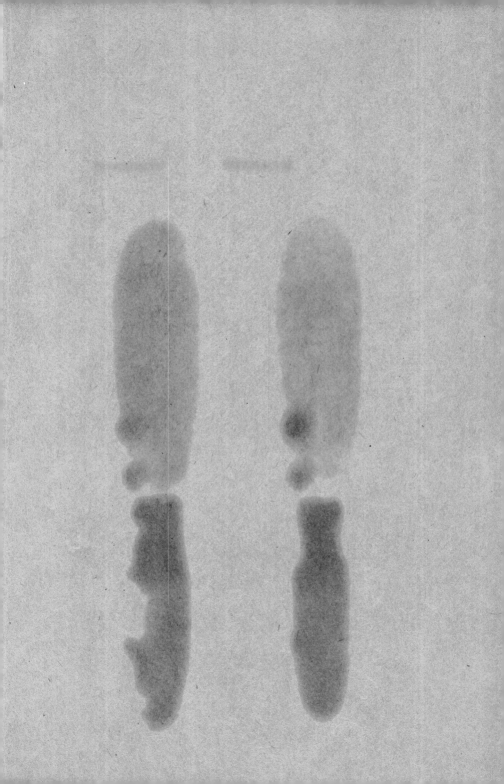